# WINSTON CHURCHILL
# ON JEWISH PROBLEMS

# WINSTON CHURCHILL
# ON JEWISH PROBLEMS

## BY OSKAR K. RABINOWICZ

NEW YORK • **Thomas Yoseloff** • LONDON

Published 1960

THOMAS YOSELOFF, *Publisher*
11 East 36th Street
New York 16, N. Y.

THOMAS YOSELOFF LTD.
123 New Bond Street
London W. 1, England

Library of Congress Catalog Card Number: 60-11320

Published under the joint sponsorship
of the World Jewish Congress

Printed in the United States of America

TO THE MEMORY

OF MY PARENTS

YEHUDAH ARYEH & GANANDEL RABINOWICZ

AND MY SISTER

ROSA

MARTYRED BY THE NAZIS

# ACKNOWLEDGEMENTS

I wish to express my appreciation of the valuable advice given to me by Mr. Stephen W. Pollak, Assistant to the Political Director of the World Jewish Congress, Dr. Cecil Roth, Reader in Jewish Studies, the University of Oxford, and Mr. Harry C. B. Underdown, while painstakingly reading my manuscript.

The compilation of a book of this nature causes an accumulation of many debts of appreciation. Limitation of space does not permit me to enumerate them all. I should like, however, to record my gratitude to all those who helped me at various times.

I also wish to acknowledge with thanks the permission of the following individuals and publishers to quote from the books listed:

CASSELL & COMPANY LTD.: Winston S. Churchill, *The Second World War*, Vol. I-VI, 1948-1954; *Into Battle*, 1941 (Compiled by Randolph S. Churchill); *The Unrelenting Struggle*, 1942; *The End of the Beginning*, 1943; *Onwards to Victory*, 1944; *The Dawn of Liberation*, 1945; *Victory*, 1946. (All compiled by Charles Eade.) *The Sinews of Peace*, 1948; *Europe United*, 1950; *In the Balance*, 1951; *Stemming the Tide*, 1953. (All edited by Randolph S. Churchill.) *Winston Spencer Churchill, Servant of Crown and Commonwealth*, 1954. (Edited by Sir James Marchant, K.B.E.)

VICTOR GOLLANCZ LTD.: Kingsley Martin, *Harold Laski*, 1953.

HAMISH HAMILTON LTD.: *Trial and Error, The Autobiography* of Chaim Weizmann, 1949.

HOUGHTON MIFFLIN COMPANY (BOSTON): Winston S. Churchill, *The Second World War*, Vol. I-VI 1948-1953.

HUTCHINSON & CO. (PUBLISHERS) LTD.: *Churchill by his Contemporaries*, edited by Charles Eade, 1953.

IRA A. HIRSCHMANN from his book *Life Line to a Promised Land*. (The Vanguard Press Inc.). New York, 1946.

McCLELLAND AND STEWART LTD. (TORONTO): Winston S. Churchill, *Blood, Sweat, Tears,* 1941.

ODHAMS PRESS LTD.: Winston S. Churchill, *My Early Life,* 1941; *The Aftermath,* 1941; *Step by Step,* 1942; *Thoughts and Adventures,* 1942 (all four volumes in the Macmillan edition); *Great Contemporaries,* 1949.

G. B. PUTNAM'S SONS (NEW YORK): Winston S. Churchill, *Blood, Sweat, Tears,* 1941; *Step by Step,* 1939; *Great Contemporaries,* 1937.

CHARLES SCRIBNER'S SONS (NEW YORK): Winston S. Churchill, *A Roving Commission,* 1940; *The Aftermath,* 1929; *Amid These Storms,* 1932.

SECKER AND WARBURG LTD.: Jon and David Kimche, *The Secret Roads,* 1954.

WEIDENFELD AND NICOLSON LTD.: Harry Sacher, *Israel, the Establishment of a State,* 1952; Barnet Litvinoff, *Ben-Gurion of Israel,* 1954.

I record my thanks to the editors of *The Daily Telegraph, The Jewish Chronicle, The Jewish Observer and Middle East Review, The Manchester Guardian* and *The Times* for permission to quote from their periodicals.

# CONTENTS

# WINSTON CHURCHILL ON JEWISH PROBLEMS

## Part I

## THE DIASPORA

# PREFACE

This study has a twofold object: it tries both to fill a
gap in the biographical literature on Sir Winston Churchill
and to determine the place due to him in Jewish history.

Biographers and historians mention Churchill's connection
with Jewish matters only incidentally, if at all. On the rare
occasions when such a reference is made, it usually applies
to the time when, as Colonial Secretary, he defined the basic
principles of Britain's Palestine policy in the *White Paper*
which bears his name. In addition we are sometimes told
how he condemned the Government decision of 1939 which
turned its back on the Zionist solution of the Jewish problem.
These scanty references virtually exhaust what Churchill's
biographers on the one hand and the Jewish historians on the
other feel it necessary to say in this connection.

It is surprising that Churchill has not yet been allocated
his appropriate place in Jewish history in general, and in
Anglo-Jewish history in particular. Not even his repeated
statements that throughout his life he has been a friend of
the Jews and an ardent Zionist have tempted a single historian
to study his stand in matters decisively affecting Jewry. It is
this omission that has prompted me to embark upon my task.
For it seemed to me as if a page, of which he himself often
spoke with pride, had been torn out of the chronicle of
Churchill's life.

This book is not intended to describe the history of the Jews
in the first half of our century. It records only the events and
problems in Jewish life about which Churchill expressed his
opinion at one time or another, or to the solution of which
he contributed by word or action. On some occasions it was
felt necessary to describe at some length events to which
Churchill referred only briefly, in order to enable the reader
to grasp their full significance. On other occasions, some

15

description of happenings to which Churchill made no direct reference seemed to me essential, as shedding light on the attitude adopted by the Government which he headed. This applies, for instance, to the stories of the Bermuda Conference, the *Struma* tragedy and the " illegal " immigration into Palestine. In some instances they serve to illustrate the difference between his personal attitude and the compromise attitude resulting from collective responsibility.

The tracing of the pattern of Churchill's intervention in such matters was not always easy, and involved a great amount of research. While his writings and published speeches are readily accessible, they do not in themselves do justice to his deep interest in Jewish affairs. In order to gain an adequate picture of the extent of this interest it has been necessary to scour the Press and political literature of half a century, often without the aid of an index. This search, begun in 1940, proved to be rewarding not only from the point of view of historical research; it also confirmed the author in his view that Sir Winston is one of the giants of our time, and that he ranks among the greatest friends the Jewish people has had in its long history of suffering and achievement.

The vast mass of material that has come to light during this investigation has made necessary its publication in two parts, the present one dealing exclusively with problems of the Diaspora, while a later one will focus on the problems of Palestine and the Zionist movement. Needless to say, these two vast, closely related subjects overlap in more than one instance. It has therefore not always been easy to draw a clear dividing line between endeavour and achievement, between tragedy and catharsis, between trial and deliverance. For clearly the fate of a hunted European Jewry had become so inextricably linked with the problem of a Palestine that was its only remaining refuge that any division must necessarily appear artificial. Thus, to a certain extent, such issues as the Jewish Brigade, the *White Paper* of 1939, or the Palestine immigration policy had to be included in Part I. Nevertheless it may be said with some measure of justification that Churchill the Humanitarian is reflected in the pages of this first part, while Churchill the Zionist will be foremost in the pages of the second.

Throughout this study it has been my endeavour to let Churchill express his thoughts in his own inimitable way. I have confined myself to sketching in their background, and occasionally commenting on them. This I regarded as the most appropriate form, for the fundamental aim of this study is to convey the views of Churchill, and of nobody else, on the issues in question. In any case, it would border on presumption to comment on expressions of thought and sentiment put with the brilliance of one of the world's greatest masters of the written and spoken word. The result is a book full of quotations from his writings and speeches which will, I hope, assist the student of history, and of Churchill in particular, to discern a facet of his life which has hitherto largely been buried in forgotten files—and in the minds of a few privileged actors on the stage of recent history.

O. K R.

# CHAPTER I

## JUDAISM AND JEWS

WINSTON CHURCHILL has written no detailed study of Judaism and its distinct features, nor has he, where he has dealt with Jews, made any deep analysis of the subject. He sees the Jews as a phenomenon encountered by anyone who, in this twentieth century, engages in current politics whether nationally or internationally. He views Judaism as he does every other spiritual, national and political phenomenon, from the vantage point of an impartial observer—one, however, who is both just and sincerely disposed towards his object.

In the course of his observations, which are based throughout on a deep understanding of the problems involved and on sound knowledge of the facts—the most important factor in dealing with so complex a subject—he often relinquished the position of the " impartial observer " to become on some occasions a merciless rebuker; but he was more often a professed admirer, especially when he came to speak of Jewry's spiritual and ethical potentialities. Whichever was the case, his utterances were undeniably permeated by a spirit of respect and friendliness. He could rightly say at a Jewish gathering in London in 1926:[1]

> Almost continuously in my political life I have been on friendly, pleasant relations with the Jewish community.

## (A) JUDAISM

To Churchill, Judaism is not a phenomenon that he approached in a philosophical spirit or with the philosophical method. As a matter of fact Churchill is no philosopher in the common meaning of the term; his is rather a " philosophy in a looser sense ", as Professor Joad once defined it,[2] " in

which a man who has touched life at many points may comment at large upon men and things, distilling in aphorisms
and epigrams, in maxims and exhortations, the ripe fruits
of his mellow experience. The philosopher so conceived is
akin to the sage or wise man of the East; experience has
ripened in him a faculty of insight which enables him to see
farther into things than his fellows, and to embody what he
has seen in pregnant observations." It is precisely from this
aspect that he treats Judaism, and he does so in his own
plain, straightforward way. A newspaper article where he
speaks of Judaism, its characteristics, its spiritual potentiality
and social structure, opens with the words:[3] " Some people
like Jews and some do not."

Churchill made no attempt to analyse these opening words,
nor even to explain to his readers what sort of man likes
Jews, and why, or the causes and manifestations of Jew-
hatred. He simply formulates an axiom and builds his
conclusions on it. Yet he does not leave his readers long
in suspense as to his own opinion. He goes on:

> No thoughtful man can doubt the fact that they are the
> most formidable and the most remarkable race which
> has ever appeared in the world.

Churchill realises that this thesis which he sets before his
readers will not always be accepted without criticism or challenge. He is, therefore, driven to provide the evidence. The
trend of his reasoning is based on the spiritual and ethical
potentialities of Judaism, and it is in this sense that he lays
his evidence before us.

The basis of his reasoning is his conception of Christianity,
to which Churchill repeatedly refers in his writings and
speeches. This conception underwent a number of phases
during his life until it crystallized into his present-day Christian outlook. His religious upbringing in his parental home
does not seem to have been too strict. It was the adherence
of his nurse, Mrs. Everest, to Low Church and " her dislike
of ornaments and ritual " that caused him to think likewise
during his childhood until he became a " passive conformist "[4]
at the age of ten, when at school at Brighton.

Still, his father's influence on him in religious matters, as
in so many others, cannot be denied, though it seems to have

made itself felt only after Lord Randolph's death.[5] Lord Randolph Churchill, " the man with that strong religious strain in his nature ",[6] during his public career very often gave expression to his religious views—in particular, during the controversy with Charles Bradlaugh, the Freethinker, over the question of taking the Parliamentary Oath.[7] But in this respect Lord Hugh Cecil's (now Lord Quickswood) influence seems to have imprinted itself more strongly upon the young Churchill during his first years in Parliament;[8] in particular during the debate on the Bill of 1901, which aimed at allowing a man to marry his deceased wife's sister. When one reads Churchill's description of Lord Hugh's exposition of the " profound reasons underlying the Ecclesiastical Law " one still feels the deep impression that this man—only five years his senior—must have exercised upon the new 26-year-old M.P. :

> Dethrone the principle of prohibited degrees, and in hundreds—nay in thousands—of households the position of these devoted women, hitherto unquestioned, would become a target for comment and calumny. All this, in itself important, was only a single instance of our duty to preserve the structure of humane, enlightened, Christian society. Once the downward steps were taken, once one's moral and intellectual feet slipped upon the slope of plausible indulgence, there would be found no halting-place short of a general Paganism and Hedonism, possibly agreeable from time to time in this world of fleeting trials and choices, but fatal hereafter through measureless ages, if not indeed through eternity itself.

This eternity of the Christian concept, which does not permit of any compromise for political expediency or practical convenience, often finds expression in Churchill's utterances. Nevertheless, while he fought the Bill of 1901 ardently on the side of the Hughlighans (so named after Lord Hugh Cecil), he confesses in the same essay that he was ultimately induced to acquiesce in the measure which he had so strenuously opposed. He attributes this change of front to the " growing tolerances of the age ", but adds as a kind of credo :

> Hugh Cecil's point of view, although superseded by irre-

sistible mass movements towards an altogether easier and more indulgent state of society, is one which may crop up again some day.

The influence that his father or Lord Hugh Cecil exercised on him in the religious field was reinforced by Churchill's own great interest in the subject, which induced him to turn to literature on religious topics. He did so at the very critical age of 22 (critical for any young man) when not only religious questions but " a dozen similar mental needs now began to press insistently upon me ". He read Winwood Reade's *Martyrdom of Man*, a harsh work throwing down a challenge to all religions, and having found that Gibbon and Lecky, both of whose works he read with admiration, held similar views, he turned agnostic and a protagonist of what he termed " The Religion of Healthy-Mindedness ".[10]  But it was life itself that brought him back to God:[11]

> As it was I passed through a violent and aggressive anti-religious phase which, had it lasted, might easily have made me a nuisance. My poise was restored during the next few years by frequent contact with danger. I found that whatever I might think and argue, I did not hesitate to ask for special protection when about to come under fire of the enemy: nor to feel sincerely grateful when I got home safe to tea.

It was quite natural that in the course of his reasoning and self-education on religious matters he would be induced to turn to the source of Christian Religion—the Bible. Churchill's writings and speeches betray a thorough knowledge of the Bible. " Its strict austerity has often been notable in Churchill's praise and condemnation ", says Ivor Brown,[12] and indeed many a phrase or description shows Scriptural origin. But it is of particular interest to note that his expositions, quotations and analogies are in so many, if not in most, cases derived from the Old Testament. Thus, in one of the great moments in his life, when in October 1911 he was appointed to the Admiralty, and was still under the impression of the news he had received about Germany's preparations for war, he describes how, on that same evening, before going to bed, he opened a large Bible in his bedroom and read verses 1 to 5 in the 9th Chapter of Deuteronomy:

Hear, O Israel: Thou art to pass over the Jordan this day, to go in to possess nations greater and mightier than thyself, cities great and fenced up to heaven.
2. A people great and tall, the children of the Anakims, whom thou knowest, and of whom thou hast heard say, Who can stand before the children of Anak!
3. Understand therefore this day, that the LORD thy God is he which goeth over before thee; as a consuming fire he shall destroy them, and he shall bring them down before thy face: so shalt thou drive them out, and destroy them quickly, as the LORD hath said unto thee.
4. Speak not thou in thine heart, after that the LORD thy God hath cast them out from before thee, saying, For my righteousness the LORD hath brought me in to possess this land: but for the wickedness of these nations the LORD doth drive them out from before thee.
5. Not for thy righteousness, or for the uprightness of thine heart, dost thou go to possess their land; but for the wickedness of these nations, the LORD thy God doth drive them out from before thee, and that he may perform the word which the LORD sware unto thy fathers, Abraham, Isaac and Jacob.

On referring to this incident Churchill recalls:[13]

It seemed a message full of reassurance.

On another occasion,[14] when discussing the problem of prophecy, he quoted Tennyson's "Locksley Hall" whose six couplets of prediction (conquest of the air for commerce and war, the League of Nations, the Communist movement) had been fulfilled eighty years after being written. Comparing them with Biblical prophecies, he again remained exclusively within the orbit of the Old Testament:[15]

We may search the Scriptures in vain for such precise and simply-vindicated forecasts of the future. Jeremiah and Isaiah dealt in dark and cryptic parables pointing to remote events and capable of many varied interpretations from time to time. A Judge, a Prophet, a Redeemer would arise to save his chosen People; and from age to age the Jews asked, disputing, "Art thou He that should come or do we look for another?"

But his respect and belief in the holiness of the Bible is not impaired even by problems to which he knows no answer. On the contrary, he challenges[16]

some of our Bishops and clergy making heavy water about reconciling the Bible story with modern scientific and historical knowledge.

There seems to him to be no necessity or justification for such efforts of reconciliation:[17]

Why do they want to reconcile them? If you are the recipient of a message which cheers your heart and fortifies your soul, which promises you reunion with those you have loved in a world of larger opportunity and wider sympathies, why should you worry about the shape or colour of the travel-stained envelope; whether it is duly stamped, whether the date on the postmark is right or wrong? These matters may be puzzling, but they are certainly not important. What is important is the message and the benefits to you of receiving it.

This is indeed harsh handling of Bible critics. He returns to the charge in his essay on " Moses ":[18]

We reject, however, with scorn all those learned and laboured myths that Moses was but a legendary figure upon whom the priesthood and the people hung their essential social, moral and religious ordinances. We believe that the most scientific view, the most up-to-date and rationalistic conception, will find its fullest satisfaction in taking the Bible story literally, and in identifying one of the greatest of human beings with the most decisive leap-forward ever discernible in the human story.

But his final reckoning with the critics of everything Biblical comes at the end of this essay in which he says:

Let the men of science and of learning expand their knowledge and probe with their researches every detail of the records which have been preserved to us from these dim ages. All they will do is to fortify the grand simplicity and essential accuracy of the recorded truths which have lighted so far the pilgrimage of man.

In the light of what has been said about Churchill's deeper and inner relationship to the Bible one can understand the moving words which he once spoke on Mount Scopus in Jerusalem on receiving a Scroll of the Law from the late Chief Rabbi of Mandatory Palestine, Abraham Isaac Kook, in 1921. He turned to the thousands of Jews assembled and, holding the Torah, said: [19]

> This sacred book which contains truth accepted by Jews and Christians alike is very dear to me, and your gift will remain in my family as an imperishable souvenir.

It is, therefore, through a deep insight into the eternal religious values that he came to the conclusion[20] that

> we owe to the Jews in the Christian revelation a system of ethics which, even if it were entirely separated from the supernatural, would be the most precious possession of mankind, worth, in fact, the fruits of all other wisdom and learning together.

Stressing thus the importance of Christian ethics in the contemporary world and its roots in the *system* of ethics and the *faith* of the Jews, Churchill crowns his argument in this same essay with the affirmation:

> On that system and by that faith there has been built out of the wreck of the Roman Empire the whole of our existing civilisation.

He also comes to the same conclusion in his essay, " Moses ", to which reference has already been made. In it he speaks of the great message conveyed to Moses out of the burning bush, the message of liberation, for the accomplishment of which Moses was endowed by God with supernatural power. This power—the power embodied in Judaism—consists, so he writes, of (a) man's belief in God, who proclaims the message of freedom, and (b) man's belief in himself as the carrier of the religious ideal. This mission finds its climax on Mount Sinai, where

Moses received from Jehovah the tables of those fundamental laws which were henceforward to be followed,
with occasional lapses, by the highest form of human
society.

It is, as pointed out, on the basis of this recognition of the
primal as well as historical origin of Jewish religion and ethics
that Churchill arrives at his conclusions on the rôle of
Christianity as not reaching beyond, not superseding, but
complementing Judaism. He says: [21]

Unluckily the stresses of the Exodus, the long forty years,
or whatever the period may have been which was needed
in the wilderness to sharpen the Children of Israel from
a domesticated race into an armed force of conquering
warriors, led them to make undue claims upon Jehovah.
They forgot the older tradition which the Pentateuch
enshrines. They forgot the enlightened monotheism which
under the heretic Pharaoh Akhnaton had left its impression upon Egypt. They appropriated Jehovah to themselves. In Renan's words, they made Him revoltingly
partial to the Chosen People. All Divine laws and
ordinary equity were suspended or disallowed when they
applied to a foreigner, especially to a foreigner whose
land and property they required.

But these are the natural errors of the human heart
under exceptional stresses. Many centuries were to pass
before the God that spake in the Burning Bush was to
manifest Himself in a new revelation, which nevertheless
was the oldest of all the inspirations of the Hebrew
people—as the God not only of Israel, but of all mankind who wished to serve Him; a God not only of justice,
but of mercy; a God not only of self-preservation and
survival, but of pity, self-sacrifice, and ineffable love.

For Churchill Judaism as the spiritual foundation of
Christianity and of Western Civilisation does not lie merely
in an abstract spiritual sphere. As a statesman he carries it
into practical life, and employs it as a measuring-rod to be
applied to the events of the day insofar as they embrace Jews
and Judaism. When Hitler and his Government launched
the wholesale Jewish persecution in Germany, few realised

the real trend and purpose underlying this brutality.[22] Yet, when the persecution of the Catholic priesthood and Protestant clergy began, accompanied by a revival of the old nordic pagan gods and by the creation of a " new Germanic religion ", it became clear to some observers that anti-Judaism had been chosen only as the starting-point for a movement aiming at the destruction of all other religions and ethical values, and consequently of Western Civilisation as a whole. One of the first to listen intently to this tumult of German national iconoclasm was Churchill, and he did his best to warn the world. He proclaimed with unambiguous clarity:[23]

This hatred of the Jews led by a logical transition to an attack upon the historical basis of Christianity.

But history has taught time and again that spiritual values cannot be destroyed by the sword, and the very fact of the existence of the Jewish race to this day constitutes the most striking proof of this truth. However violent the attacks made upon it in the course of its history, Judaism could never be annihilated. But this is only the negative aspect of the story: Judaism did not remain static in the course of the assaults from which the people suffered. On the contrary, as Churchill admiringly told a Jewish meeting in London in 1926,[24] in spite of all, it has survived

and reserved its strength, its destiny, its power for good, its power to develop and to guide and aid by its development the march of the human mind.

There is only one other nation that Churchill considers possessing similar qualities for suffering and surviving like the Jews, namely the Greeks. In his *War Memoirs*, when speaking about the Greek ordeal, he wrote:[25]

No two races have set such a mark upon the world. Both have shown a capacity for survival, in spite of unending perils and sufferings from external oppressors, matched only by their own ceaseless feuds, quarrels and convulsions. The passage of several thousand years sees no change in their characteristics and no diminution of their trials or their vitality. They have survived in spite of all that the world could do against them, and all they could do against themselves, and each of them from angles so different have left us the inheritance of their genius and wisdom. No two cities have counted more with mankind than Athens and Jerusalem. Their messages in religion, philosophy and art have been the main guiding lights of modern faith and culture. Centuries of foreign rule and indescribable, endless oppression leave them still living, active communities and forces in the modern world, quarrelling among themselves with insatiable vivacity. Personally, I have always been on the side of both, and believed in their invincible power to survive internal strife and the world tides threatening their extinction.

It is, of course, stressed in this quotation that these analogies are derived from "angles so different". Indeed, even in this formal comparison the fundamental differences in the extent of suffering as well as in the art. of survival are not stressed sufficiently; for the Greeks remained in their homeland while Jewry was scattered all over the globe. The different angles, however, are most striking in the spiritual field, and in this connection there is no doubt that Churchill does not wish to obscure the distinguishing lines. For he says in his " Moses " :[26]

At any rate there is no doubt about one miracle. This wandering tribe, in many respects indistinguishable from numberless nomadic communities, grasped and proclaimed an idea of which all the genius of Greece and all the power of Rome were incapable.

He could, therefore, arrive at the conclusion,[27] which is so often adumbrated in his writings, that

the thought, the inspiration and the culture of the Jews has been one of the vital dominants in world history. There are none of the arts or science which have not been enriched by Jewish achievements.

This very fact, based on his knowledge of history and on a thorough understanding of the spiritual trends that shaped human progress, induces him to expect also in future important contributions in all fields of activity—the pre-requisites of which are talent, vision and ability to realise them—to be brought about by the genius of the Jewish people. In this sense at least he visualises the mission of an institution like the Hebrew University in Jerusalem, giving expression to his expectations in the message referred to above:

> I hope and believe that as it stands aloft on Mount Scopus it will cast a mellow, shining light around it, and proclaim to a distracted generation true progress, not only in literature, scholarship and science, but in those tolerant, comprehending humanities, without which all the rest is only mockery to human beings.

His belief in the spiritual capacity of the Jews did not find its expression only in theory. As in many other respects he draws his practical conclusions wherever reality calls for them. Thus he was well aware that World War II was not merely a matter of fighting on battlefields, for the creative spirit would have the last word in achieving victory. In a message to the International Conference on Science and World Order meeting in London he reiterated this conviction when he said that[28]

> Superiority in scientific development is a vital factor in the preparation for victory.

In this respect he saw Germany at a disadvantage and did not hesitate to hold this up to the civilised world as a ray of light in the dark months after the collapse of France. The creative spirit of the Jews, in his view, would benefit not the Germans but the Powers fighting against the evil of National Socialism :[29]

> Since the Germans drove the Jews out and lowered their technical standards, our science is definitely ahead of theirs.

And when on the occasion of his 80th birthday Anglo-Jewry honoured him by naming after him a group of buildings in the new Technion City to be erected on Mount Carmel, he readily accepted this honour and in his message,[30] stressing the gift and ability of Jewish scientists, he expressed his thanks

that my name will be associated with an undertaking devoted to the advancement of knowledge and human well-being . . .
I am sure that the Israeli Institute of Technology has a great contribution to make to Israel's future prosperity and that Israel's prosperity cannot but be of great benefit to other countries as well.

It is, therefore, quite natural that, in view of this inexhaustible capacity of the Jews the question should arise in Churchill's mind: What power achieved all this? Wherein lies the source of this unique manifestation? As far back as 1906 he seems to have understood the problem, when, addressing a Jewish gathering in Manchester, he said that[31]

he was quite sure of this, that if we were to have the higher corporate life we must have the higher corporate incentive, we must have the larger spirit, the larger driving power. He did not think, however, that people could unite in communities unless they possess some guiding principle. The Jews were a lucky community, because they had the corporate spirit of their race and faith.

On the other hand we know that he was often confronted not with a " united community ", as is stressed above as the ideal aim, but was to witness internal strife and quarrels among Jews, which assumed particularly pernicious forms during the period of the British Mandate in Palestine.[32] Reference has already been made to a certain proneness to quarrel which Churchill dislikes in the Jewish community,[33] and which—like some other characteristics—he finds are common to both Jews and Greeks:[34]

The Greeks rival the Jews in being the most politically-minded race in the world. No matter how forlorn their circumstances or how grave the peril to their country, they are always divided into many parties, with many leaders who fight among themselves with desperate vigour. It has been well said that wherever there are three Jews it will be found that there are two Prime Ministers and one leader of the Opposition.

These are harsh but true words, and Churchill feels that these negative qualities are apt to obscure the true greatness of Jewry and Judaism. This seems to me one of the reasons why he so often stresses the importance of " corporate unity " and the unifying bond of Jewish spirituality. Already some fifty years ago he gave expression in a few pregnant words to his belief,[35] that Jewry's survival, spiritual and physical

would never have been achieved or completed but for the main sheet-anchor to which the Jewish people have been attracted, unshakable in their unswerving adherence to the faith of their fathers.

This is the spirit which Churchill so sincerely admires in the Jews, and arising from it is his belief in the miracle of the continued existence of Judaism.

It is a precious thing, a bond of union, an inspiration and a source of great strength,

he declared at a gathering at the Manchester Jewish Working Men's Club;[36] and in his closing words at this same assembly he cried to his audience:

Guard and keep that spirit!

as though an ancient Hebrew prophet had risen in him and was endeavouring to guide his people along the right path.

(B) INDIVIDUAL JEWS

Of course, Churchill does not regard each single Jew as a hero of the spirit, or every Jew as the dispenser of ethical teachings. He does not become a follower of anti-Semitic techniques employing the inductive method by drawing conclusions from the behaviour and actions of individual Jews. Nor is he a follower of the deductive method which seeks to apply to the individual the conclusions drawn from the community as a whole. Churchill is a realist in this matter too, his feet firmly planted in practical life. As he views it, there are all sorts of people in every country and in every race; good, bad, and, for the most part, indifferent.[37]

Churchill applies the same general standard to the Jews, but in their case he finds it of particular significance. He wrote:[38]

In a people of peculiar genius like the Jews, contrasts are more vivid, the extremes are more widely separated, the resulting consequences are more decisive.

But—he continued,

it is a great mistake, widely and frequently made, to assume that every individual has a definite share in those qualities which constitute the national character of a people. Nothing is more wrong than to deny to an individual, on account of race or origin, his right to be judged on his personal merits and conduct.

That is true for Jew and non-Jew alike.

Allusion has already been made to Churchill's essay on " Moses ", surely one of his most remarkable writings, placing the leader of the Jews in the highest possible historical position as the man who

was the greatest of the prophets, who spoke in person to the God of Israel; he was the national hero who led the Chosen people out of the land of bondage, through the perils of the wilderness, and brought them to the very threshold of the Promised Land; he was the supreme law-giver, who received from God that remarkable code upon which the religious, moral, and social life of the nation was so securely fastened. Tradition lastly ascribed to him the authorship of the whole Pentateuch, and the mystery that surrounded his death added to his prestige.

And he does not hesitate to reserve for Moses the description as

one of the greatest human beings with the most decisive leap-forward ever discernible in the human story.

Throughout his career, Churchill never departs from the order of values when assessing individual Jews or non-Jews. The Jew as such does not play any rôle whatever, only the man and his deeds. A few examples, taken at random, will provide evidence of this.

### SOLOMON DE MEDINA

When delving more deeply into his family's history

Churchill unavoidably stumbled upon the testimony in 1711 of the " Jew Medina " against Sir Winston's ancestor, the Duke of Marlborough.[39] It was mainly on the evidence of Sir Solomon de Medina, the Government's principal army contractor, with regard to payments made to the Duke in the course of Medina's supply of bread to the Army, that the great General was dismissed by Queen Anne. While a feeling of bitterness is clearly discernible in this part of Churchill's classical biography, he found no words of condemnation of Medina as a Jew, though contemporary literature could have supplied him with some sharp and colourful gibes.

## LORD BEACONSFIELD

One probably does not need to stress too emphatically Churchill's reverence, respect and admiration for " the Jew Prime Minister of England ", as he once called Lord Beaconsfield,[40] the man " who was always true to his race and proud of his origin ". They have often been mentioned by Churchill himself as well as by his biographers. He was actually brought up in an unswerving belief in everything that " Dizzy " did and taught;[41] and remained throughout his political career an apostle of the Tory Democracy which had once knitted his father, Lord Randolph, so closely to Lord Beaconsfield. One is almost tempted today—after his resignation—to read into Churchill's characterisation of Lord Beaconsfield a kind of self-portrait:[42]

> His character and the hard experiences of his earlier years made him seek eagerly for the first signs of oncoming power. He was an old man lifted high above his contemporaries and he liked to look past them to the new generation and to feel that he could gain the sympathy and confidence of younger men.

## SIR ERNEST CASSEL

Sir Ernest Cassel was an old friend of Lord Randolph's[43] and to the end of his life was on intimate terms with his son. It was to him[44] that Winston Churchill turned after making £10,000 profit out of his lectures on his experiences in the Boer War, and asked Sir Ernest to invest £6,000 of the money and to

'Feed my sheep.' He fed the sheep with great prudence. They did not multiply fast, but they fattened steadily, and none of them ever died.

Also, on another occasion, when as a result of his biography of Lord Randolph, he found himself with a profit of £8,000, Churchill again invested the greater part through Sir Ernest Cassel. This and other incidents in their relationship became known to a wider public during Churchill's libel action against Lord Alfred Douglas[45]—to which reference is made in another connection.[46] In the course of his testimony Churchill confirmed[47] the Attorney-General's contention of " Sir Ernest Cassel's friendship with his father " and stated that " shortly after Lord Randolph's death in 1895, he got to know Sir Ernest very well."

In the course of the cross-examination by defence Counsel, Mr. Cecil Hayes, the following interchange took place:[48]

> Hayes: In 1907 you were on close terms of friendship .with Sir Ernest Cassel?
> Churchill: Yes, on terms of honourable friendship.
> Hayes: You were grateful to him in 1907?
> Churchill: He was a very great friend of mine.

### LEON BLUM

Conscious of the " fiery French Premier's "[49] merits, Churchill expresses his admiration for Léon Blum's " genial and friendly " attitude at a time of his own " political wilderness ", and is full of praise for Blum's self-effacing behaviour "[50] in World War II.

Churchill gave particular emphasis to his appreciation of Blum in his description of the critical pre-war years, for he believed[51] that

> the action and influence of the Blum Government has been successful, or at least beneficial. There never was a time since the war [i.e., World War I] when closer and better relations existed between the French and British Governments. Nor was there ever a time when the two western democracies worked more smoothly together in the common cause of peace and freedom.

But Blum's personal effort and standing in those days comes in for much higher praise and appreciation on the part of Churchill:

> If the scene has darkened, the atmosphere has become more clear, and the shape of objects more sharply defined. In all this rallying of the forces which stand for peaceful and tolerant solutions of world problems, M. Blum has rendered a high personal service. Indeed, it was not in the power of any other Frenchman at this particular time in the life of France or Europe to do so much for the common good.

Blum was one of the survivors of Nazi occupation in France. On his release Churchill wrote to him on May 9, 1945, a letter in moving terms:[52]

> I send you my warmest congratulations on your liberation. I need not tell you how often my thoughts were with you during the long years of your captivity, nor how glad I am to be able to rejoice with you on this day of victory.

### PIERRE MENDES-FRANCE

In the relatively short period of time during which M. Mendès-France was in charge of the French Government a number of issues of world-wide significance had to be dealt with, which demanded both vision and courage. No issue, however, was more complicated and difficult to get past the French National Assembly than the Paris Agreements to bring Germany back into the concert of nations. Even in that short period the British Prime Minister was able to establish close and friendly contact with the French Premier, which developed into a relationship of mutual admiration. In one of his letters to Mendès-France Churchill gave eloquent expression to his sentiments:[53]

> I renew my congratulations to you on your success in the Chamber. I feel that your difficulties in dealing with all the vehement and self-centred groups must be enormous. Your courage and vitality have given me an impression of French leadership which I had not sus-

tained since the days of Clemenceau. Pray accept my earnest compliments.

### DR. CHAIM WEIZMANN

Churchill also repeatedly refers to Dr. Chaim Weizmann as " an old friend of mine for many years ",[54] to whom he was introduced as far back as 1905 when, at the end of a great meeting in Manchester against the Russian pogroms at which Churchill spoke,[55] Dr. Weizmann seconded a motion moved by Barrow I. Belisha calling for the establishment of a World Jewish Parliament. After that meeting, the chairman, Nathan Laski, gave a dinner party in honour of Churchill to which Dr. Weizmann was invited.[56] During his campaign against Bolshevism in 1918-20, Churchill contrasted " the fiery energies of Dr. Weizmann, the leader, for practical purpose, of the Zionist project ",[57] with Jewish Communists, and strongly advised Jewry to follow the former. Many years later, in one of his post-war speeches in Parliament he spoke[58] of

the figure of Dr. Weizmann, that dynamic Jew whom I have known so long, the ablest and wisest leader of the cause of Zionism, his whole life devoted to the cause, his son killed in the battle for our common freedom.

On Dr. Weizmann's death Churchill said at the Lord Mayor's Banquet:[59]

Here was a man whose force and fidelity were respected throughout the free world, whose son was killed fighting for us in the late war, and who, it may be rightly claimed, led his people back into their promised land, where we have seen them invincibly established as a free and sovereign State.

In March 1954 the Manchester Zionist Council organised an exhibition " Manchester and Israel—a city's contribution to the birth of a State ", which coincided with the fiftieth anniversary of Dr. Weizmann's settlement at Manchester. Sir Winston sent the following message:[60]

The City of Manchester may be proud of its connection with Dr. Weizmann, a man of vision and of genius, whose lasting memorial will be the vigour and the prosperity of the State of Israel, which he did more than any other single man to inspire and create. I am indeed glad that Manchester should commemorate the 50th anniversary of this great man's arrival in our country, and I send my best wishes for the success of the exhibition which is being held.

### BERNARD BARUCH

Outstanding among those who came close to Churchill as friends, advisers and counsellors, is no doubt Bernard Baruch, the American statesman and financier. Their first contact took place in World War I when both, while in charge of the departments of munitions in their respective countries, concluded an important agreement for the supply of guns, without knowing each other.[61] When ultimately they met, they became, and have remained to this day, intimate friends. Baruch, in his "Birthday Letter" on the occasion of Churchill's eightieth birthday,[62] gave eloquent expression to this remarkable friendship.

### NATHAN LASKI

Nathan Laski, father of Harold and Neville, was one of the Churchill stalwarts in Manchester. It was to him that Churchill addressed his letter on the Aliens Immigration Bill,[63] and it was in Laski's house that Churchill was entertained as "Liberal candidate for North-West Manchester" on June 16, 1904, soon after he joined the Liberal party.[64] This was of considerable importance, as Laski was the President of the Manchester Hebrew Congregation, and Churchill's constituency was densely peopled by Jewish residents, so that his great victory in the 1906 election "was in considerable measure due to the support of the Jews."[65]

Churchill gave dignified expression to his regard for Nathan Laski in a letter, addressed to Harold, on the former's death in 1941:[66]

> He was a man whose heart overflowed with human feeling and whose energies were tirelessly used for other people and large causes. I feel I have lost a friend; and all my memories of Manchester and Cheetham are veiled in mourning.

### PROF. HAROLD LASKI

Nathan Laski's son, Harold, knew Churchill from his boy-hood and " used to recall that Winston Churchill . . . stayed at his father's house and sat on his bed to talk to him "[67] during the by-election campaign in 1908. Harold Laski was then a boy of fifteen, but it was only from about 1914 onwards that a correspondence developed between them which, though conducted spasmodically, continued until 1945.[68] During the general election of that year Churchill, in his attacks on the Labour party, inevitably had to deal with Harold Laski, who then held the post of Chairman of the Party and though him-self not an M.P. intervened in matters confined to Parlia-ment.[69] His biographer tells us[70] that Prof. Laski felt terribly hurt by what Churchill called " The Laski episode ".[71] In view of their long acquaintance it is strange that Churchill should have referred to Laski as " this hitherto almost unknown person ",[72] but read in its context this presumably applied to his being unknown in Parliament. For the sentence in Churchill's speech containing this phrase continues that Laski,

> who has never sought to face the electors and sits at the head of what is called ' the National Executive Com-mittee ', of which the larger part are not even members of Parliament, that he should have the right—I can but call it the presumption—to lay down the law to the publicly-proclaimed leader of the Labour Party, etc.

Whatever the merits of the case, this " episode " brought to an end the " affection and respect going back to childhood which Harold always felt for Churchill ",[73] a relationship which Churchill had once defined as follows in a letter to Laski:[74]

> I have always accounted you a friend rather than a follower.

### LORD READING

Churchill's relations with Rufus Daniel Isaacs, First Marquess of Reading, certainly deserve mention in this connection. The present Lord Reading records[75] that Chur-chill was one of those men " with whom his [Rufus Isaacs'] personal relations were most cordial." Sir Winston admired in him the multiplicity of functions he held (which also characterise Churchill's own life) and his ability to master them all:[76]

> Advocate, judge, ambassador, Viceroy—all these great functions had fallen to him, and there was not one of them that he had discharged up to the present which he had been found in any degree or respect unequal.

But it was the cordial personal relationship between them which Churchill on this occasion wished to underline:[77]

> He worked with him as a colleague and friend for many years, and they had had good days—and days less good. They had had anxious times and then again brighter times. Always had he admired his distinguished and in many respects incomparable, gifts, always had he known him for a true man, and a wise and faithful friend.

*  *
*

In the case of all these individual Jews selected at random as well as many others to whom no reference can be made owing to lack of space, Churchill's approach, respect and admiration, are based solely on his evaluation of their merits. No racial, religious or other consideration ever apparently enters his thoughts.

As I pointed out before, he applies these same standards also in cases where he disapproves of people or their teachings; and no prejudice mars his assessment even in such cases.

### DOV GRUNER

Thus during the bitter struggle of the Irgun Zvai Leumi in Palestine against the British forces, a young man, Dov Gruner, was condemned to death, and Churchill raised the case in Parliament:[78]

> He was going to hang I think the next morning, and the terrorists seized a judge of the bench and an officer in the street and took them off, saying they would kill them if the sentence was carried out. And sentence was not carried out. We were immediately told that the prisoner had appealed to the Privy Council. That was

not true. It was an excuse and a procedure vamped up; the Jewish Agency were brought in to make some suggestions and, as far as I can gather from the accounts, he was persuaded only with great difficulty to make an appeal.

But Gruner withdrew his appeal into which he had been coaxed. While demanding in the same speech that a sentence once pronounced be carried out, Churchill who, very characteristically, referred to him as "Mister" Dov Gruner could not suppress admiration for his stand:[79]

> The fortitude of this man, criminal though he be, must not escape the notice of the House.

\*    \*
\*

### COMMUNIST JEWS

Whenever he is compelled to condemn people Churchill applies the same measuring-rod of merit and character only. If they are Jews, it is worthy of notice that he stresses their Jewish descent, but simultaneously points emphatically to the fact that these men and women have for the greater part become stateless and unbelieving internationalists, who were[80]

> reared up among the unhappy populations of countries where Jews are persecuted on account of their race. Most, if not all, of them have forsaken the faith of their forefathers, and divorced from their minds all spiritual hopes of the next world.

He mentions in this connection the names of Communist leaders, who long since have either died or have been later purged during the Bolshevik trials in the thirties, such as Rosa Luxemburg, Emma Goldman, Bela Kun, Zinoviev, Radek, etc.

### LEON TROTSKY

It is pity rather than hatred that moves Churchill when viewing these people. One short but very characteristic extract from his essay on Trotsky shows this clearly:[81]

> Trotsky was a Jew, he was still a Jew. Nothing could get over that. Hard fortune when you have deserted your

family, repudiated your race, spat upon the religion of
your fathers, and lapped Jew and Gentile in a common
malignity, to be baulked of so great a prize for so narrow-
minded a reason! Such intolerance, such pettiness, such
bigotry were hard indeed to bear. And this disaster
carried in its train a greater. In the wake of disappointment loomed catastrophe.

*

His father—old Bronstein—died of typhus in 1920 at
the age of 83. The triumph of his son brought no comfort to this honest, hard-working and believing Jew.
Persecuted by the Reds because he did not change his
belief, persecuted by the Whites because he was Trotsky's
father, and deserted by his son, he was left to sink or
swim in the Russian deluge, and swam on steadfastly to
the end. What else was there for him to do?

*

It may be that in these future years, Trotsky will find as
little comfort in the work which he has done, as his father
found in the son he had begotten.

Churchill despises these figures, but he does not draw any
conclusions from their acts to be applied to Jewry as a whole.
In this case too he judges the men according to their own
merits and also gives praise where he feels it is due. This is
the case with Maxim Litvinov, " the eminent Jew ", the one-
time Soviet Foreign Secretary, to whom reference is made in
another connection.[82]

* *
*

Churchill does not leave us in any doubt that his admiration
is for Jews who stand by their Judaism. Whenever he
expresses an opinion on this question he links with it an
appeal to Jews to remain loyal to their Jewish faith. Thus
he said in his Manchester speech already referred to:[83]

That personal and special driving power which they
possessed would enable them to bring vitality into their
institutions, which nothing else would ever give. If they
would allow him he would say, ' Let them be good Jews,

cultivate a higher type of individual, to fit them for a
more elevated status in the community '. As he had said
at the Club [the Working Men's Club in Manchester]
that morning, his advice was, if he might say it without
disrespect, ' Be good Jews! A Jew cannot be a good
Englishman unless he is a good Jew.'

It is the larger community which Churchill has in mind to the
good of which, he thinks, the common effort of individual
Jews should serve; for that would benefit not only the Jewish
community but through it those people among whom Jews
live. He applies this particularly to the Jewish community
in Britain:

> The higher the type of individual the greater the eleva-
> tion of the community, and the greater the elevation of
> the community the greater the glory, the power, the
> splendour and the assurance of permanent dominion of
> the Empire in which those communities are woven
> together.

It is therefore quite natural that, having attributed to the
Jewish community such a high and important mission,
Churchill should turn his attention also to the trends inform-
ing that community.

## (C) THE JEWISH COMMUNITY

Churchill sees two conceptions in the Jewish community
which he respects: the " national " Jews and Zionism.
The " national " Jews he describes as follows: [84]

> These are the Jews who, dwelling in every country
> throughout the world, identify themselves with that
> country, enter into its national life, regard themselves as
> citizens in the fullest sense of the State which has received
> them.

He regards this faithful loyalty as one of the characteristics
of the Jewish people, which its members feel even in countries
where they are persecuted as for instance in pre-Bolshevik
Russia: [85]

> Even in Czarist Russia, the country where the Jews in
> the past have suffered so much, the national Russian

Jews have managed to play an honourable and useful part in the national life of Russia, and in political life they were for the most part active in the Liberal and Progressive parties, and were among the staunchest upholders of friendship with France and Great Britain.

On many an occasion after Hitler's accession to power Churchill pointed in his speeches and writings to the patriotism of the Jews towards Germany or Austria[86] throughout the centuries of their settlement there, to the affection they felt and the sacrifices they brought for the peoples among whom they lived, and to their work for the well-being of these States. He contrasted this with Nazi Germany's response —the wholesale murder of Jewish subjects.

In Churchill's view, that same loyalty exists also in other countries where Jews live and merge into the national life; it applies particularly to Great Britain, where the Jews are faithful to their religion, loyal to the country, and have adapted themselves to the general national life. In the Churchillian definition, such a Jew would say (and these are his own words): [87]

I am an Englishman practising the Jewish faith.

Churchill respects and honours this conception, describing it as

a worthy conception and useful in the highest degree.

And he regards it as a blessing that the Jews of Britain have been able to maintain that loyalty and to create at the same time a strong, unified community of their own.[88] On another occasion he said: [89]

I was very glad to have had the experience of watching the life and work of the Jewish community in England; there is a high sense of the corporate responsibility in the community. There is a great sense of duty, which was fostered on every possible occasion by their leaders.

There is no doubt in Churchill's mind that no loyalty or patriotism alone would suffice to create such happy conditions, free from bias and suspicion, were it not for the principles that govern the State where these Jews live. He quoted twice in his public career the words imputed to Disraeli " The

Lord deals with the nations as the nations deal with the Jews."[90] The first occasion was in 1905[91] when he prefaced this quotation with the statement that the Jews

> enjoyed in this country a position in which they had prospered greatly, living as peacable, law-abiding citizens, who are an honour and a credit to any country.

The second occasion was in an article,[92] written at a critical political moment after World War I, where he again contrasted the life of Jews in a country like Russia, where they were most cruelly treated,

> with the fortunes of our own country, which seems to have been so providentially preserved amid the awful perils of these times [and] we must admit that nothing that has since happened in the history of the world has falsified the truth of Disraeli's confident assertion.

Yet for all his respect for the " national " Jews in Britain and elsewhere, Churchill sees a limitation cramping their conception, and merely a " negative resistance ", as he calls it, in their activities—which is not enough:[93]

> It cannot suffice to protest as Jews and alienate themselves from those whose actions they do not approve. It is essential to have a positive programme for the Jews. Positive and practicable alternatives are needed in the moral as well as in the social sphere.

And looking round in his search for such a " practicable alternative " he finds it in that " sphere of political conception " to which he ascribes the most important task in Jewish life—Zionism.

This is not the place to describe Churchill's conception of Zionism and its importance for Jewry, as this is dealt with in another section of this study.[94] In this general outline of his views on the two most important and worthy conceptions in the Jewish community it is, however, opportune to emphasise the fact that Churchill does not see any incompatibility in the two, but believes and actually recommends that all Jews should support Zionism and[95]

> enter upon an inspiring movement, which directs the

energies and hopes of Jews in every land towards a simpler, a truer and far more attainable goal.

It does not enter his mind therefore to enquire whether Zionist ideology, in affirming the existence of a Jewish nationality, conflicts with the obligations of a citizen of the State in which the Zionist lives. For Churchill this question simply does not exist. To quote again from this same essay, he regards Zionism as a conception

of deep significance for the whole, on which so many blessings rest,

and that to adhere to it or support it leaves no room at all for any negative or harmful manifestations, either for Jews or Gentiles. Churchill sees no element of contradiction intervening between Zionism and the duties of a Jewish citizen, say, in Britain, for the simple reason that Zionism[96]

would from every point of view be beneficial, and would be especially in harmony with the truest interests of the British Empire.

But not only with these interests. Such confines would be too narrow for a world-embracing Zionism and the Zionists who live among other peoples and in other countries. The importance of Zionism far exceeds these interests, for in Churchill's own words, it is a[97]

great event in the world's destiny, and its cause is one which carries with it much that is good for the whole world and not only for the Jewish people.

*    *
*

This brings to a conclusion the theoretical part of Churchill's views on the philosophy of Judaism, on individual Jews and on the conceptions informing the Jewish community. It constitutes the background against which Churchill's stand in Jewish matters, as described in the following pages, should be read and studied, for without even a cursory glimpse of his basic approach to Judaism and the Jews his subsequent words and deeds could scarcely be understood or appreciated.

What follows is the practical part of Churchill's reaction to events concerning Jewry as they arose in his daily routine during the fifty years of his public life.

# CHAPTER II

## THE ALIENS QUESTION

THE influx of Jews from Russia and Roumania into Britain in the two decades beginning in the early eighteen-eighties, when the first great anti-Semitic outbreaks in Russia and the discriminatory policy of the Roumanian Government drove the Jews to emigration, was bound before long to cause a reaction on the part of the British population. It was particularly after the Boer War that agitation against the admission of foreigners into Britain assumed serious proportions and led to the establishment of a number of anti-alien associations, the most important being the " British Brothers' League " founded by Major William Eden Evans-Gordon. Its agitation was based on the pleas that the aliens arriving in Britain included " criminals, anarchists and immoral persons ", that they inundated the labour market with cheap labour and occupied the scanty living-space in London's already overcrowded East End. The aim of this agitation was to induce Parliament to enact legislation to control the hitherto unrestricted immigration. As a result of this ever-increasing campaign, the " Royal Commission on Alien Immigration " was appointed on March 21, 1902, consisting of the following members: Lord James of Hereford, Chairman; Sir Kenelm Digby, K.C.B.; Major William Eden Evans-Gordon, M.P.; the Hon. Alfred Lyttelton, M.P.; Henry Norman, M.P.; Lord Rothschild, and William Vallence (who for many years had acted as Clerk to the Whitechapel Guardians).

The terms of reference of the Commission were " to inquire into and to report upon the character and extent of the evils which are attributed to the unrestricted immigration of aliens, especially in the Metropolis; and the measures which have been adopted for the restriction and control of Alien Immi-

46

gration in foreign countries, and in British Colonies ". The Commission sat for many months in public, examined witnesses, and collected material for their report, which was finally published on August 14, 1903.[1] The most prominent witness to plead for restrictive measures before the Commission was Arnold White, one of the leaders of the " British Brothers' League " and chief protagonist of the anti-alien agitation. In his testimony he went beyond the question of alien immigration into Britain and dealt with the root of the general Jewish problem, basing his thesis on the biased assumption that Jews cannot be loyal citizens to the country of their adoption if they remain loyal Jews. He asserted that whatever was wrong with the condition of the people in Great Britain was a result of the presence of Jews, who drew for their increasing numbers upon alien immigration, and accordingly demanded that this influx should be halted by legislation. Most of the anti-alien witnesses followed a similar negative line. On the whole, reading this voluminous Report, one is astonished to find that none of the 175 witnesses who gave evidence had any practical proposal or positive solution to submit with the exception of Dr. Theodor Herzl, the founder and president of the World Zionist organisation, who was invited to testify and who alone offered a policy. " Nothing will meet the problem the Commission is called upon to investigate and advise upon ", he said, " except a diverting of the stream of migration that is bound to go on with increasing force from Eastern Europe. The Jews of Eastern Europe cannot stay where they are—where are they to go? If you find they are not wanted here, then some place must be found to which they can migrate without that migration raising the problems that confront them here. Those problems will not arise if a home be found for them which will be legally recognised as Jewish."

As was to be expected, the Royal Commission suggested some restrictive measures, especially with regard to the exclusion from entry into Britain of certain undesirable categories of immigrants. The Commission's recommendations for legislation made in the Report may be summed up as follows:

1. That the immigration of certain classes of aliens be subjected to State control;

2. That a Department of Immigration be established;

3. That correct statistical returns relating to Alien Immigration be secured;

4. That legislative power be obtained for the purpose (a) of making and enforcing orders and regulations, applicable to immigration generally, and (b) that immigration officers to have the power to inquire into the background of " undesirable " immigrants, (c) to report on their findings to the Immigration Department, which (d) must act upon any information thus obtained. (e) Any alien immigrant who, within two years of his arrival, is ascertained " undesirable " or shall become a charge on public funds, except from ill-health, or shall have no visible means of support, may be ordered by a court of summary jurisdiction to leave this country.

5. Every effort should be made (a) to enforce with greater efficiency the law dealing with overcrowding, the existence of which (b) in any area be investigated, and (c, d, e) if it be found that the immigration of aliens has substantially contributed to any overcrowding, such area may be declared to be a prohibited area. (f) All alien immigrants on arrival to be registered, and change of residence during the first two years of stay in this country to be notified. If within that period (g) any alien shall be found resident within a prohibited area he shall be removed therefrom, and shall be guilty of an offence.

6. Upon conviction of any felony or misdemeanour, upon indictment, the judge may direct as part of the sentence that the alien thus convicted shall leave the country. If such direction be disobeyed, the alien may, on summary conviction, be punished as a rogue and a vagabond.

7. That further statutory powers shall be obtained for regulating the accommodation upon and condition of foreign immigrant passenger ships.

From these recommendations Sir Kenelm E. Digby, as well as Lord Rothschild, dissented. Both felt that the restrictive measures aimed at " undesirables " would unavoidably affect deserving and honest people; nor did the "overcrowd-ing" demand such drastic legislative measures as the majority of the Commission suggested.

However, a study of this Report cannot leave the reader in doubt that, while the Commission was ostensibly inquiring into the general subject of immigration, it was in fact con-cerned only with the Jewish aspect of the problem, "for it is either incomprehensible blindness or the merest cant to deny that the recommendations and the proposed legislation are directed against Jews ".[2]

## (A) THE ALIENS BILL OF 1904

Whatever the merits or demerits of this Report, its recom-mendations were so specific and emphatic that the Govern-ment felt that it had to consider some measure to be brought before Parliament. Seven months later, on March 29, 1904, Akers-Douglas, the Home Secretary in Balfour's cabinet, introduced in the House of Commons a "Bill to make pro-vision with respect to the Immigration of Aliens, and other matters incidental thereto ", which was "backed" by the Colonial Secretary (Alfred Lyttelton), the President of the Local Government Board (Walter Long) and the Parliamen-tary Under-Secretary at the Home Office (Thos. H. A. E. Cochrane). The Aliens Bill of 1904, as it was subsequently to become known, was the cause of Winston Churchill inter-vening for the first time, and very prominently, in a problem affecting Jews. The Bill's numerous recommendations were inevitably based on the Report of the Royal Commission. In short, it provided that

(1) The alien arriving in Britain might be required to furnish a certificate and particulars with respect to his character and antecedents, to his proposed place of residence and to his identification;

(2) "Undesirables" might be refused permission of entry;

(3) The Home Secretary should consider and finally deter-mine any case of detention and refusal to grant leave to land;

(4) Power (without details of its scope or limitations) should be given to the Secretary of State to exclude criminals;

(5) The dwelling or residence of aliens in a "prohibited

area " (i.e. one overcrowded according to any sanitary authority) might be either prohibited or regulated.

The Bill was introduced under the ten minute rule, which only permits two short speeches to be made in the House, and was given a first reading without a division on March 29, 1904. On April 25, 1904, the Bill passed the second reading by a majority of 124. Winston Churchill, although still officially a Conservative, then abstained from voting as the division list shows. During the second reading, Walter Long, President of the Local Government Board, told the House that the Government were not foolish enough to ask that their proposals should not be subject to amendment. " We are quite ready ", he said,[3] " to consider any suggestion which would have for its object the improvement of this Bill in order to secure the end that we all have in view ". Referring to this statement, the *Jewish Chronicle* in an editorial[4] called the attention of the Jewish leaders to this fact and pointed out that " it is necessary to make the most of the Government's accommodating disposition ". Nor did the leadership of Anglo-Jewry deal lightheartedly with the Bill and its possible anti-Jewish implications. All necessary preparations were made for the battle, the situation was surveyed, material (statistical, factual and other) was gathered and incorporated in a memorandum. On May 19, 1904, a deputation of the Board of Deputies, introduced by Lord Rothschild, was received by T. H. A. E. Cochrane, the Parliamentary Under-Secretary to the Home Office, and it put before him the Jewish objections to certain parts of the Bill. On this occasion speeches were delivered by Lord Rothschild, Sir Samuel Montagu (later Lord Swaythling), David L. Alexander, K.C. (President of the Board of Deputies), Claude Montefiore (President of the Anglo-Jewish Association) and Stuart M. Samuel, M.P.[5] Shortly after this, Winston Churchill participated publicly for the first time in the controversy on the Aliens Bill. In a letter to the President of the Old Hebrew Congregation in Manchester, Nathan Laski, he wrote:[6]

Dear Sir,—What has surprised me most in studying the papers you have been good enough to forward me is how few aliens there are in Great Britain. To judge by the talk there has been, one would have imagined we were being overrun by a swarming invasion and "ousted" from our island through neglect of precautions which every wise foreign nation has adopted. But it now appears from the Board of Trade statistics that all the aliens in Great Britain do not amount to a 140th part of the total population, that they are increasing less than 8,000 a year on the average, and that—according to the reports of the Alien Comimssion—Germany has twice as large and France four times as large a proportion of foreigners as we have. It does not appear, therefore, that there can be any urgent or sufficient reasons, racial or social, for departing from the old tolerant and generous practice of free entry and asylum to which this country has so long adhered and from which it has so often greatly gained.

While good cause for such a change is wanting, the machinery of enforcement is dangerous both in principle and detail. Parliament has always declined to confer upon police or customs officers acting under the Executive Government the kind of powers accorded by Clauses 1 and 2.[7] No one can tell how much bullying and blackmail might result from their application, or what an instrument of oppression they would furnish to the hand of an intolerant or anti-Semitic Home Secretary. The custom in England has hitherto been to allow police and Customs officers to act and report on facts, not to be the judges of characters and credentials. The objections against the new procedure have been very clearly stated by Lord Rothschild, a supporter of the present Government, in a recent speech.[8] He said: "The Bill introduced into the House of Commons proposes to establish in this country a loathsome system of police interference and espionage, of passports and arbitrary power exercised by police officers who in all probability will not understand the language of those upon whom they are called upon to sit in judgment. This is all contrary to the recommendations of the Royal Commission".

The machinery, though highly objectionable in its character, is, according to Sir Kenelm Digby, likely to prove largely unworkable in practice.[9] As it is admittedly impossible to apply the provisions of the Bill at all the ports of entry, the professional thief, anarchist, or prostitute — often well supplied with money — have only to pick their route with caution, and can pass in as easily as before. The simple immigrant, the political refugee, the helpless and the poor—these are the folk who will be caught in the trammels of the Bill, and may be harassed and hustled at the pleasure of petty officials without the smallest right of appeal to the broad justice of the English courts. When we come to such provisions as that contained in Clause 2, subsection 3,[10] which provides for the banishment of an alien who is proved by the testimony of the common informer, perhaps his private enemy or a trade rival, to have received parochial relief, as late as one year after the relief has ceased, we can only wonder that an English gentleman should make such proposals to the House of Commons in the 20th century.

The whole Bill looks like an attempt on the part of the Government to gratify a small but noisy section of their own supporters and to purchase a little popularity in the constituencies by dealing harshly with a number of unfortunate aliens who have no votes. It will commend itself to those who like patriotism at other people's expense and admire Imperialism on the Russian model. It is expected to appeal to insular prejudice against foreigners, to racial prejudice against Jews, and to labour prejudice against competition; and it will no doubt supply a variety of rhetorical phrases for the approaching election. The same men who are obstinate opponents of trade unionism will declaim about "the rights of British labour". Those who champion the interests of the slum landlords will dilate on the evils of overcrowding. Those who have been most forward in bringing Chinese into Africa will pose as the champions of racial purity at home. I take leave to doubt the wisdom of this Bill even as a political manœuvre. In spite of militarism and false ideas about trade, there is a growing spirit of fraternity between democracies. English working men are not so selfish as to be unsympathetic towards the victims of circumstances or oppression. They do not respond in any marked degree to the anti-Semitism which has darkned recent continental history; and I for one believe that they will disavow an attempt to shut out the stranger from our land because he is poor or in trouble, and will resent a measure which without any proved necessity smirches those ancient traditions of freedom and hospitality for which Britain has been so long renowned.

Yours very truly,

WINSTON S. CHURCHILL.

This letter gives a comprehensive summary of Churchill's opinion of the Bill. The *Jewish Chronicle*, in commenting on it, said[11] that "the community at large, Jewish and Christian alike, owe a debt of gratitude to Sir Kenelm Digby[12] and Mr. Winston Churchill for their searching and outspoken criticism of the Restriction Bill". At that time Churchill, who was a member of Parliament for Oldham, had taken an important political step by joining the Liberal Party. A seat was offered to him in North-West Manchester and in May 1904, at a meeting in the Free Trade Hall, he pronounced himself a supporter and follower of Richard Cobden, the Free Trade apostle.[13] Two weeks later he took his seat on the Liberal benches. Just then, on June 8, 1904, the Home Secretary moved in the Commons that the Order for Committee on the Aliens Bill be read and discharged, and that the Bill be referred to the Standing Committee. This was regarded by the Opposition as an attempt to avoid discussion in Committee of the House, and on this occasion Churchill, making his first speech from the Opposition benches, attacked this procedure by pointing out[14] that

The Home Secretary was the only person he had heard describe this Bill as non-contentious. What was meant by a non-contentious measure? Was it a Bill which could not be contended against, or to which no objection could be taken? If so, surely it could not be said this Bill came within that category. It raised all kinds of bitter and angry feelings in various parts of the country; it brought up questions of prejudice and passion. Many loyal supporters of the Government objected to the Bill, and Lord Rothschild himself had introduced to the right hon. Gentleman a deputation which complained of the Bill in moderate but powerful terms.[15] It was an abuse of language to describe the Bill as non-contentious, and nobody, except for Party purpose, would have made such a statement.

The present Bill bristled with questions of police, the liberty of the subject, race, and religion, and a multiplicity of detail, and, after all, detail was a matter of principle when a measure was wholly objected to. This Bill appeared to contain a sufficient number of clauses to make it an unpleasant, disagreeable and ill-tempered operation in Grand Committee, and moreover, if it passed the Grand Committee the whole business might be gone over again on Report. He thought the proposal showed that the Government were not in earnest. He had long suspected it because there were forces at work in the Government Party against the measure. If the Government intended to carry it they need not propose to send it to a Committee where the ordinary machinery for closure by compartments was not at their disposal. He thought this Bill was intended to deal with certain constituencies in the East End of London at the next Election. He ventured to say it then, and he said it again, that the Government was not in earnest about that Bill, and did not desire to pass it. They brought it forward in order to have an opportunity of saying they wished to deal with the subject, and in order to satisfy a demand made by those who were behind them. A variety of forces had acted upon the Government in regard to the Aliens Bill. His hon. and gallant friend the Member for Sheffield[16] had all his life been advocating this kind of legislation; there were those associated with the protectionist movement who thought it akin to their general line of political thought, and there was in his own Party opposition from wealthy Jewish supporters—very proper opposition—and consequently the Prime Minister was forced to choose between the different conflicting forces. The Government decided to make a show, and on the very first excuse made haste to drop it.

The *Jewish Chronicle,* welcoming Churchill's speech, observed in a leading article:[17] " It is tempting to accept the suggestion of Mr. Churchill that the Government is no longer in earnest about the measure, since upon its shaping in Committee depends whether the Bill shall work the revolutionary changes, which many speakers deprecated, or shall merely empower criminal judges to make the useful addition of banishment to sentences passed after a fair trial in open court."

The Bill was, on the Home Secretary's motion, committed to the Standing Committee on Law to which shortly afterwards a number of members were added by the Selection Committee, among them being Winston Churchill.[18] The Committee's scope was limited, for it could competently deal only with reshaping innocuous parts of the Bill which aimed at the repatriation of aliens; it could not investigate such questions as " prohibited areas " or the arbitrary power proposed to be conferred on inspectors at the landing places or on the Home Office to exclude or expel aliens without the formalities of a trial.

## THE BILL IN GRAND COMITTEE

The Grand Committee commenced its sittings on June 20, 1904, and sat until July 7. On a number of occasions heated debates took place, and dramatic scenes were not lacking. Churchill played a dominant rôle in these proceedings, and the survey published at the time in the *Jewish Chronicle*[19] conveys, better than a verbatim report may ever achieve, the atmosphere of the deliberations. It also illustrates accordingly much more vividly Churchill's fiery and courageous stand in this battle of words. It would require almost a volume of its own, to publish such a survey in this study, whereas it is possible to include only a brief and unavoidably inadequate summary.

The dominant impression to be gained from reading these reports is that it was mainly a battle for every sentence, every word, in the clauses under discussion, which filled the sessions of the Standing Committee. The battle (after the debate on Clause I had been postponed) commenced round Clause II of the Bill which read as follows:

If, on any inspection in pursuance of regulations made under this Act, it appears to the inspecting officer that any passenger who is being brought to the United Kingdom is an alien and—

(a) Comes under any of the categories set out in Part I of the Schedule to this Act; or

(b) Is suffering from any infectious or loathsome disease, or from any mental incapacity; or

(c) Refuses to furnish the prescribed certificates, particulars, or means of identification;

the inspecting officer may prohibit the landing of that passenger pending the decision of the Secretary of State on the case, or detain him pending such decision, and shall report the case to the Secretary of State.

The opposition to the Bill, headed by Sir Charles Dilke, C. P. Trevelyan, W. Runciman and Winston Churchill, expressed itself in the moving of a great number of amendments, each of which was hotly contended, debated at length, and finally voted upon. If a situation can arise where it takes hours to air all the pros and cons as regards the omission of the words " in pursuance of regulations made ", and more hours' quibble whether to omit the words " made under this Act " and insert in their place " to be hereafter set forth ", one is not surprised to read that as the hours passed by resentment rose against those who submitted such amendments and uncompromisingly fought for them. Particularly this applied to Winston Churchill, for not only had he joined the Liberal Opposition shortly before these debates, but he was also the mover or seconder of the Opposition amendments. The most conspicuous fact in this connection is the complete absence in a number of Committee meetings of any speeches on the part of the advocates of restrictions, so that the discussion was almost entirely confined to the Opposition. Commenting on this, Churchill remarked at one of the meetings: [20]

The truth was that the champions of the Bill sat stolidly silent. Throughout the whole sitting not a single sentence escaped the lips of Major Evans-Gordon or Sir Howard Vincent, and the Restrictionist party, with the exception of three or four brief interventions, remained wilfully dumb.

On the other hand the continuous intervention by Opposition members made the deliberations a rather one-sided affair which on some occasions displeased the Restrictionists, Churchill becoming a welcome target in this respect, too. Thus in one of the meetings, when an amendment put forward by Walter Runciman was under consideration, Churchill pressed the Home Secretary for a reply as to whether or no he was in favour of this amendment, but was interrupted by E. A. Goulding: " Can an hon. member speak seven times on the same amendment?" The paper at this point records[21] " loud laughter, and cries of ' Yes ' ", and Churchill's reply that " of course he could ". On a subsequent occasion Churchill was again attacked for speaking too often. By then, several days of protracted discussion had passed, the arguments having become more heated and the words less carefully chosen. Thus after a short remark Churchill was interrupted:[22]

> *Mr. Ridley* said that the repetition of the same arguments persistently, especially by the hon. member for Oldham,[23] could not be for any other purpose than that of wasting the time of the Committee. (Uproar.)

The Chairman called Ridley to order for this remark. Nevertheless, in the course of a subsequent intervention he repeated it, branding Churchill's attitude as " the avowed intention of wasting time ".

Such scenes could, of course, not remain without any influence on the smooth flow of the deliberations, and both parties were trying to find fault with the other whenever a chance arose. Thus while Churchill was attacked for having spoken too much and too often, he in turn asserted a conspiracy of silence on the Restrictionist side. During a speech by Churchill on an amendment, the leader of the Restrictionists, Major Evans-Gordon, conversed with some members of the Committee[24]

> which drew from Mr. Churchill the taunt that while the member for Stepney appeared anxious to reply, his friends were excitedly urging him to say nothing. This sarcastic remark was greeted with some commotion and cries of " You are quite wrong!" " Nothing of the kind."

With the deliberations dragging on without any noticeable results, a personal note crept increasingly into the debate. This reached a climax at the last meeting when finally Major Evans-Gordon explained the reasons for his silence during the discussions. His argument was[25] that the Opposition from the outset was out " to end, not mend, the Bill " and to " choke it with words till the time limit was reached ". But the sharpest rebuke he kept for Churchill who, he said, " was faithfully carrying out the instructions he had received from the party for which he was acting. He did not say for anybody in particular ". This brought Churchill immediately to his feet and, interrupting Major Evans-Gordon, he

> asked the hon. member whether he suggested that he had come there under instructions? Mr. Churchill referred to a suggestion made in the *Sun* newspaper that he was acting under instructions from Lord Rothschild, and said that he regretted that so foul a slander should be repeated here.[26]

Major Gordon replied that he had not seen the article in the *Sun*, and had no intention of attributing any such thing to him. He then withdrew the word " instructions ". When shortly afterwards Churchill spoke for the last time in the Committee, he remarked that he did not deny Major Gordon's sincerity in his rôle as the chief mourner for the Bill, but that the characteristic feature of the Bill in Grand Committee was[27]

> that the Government were torn between the wish to please those who were asking for the Bill, and the desire to conciliate those powerful and wealthy supporters of the Conservative Government in the country who were opposed to the Bill, and were using their influence to bring it down.

At this point Major Evans-Gordon interrupted the speaker saying that he supposed " that the hon. member was referring to the powerful Jewish supporters of the Government. But ", he continued, " he did not know that that was so. Some had brought influence to bear—by no means all—but what that influence was, he left to the hon. member."

Churchill's reply to this interruption is not fully recorded in the report, as the disorder that followed probably made it inaudible. Thus all we are told is that

> Mr. Churchill argued that the Government had been influenced by those desiring this legislation, and by powerful supporters whose support it was anxious to receive and who desired that it should not legislate. While anxious to solace wealthy Jewish supporters . . . (Disorder, Sir Harry Samuel exclaiming " Monstrous! Absolutely monstrous!") The hon. member proceeded to contend that the withdrawal of the Bill was a matter of Government responsibility.

At that particular moment the main argument centred round the question as to who caused the Bill to be abandoned. For at the beginning of this meeting the Home Secretary had announced[28] its withdrawal, since by the seventh day of its meetings the Committee " had taken only three lines of one clause. There were eleven clauses in the Bill, and something like 240 lines ". The time factor alone would make it impossible to have the discussion completed during the session, and therefore he suggested that the Committee should not proceed with the consideration of the Bill. Charges that Churchill was guilty of having " killed the Bill " were then proferred more and more vociferously, and found their most outspoken expression in the speech of the Attorney-General, Sir Robert Finlay, K.C., who said[29] that Churchill " really had one principle—to kill the Bill ". This charge remained for a long time to come an oft-repeated slogan in the subsequent controversies and debates on the question of alien immigration. True, Churchill cannot be altogether absolved from blame. While he denied strongly that the killing of the Bill was his object, the following interjection at a previous meeting is recorded: [30]

> *Attorney General*: I accept the assurance of the hon. members opposite that they do not desire to wreck the Bill.
> *Mr. Churchill*: Don't accept that from me. (Laughter.)

In addition to these controversies and quibbles, the report on the deliberations in Grand Committee brought to light a phenomenon which so often appeared in Jewish history to the detriment of Jewish interests — the rôle of the self-appointed Jewish spokesman. It has been mentioned that Sir Harry Samuel interrupted Churchill during his last speech in Committee. Shortly afterwards Sir Harry outlined his own view of the problem by pointing out[31] that " in East London a large number of foreigners belonging to his race had settled in a compact mass and driven many Britishers from their homes . . . He had, unfortunately, been an eyewitness, day after day, of foreigners who had landed and made money here, buying up whole streets and sub-letting only to those of their own race." And in order not to leave his listeners in doubt Sir Harry said that in taking this attitude " he felt that he was doing his duty as an Englishman—his family had lived here for generations—and a Jew." It is worthy of note in this connection that no other speaker in Grand Committee throughout the seven days of its deliberations had ever used any such language on Jewish aliens as did Sir Harry Samuel. It is, therefore, not surprising that a little later, when a number of speakers rose in order to catch the chairman's eye, there were cries, particularly from Sir Howard Vincent, one of the leaders of the protagonists of the Bill, for Stuart M. Samuel, the other Jewish member of the Committee (and no relation to the former). In his speech Stuart Samuel disposed of Sir Harry Samuel's attack in three sentences:[32] " Sir Harry Samuel had referred to the attitude of the Jewish community. He could assure the Committee that Sir Harry Samuel was the only member of the Jewish community, at all well-known, who had ever appeared on any platform convened by the member for Stepney[33] and his friends. That he thought, completely disposed of the question of the attitude of the Jewish community."

There is no indication in the report how Churchill (or any other members) reacted to the internal Jewish strife thus brought into the open. Nevertheless, in view of what Churchill has to say about the quarrels within the Jewish community,[34] one can assume that incidents such as that referred to here did not fail to leave an impression on one who took such a courageous stand on behalf of Jewish immigrants. For it was particularly the Jewish immigrants whom Churchill had at heart and whose right to come to Britain he defended.

As he made clear to the Committee[35]

> He did not wish to close the door against the unfortunate Hebrew coming from the Continent.

The underlying principles of his fight against the Bill as expressed in his numerous short speeches when dealing with the various amendments, can be summarized from his last speech:[36]

> Mr. Churchill went on to contend that the opposition to the Bill was based on broad, general principles, long held in veneration in this country. There were three main objections to the measure. It endangered the right of asylum to political offenders and the poor and unfortunate. It allowed a police officer or Customs House officer to pronounce on matters of opinion, and it created a different status for people living together in this country, an enactment which he described as impossible and improper. All should be free and equal before the law of the land.

## THE AFTERMATH

The speeches in the last session of the Grand Committee had set the theme for Government and Opposition to justify their respective attitudes towards the Bill in the eyes of the public. Major Evans-Gordon's forecast that " the Bill was dead but that the agitation would remain "[37] was soon to prove true. Newspapers analysed the pros and cons of the aliens question, and meetings took place all over London and the country.[38] As was to be expected, Churchill came under heavy attack. A Mr. A. T. Williams did not hesitate to call him publicly " the renegade Churchill "[39] and other speakers found other no less abusive epithets for him. The *Jewish Chronicle* did not fall into the other extreme, but in a cool evaluation of the situation stated in a leader:[40] " Not for the first time in modern history an Aliens Bill has failed to pass the Legislature. The measure which was abandoned yesterday week was not afforded a reasonable chance of passing by those who were responsible for its production. We dismiss the suggestion of Mr. Churchill that the Government were never in earnest about it, and that their lukewarmness was due to weighty Jewish influences. The member for Stepney[41] and his friends, who brought such undisguised pressure upon the Government in favour of this legislation, could not object to the exertion of contrary influences. But it is not necessary to assume that there has been any ' Jewish ' pressure. The delay in the passage of the Aliens Bill has been no greater than that which has occurred in the case of the Licensing Bill, the Port of London Bill and other measures. The situation in all these cases can be accounted for by a variety of causes into which one need not enter in detail here."

Churchill took no part in the public hair-splitting about words that followed the abandonment of the Bill. Only once, in a letter to a correspondent, summarising his stand in the matter, he said, *inter alia*:[42]

If the Government had been in earnest about the Aliens Bill, they would never have sent it to a Grand Committee, but would have kept it in Committee of the House itself, where they could have used the Closure, have sat up late, and where their large majority would have been effective. Had they chosen to do this they could certainly have passed the whole thing in eight or ten days. No doubt those members who resisted the Bill in Grand Committee would equally have resisted it in the House. But the fortunes of the Licensing Bill are sufficient proof that they would have met with a very different measure of success. I was myself astonished at the decision to send the Bill upstairs, and I said so at the time in debate. Since studying its details more closely I no longer wonder that the Government did not care about passing it. For, quite apart from the principles involved, many of its provisions were bound to prove quite unworkable in practice. But the truth is that Ministers have been playing with this subject for years under the influence of conflicting forces. First the pressure in its favour from the East London members and from the protectionists who regard this kind of legislation as a part of the Birmingham-Sheffield programme. Secondly, the resistance of some of their most influential Jewish supporters, who—to their honour as I think—are opposed to the Bill. In these circumstances the Government seem to have decided to toss the Bill to the Grand Committee on Law, to make just enough show of fight to satisfy its supporters, and then at the first excuse to withdraw the Bill and try to throw the blame on the Opposition.    This, no doubt, explains why they refused a compromise which would have enabled them by general consent to exclude criminals from our shores, and to banish foreigners who by conviction for serious offences are proved to have abused the hospitality they have received.

There was one last occasion when Churchill intervened officially in matters relating to the abandonment of the Bill. When the Prime Minister, Arthur James Balfour, announced in Parliament the withdrawal of the Bill and indicated that no time would be wasted by making an effort to pass restrictive legislation, Churchill rose and again put his case in a short passage,[43] repeating the arguments which led him to conclude that the Government was not in earnest about the Bill and was finally quite pleased to drop it.

Thus ends the story of the Aliens Bill of 1904.

*

It is not without irony that during the period covered in this chapter, on August 14, 1903—the very day of the publication of the *Report of the Royal Commission on Alien Immigration*—the British Government submitted to Herzl's London representative, J. L. Greenberg, an offer for the establishment of an autonomous Jewish settlement in the East African protectorate; and that on the very first day of the meeting of the Grand Committee which considered the Aliens Bill—June 20, 1904—Parliament debated this offer. The president of the Zionist Organisation, Dr. Theodor Herzl, one of the most prominent witnesses to appear before the Royal Commission, died during the deliberations of the Grand Committee, on July 3, 1904.    Four days later, on the day of his burial, the Aliens Bill was withdrawn. Israel Zangwill, speaking on that day at a memorial meeting at the Great Assembly Hall in London, said:[44] " Who can say where Herzl will lie buried, since his living influence is everywhere? It could easily be traced, even in the withdrawal of the Aliens Bill, anent which he gave evidence—the withdrawal which, by a cheering coincidence, comes to diminish the darkness of his funeral day."

## (B)   THE ALIENS ACT, 1905

The heat of the war of words engendered by the delibera- tions in the Grand Committee on the Aliens Bill, 1904, made the ruling party blind to any suggestion emanating from the Opposition, however useful it may have been. Thus the Government's refusal of the offer of the Liberal members, to pass a short measure providing that all foreigners found guilty of crimes in Britain should be expelled, made a wide and intensive propaganda possible. While it was felt on every side, without any exception, that criminal aliens should not be admitted to Britain, the failure of the Government to provide legislation for that limited contingency and their desire to extend the stringency upon the innocent immigrant as well, made the debate on the aliens problem a renewed subject for the Press and for public meetings. Small incidents such as the imprisonment of two burglars who had only been in England a few weeks[1] were sufficient to add fury to the anti-alien propaganda. But the usual full head of steam was in the meantime raised by ministers as well as by leaders of the restrictionist movement. Joseph Chamberlain set the ball rolling with a violent anti-alien speech at Limehouse in December, 1904.[2] He spoke of the " unrestricted immigration of people " under which the inhabitants of the East End were suffering. " The evils of this immigration have increased ", he continued, " during recent years. And behind those people who have already reached these shores, remember there are millions of the same kind who, under easily conceivable circumstances, might follow their track, and might invade this country in a way and to an extent of which few people have at present any conception. The same causes that brought 10,000 and 20,000 and tens of thousands, may bring hundreds of thousands, or even millions. If that would be an evil, surely he is a statesman who would deal with it in the beginning." But he did not only plead for the introduction of a Bill restricting alien immigration. He felt it his duty also to point out that the Jewish immigrants were " driven from their homes by the grossest and most brutal persecution ", and he therefore advocated a solution in a passage full of warmth

and respect for Theodor Herzl, whom he had met in connection with the suggestions for Jewish autonomous settlements
in the Sinai Peninsula and in East Africa.[3] Chamberlain
proclaimed himself an adherent of the Zionist solution of the
Jewish problem. Herzl's warning words uttered at the last
meeting between the two statesmen on April 23, 1903, may
still have resounded in Chamberlain's ears. For when he had
informed Herzl of the possibility that an Aliens Bill might be
introduced in England, the Zionist leader exclaimed:[4] " If you
allow me to say so, Mr. Chamberlain, I should prefer for
England's glory that you do not make such a Bill. Drain them
elsewhere, but don't make an Alien Bill." In the heat of the
controversy about the alien problem only Chamberlain's anti-
alien attitude with its exaggerated figures and implications,
not his positive suggestions were remembered.

Soon afterwards the campaign for the by-election in the
Mile End Division turned " chiefly on the aliens question ".[5]
This constituency, situated almost in the heart of the aliens'
area, was called upon to express its vote for or against restrictive immigration measures. The Unionist candidate Harry
Lawson (of Jewish descent),[6] who favoured legislation on the
pattern of the withdrawn Bill of 1904, was opposed by the
Liberal candidate Bertram Stuart Strauss, a professing Jew.
The greatly reduced majority of the Unionist candidate, which
dropped from 1,160 to 78, came as a shock to the Government
which, as the Jewish Chronicle pointed out,[7] with " no casuis-
try, however laboured or tortuous, can construe this as a
mandate to proceed with a drastic measure of restriction next
session ".

Parallel with these events the Standard newspaper took the
lead in publishing anti-alien articles. The most conspicuous
series in that paper came from the pen of a special commissioner, R. H. Sherard, and aroused heated debates and a lively
controversy in the general press and particularly in the
columns of the Jewish Chronicle.[8] Other newspapers and
magazines in those days also carried articles on this problem,
and reported on meetings up and down the country calling
for restrictions or opposing them.

Churchill kept mostly aloof from the actual controversy
which followed the withdrawal of the Bill of 1904, and preceded the introduction of the new Bill. In reply to an inquiry

by a correspondent at that particular moment, he said in a short note that he thought the Government were not so much concerned with the Bill, as with the problem of their own fortunes at the next election: [9]

> The Government did not want the Bill. They wanted the grievance. They were anxious not to legislate, but to electioneer.

This referred to the election then pending in Mile End. However, this evaluation of the motives underlying the propaganda round the Bill was later seen to apply also to the general election and strikingly demonstrates Churchill's foresight in political matters. Thus on the occasion of the second reading of the new Aliens Bill Sir Charles Dilke spoke[10] of a " statement made in the country by a leading member of the Cabinet. He told his constituents that the Government could not dissolve yet, because it was necessary for them first to pass this measure." As it later turned out, soon after the Aliens Bill became the Aliens Act, the Government resigned and the general election took place.[11] It was in connection with the Mile End election that Churchill, after some interval, took again a more prominent stand in the Aliens question. The *Westminster Gazette* carried the following " Note " on the subject: [12]

> The Alien Immigration question is likely to be a prominent and burning one in the coming election in the Mile End Division, and in view of this Mr. Winston Churchill has done good service by throwing some light on the question of the Government's Alien Bill of last Session. Mr. Churchill, writing in reply to a correspondent, points out that the Government could have carried the Bill without opposition if they had dropped the controversial parts and limited it to providing for the exclusion of criminal aliens. The Government, however, would have all or none, and the Bill was lost. To accuse the Opposition, therefore, of facilitating the influx of criminal aliens into this country is unjust, although we have no doubt the statement will be freely made. What the view of those who opposed the Bill in its entirety was is thus set forth by Mr. Winston Churchill: " Shut out the alien;

if diseased, always; if immoral, when you can find out; if criminal, after you have convicted; but do not shut out persons merely because they are poor, and do not thrust upon police and Custom House officers duties which they cannot properly discharge." Undoubtedly the condition of affairs in Russia has induced an exceptional number of fugitives from military service to come here; but it seems, to judge from what one hears in certain quarters, to be deliberately " forgotten " that a large proportion of these immigrants are on their way elsewhere. We doubt whether many of those who were amongst the unemployed in the Trafalgar-square demonstration[13] yesterday could trace their lack of employment, either directly, or indirectly, to alien immigration, but in any case we agree with Mr. Churchill that it would not be in accordance with British traditions to close the doors against the unfortunates who have fled to this country.

But, as was to be expected, the Government felt impelled to do something in the matter, particularly as its prominent members one by one spoke and wrote about a new Bill to be submitted to Parliament in place of the one withdrawn in the previous session. Thus A. J. Balfour, the Prime Minister, told his party friends[14] that there would be no necessity " to trouble you and other London Unionist members to come to me on a deputation in order to urge upon the Government the necessity of proceeding with the Aliens Bill. The measure is one to which the Government attach the very greatest importance. It will be introduced on Tuesday, and I hope the second reading will be taken at the very earliest date after Easter which the general course of public business admits. You and your friends may rest assured that the Government will use their best endeavours to get it passed into law." Accordingly the Home Secretary, Akers-Douglas, on April 14, 1905, moved under the ten minute rule, for leave to bring in the new Aliens Bill.[15] It was also " backed " by Arthur James Balfour, the Prime Minister, Sir Robert B. Finlay, the Attorney General, T. H. Cochrane, Under-Secretary of the Home Office, and Bonar Law, Parliamentary Secretary to the Board of Trade.[16] The motion for the Home

Secretary was passed without a division and the Bill was read a first time.[17]

In his opening speech the Home Secretary outlined the objects of the Bill as follows: [18]

" With regard to the actual provisions of the Bill, it deals with the prevention of landing of undesirable aliens; it provides that no immigrant shall be landed from an immigrant ship except at a port where there is an immigration officer appointed under the Act, and without leave of that immigration officer given after he has made an inspection in company with a medical inspector.  In cases where leave to land has been refused the immigrant or the master of the ship may appeal to a board appointed at each port where immigrant ships may land immigrants and this Board is to consists of three persons of whom one shall be a magistrate and the others have acquaintance with Poor Law and administrative matters.  We hope thus to obtain the co-operation of the Jewish Board of Guardians in order that the interests of that community, especially in London, where it is very large, may be properly respected.  And we decide that an immigrant shall be considered undesirable, and, as such, may be refused permission to land, if he cannot show that he has —or is in a position to obtain—means to support himself in a decent condition; if he is a lunatic, or an idiot, or, owing to disease or infirmity, is likely to become a charge on the rates or otherwise a detriment to the public; and if he has been sentenced abroad for an extraditable crime, not being of a political character, or if he has been previously expelled under this Act.  The landing of an immigrant, however, shall not be refused on the ground only of means if he proves that he is seeking admission solely to avoid prosecution for an offence of a political character. That is the first part of the Bill.

" The second part deals with the exclusion of undesirable aliens who are already in our midst.  To secure this the Secretary of State may make an expulsion order requiring an alien to leave the United Kingdom within a time which he fixes, and afterwards to remain out of it, but the Secretary of State can only act on the certificate of a court of law, including the court of summary jurisdiction, if he is satisfied that the alien has been convicted of an offence for which he can be imprisoned without the option of a fine, and that the court recommends the expulsion, either in addition to, or in lieu of, the sentence which he receives. Then, again, an alien may be sent out of the country if the certificate is given to the Secretary of State of a court of summary jurisdiction within twelve months of the last entry to this country of the alien, showing that the alien has, within three months from the time the proceedings were commenced, received parochial relief of such a character as would disqualify him from holding the parliamentary franchise, which is a condition that is well-known, or that he has been convicted of an extradition crime abroad. The Secretary of State, further, has power to pay the expenses of the departure of the alien, but such expenses he can recover from the master of the ship who brought the alien if the expulsion order is made on a certificate within the six months of his landing. Further, that liability will not only extend to the shipowner, or to the master of the ship, but to that particular line of shipping. Then the obligation which falls on the master of the ship at the present time to make a return will be continued, but these returns will have to be made in a very much more exhaustive and much more accurate way, than that in which they are now made. This, very shortly, is the Bill which I ask leave to introduce."

The first reaction to this new Bill among the opponents of restriction and in the Jewish Press was one of comparison between the two proposals. No doubt was then left in the mind of readers that " the new Aliens Bill is an improvement upon its predecessor ".[19]   At the same time, the positive differences were contrasted with the old provisions in the following main clauses:[20] (a) While the last Bill was throughout full of statements about overcrowding, the new Bill was completely indifferent to this problem. (b) It therefore did not include the absurd provision concerning prohibited areas. (c) There was no provision forcing an alien to furnish "prescribed certificates and particulars with regard to his character and antecedents, and with regard to his proposed place of residence in the United Kingdom, and to furnish the prescribed means of identification ". (d) Nor was the clause retained which required aliens to keep the police informed of all changes of address during the early years of residence in this country. (e) The new Bill also differed in matters of machinery from its predecessor. No longer would the inspecting officer decide provisionally whether or not an alien came within one or the other category of " undesirables "; this was now to be entrusted to an immigration officer accompanied by a medical inspector. (f) In the new Bill the alien had the right to appeal to an Immigration Board as to his admission. It was suggested that the Jewish Board of Guardians be invited to co-operate on that Board.

After this first reaction to the Bill the debate on the second reading of the Bill brought to light a more elaborate analysis which was to guide the Opposition to a number of its provisions. The debate took place on May 2 and was opened by Sir Charles Dilke. He pointed out[21] that the whole Bill rested on the old fallacies and delusions and that the " misrepresentation which is going on is stupendous ", particularly with regard to the numbers of aliens as produced by the Government. He moved an amendment[22] " that this House, holding that the evil of low-priced alien labour can best be met by legislation to prevent sweating, desires to assure itself, before assenting to the Aliens Bill, that sufficient regard is had in the proposed measure to the retention of the principle of asylum for the victims of persecution ".

The amendment was, however, declared lost when the House divided and the second reading of the Bill subsequently agreed to without a division.[23]

Churchill is neither recorded as having participated in the debate nor is his name mentioned in the division list.[24] From his later vehement opposition to the Bill we can conclude that he was not among those " leaders of the Liberal party, [who] frightened, apparently, by that appeal from the East End Liberal members and candidates, have abstained so far from opposing the Bill ".[25] He was to become increasingly prominent in the fight the nearer the date for the Committee stage of the Bill drew.

The Bill having meanwhile been more closely analysed in the debate on the second reading and among Jewish leaders, it became apparent that, despite its improvements upon its predecessor, a number of amendments were called for to prevent the proposed new legislation becoming merely a measure against innocent immigrants. The Board of Deputies therefore met in special session on May 8, 1905, to discuss the Aliens Bill in the light of a memorandum specifically prepared for that purpose by the Immigration Committee of the Board. It constituted a detailed analysis of the new Bill and stressed the objectionable clauses simultaneously outlining suggestions for amendments.[26]

During the debate the question was considered in what way the various amendments suggested should be brought to the notice of Parliament and eventually incorporated in the final text of the Bill. Herbert Bentwich suggested an approach through various congregations all over the country to their local Members of Parliament[27] and this form of conveying the memorandum to the Members of Parliament was agreed upon. Subsequently in every Jewish community in the British Isles addresses were submitted to local Members of Parliament to acquaint them with the defects of the Bill, and requesting them either to move or support an amendment in the House. In most cases the memorandum of the Board of Deputies was used, but a form of address proposed by the *Jewish Chronicle*[28] also became very popular. It contained the following main points which called for amendments of the Bill:

1. The Bill does not make any exception in the case of victims of religious persecution.

2. No right of appeal to the ordinary courts of law is open to persons refused permission to land or who, having been allowed to land, are threatened with expulsion from the country; or to shipping companies to be burdened with the expense of their maintenance and re-shipment.

3. The Bill enables an expulsion order to be made on some grounds which are exceedingly trivial, for example, for " living under insanitary conditions due to overcrowding ".

4. The Bill throws on the shipping companies the cost of maintaining and returning aliens, who, though having once been permitted to land, are subsequently expelled for reasons over which the shipping companies have no control. The effect of this would be to stop the whole of the steerage passenger traffic.

The amendment movement spread quickly and the pages of the *Jewish Chronicle* are full of enthusiastic reports about this political offensive which did "the greatest credit to the Jewish community ".[29]

Churchill too received this memorandum and made full use of it at his first public appearance in a new crusade for the improvement of the second Bill. In a speech in Manchester on June 28 he moved the following resolution[30] which explicitly contained a reference to the "printed Statement" as published in the *Jewish Chronicle*:

> That this large and representative meeting of Manchester and Salford Citizens held in the Midland Hotel, Manchester, under the Presidency of W. Joynson-Hicks, Esq., is of opinion that the proposed Aliens Bill requires amending in the directions indicated in the printed Statement now read, and which has been issued with the circular convening this Meeting.

He motivated the resolution in a speech in which he agreed with the first impression created by the new Bill that it constituted an improvement on the last one. He expressed particular satisfaction with the results of his endeavours during the debates in Grand Committee on the old Bill, as the new Bill contained a number of alterations based on those principles for which he had stood. In his speech he said:

> We have met to discuss a matter that is doubtless urgent to North-West Manchester, and excites the greatest possible interest in that quarter, but although of the greatest importance to many, could not be considered a national question. In certain parts of London, Leeds and Glasgow likewise, the formation of certain alien communities raises a novel and peculiar problem of unusual perplexity. But as a whole to British people it is not a serious or a large question, nor a social or economic question, but entirely a political question. The number of aliens in this country is small in proportion to the population, and smaller than in any other country in Europe except Spain. Mr. Akers-Douglas last year gave large figures relating to alien immigration into England. A large number certainly landed, but it was

proved conclusively by the returns that many were en route to the United States or Canada, and only a comparatively small number remained. The total increase of the whole alien population did not exceed 7,000 or 8,000, and this can certainly not be considered large, taken with the fact that the native population increases at the rate of 400,000 per annum. The present Bill was, however, not aimed at reducing the quantity, but at improving the quality, of the aliens who reside in this country, and it is solely aimed to keep out the undesirable. All are agreed on the general principles of expulsion, and I should give large powers of expulsion to the executive against alien immigrants who abuse the hospitality of this country, likewise to those considered a nuisance or a burden in the country. Let the facts, however, be decided by a court of summary jurisdiction, not by the stroke of a pen of some official. There is no doubt a proportion of crime, prostitution and disease brought into this country by a number of aliens, but this is not due to Jewish immigrants but to American immigrants who land at western ports and at none of these ports is the Bill to have any machinery. If a plan could be devised to separate the good and the bad immigrants I should heartily welcome such plan—I want, however, to be assured that the machinery would not cost more than the advantages gained. I want likewise to feel assured that the provisions do not violate the general ideas of freedom always guarded so carefully in this country, nor lightly desecrate, those ideas of hospitality for which this country has in days gone by reaped no unworthy advantages. Last year I laid down three principles which should be regarded in dealing with alien immigration. It is not practicable to allow officials, such as coastguardsmen, Custom House officers, or the police, to form opinions upon difficult questions that deal with matters of such importance as the antecedents of immigrants, their general character, their ability to maintain themselves or their families, or their liability to disease. Secondly, mere poverty by itself should be no bar to prohibit a man entering this country. I am of opinion that a man's own personal strength, his own bodily

vigour as a man is in itself an asset to us, a valuable
commercial asset that could in itself be capitalized to an
assured amount. The want of funds should not, and
ought not, to reduce that man to the undignified position
of a pauper. Thirdly, political refugees or religious
refugees should not be deprived of an asylum on British
shores. The Bill of last year I learnt was not drafted by
experts, but was an amateurish plan known by the
department to be unworkable. I am glad to be able to
state that although I was styled obstructionist almost all
the proposals I made in Grand Committee last year have
been accepted in drafting the Bill this year. I was told
my amendments were of a partizan and farcical character, but these very amendments were those brought forward this year, and, therefore, I regard the 1905 Aliens
Bill as a great improvement on the Bill of 1904. I must
also admit that if the proposed amendments can be
humanely administered no great evil could possibly
occur, and some advantages might, perhaps, be gained.
I, therefore, do not even regret the obloquy or abuse—
foul abuse — and the indescribable letters I received
regarding my attitude in obstructing the 1904 Bill. I am
not sanguine, however, of this Bill producing very satisfactory results.

Manchester was particularly active in keeping the public
informed about the stages of the fight against the defamatory
clauses in the new Bill. For this purpose a special sub-com-
mittee was created consisting of[31] B. I. Belisha[32] (Chairman),
Nathan Laski[33] (Treasurer), Dr. J. Dulberg (Hon. Secretary),
J. Besso, S. Finburgh, and H. B. Morris. They organized
meetings, made information available to the press, and kept
in close contact with their co-religionists. A meeting of all
congregations on July 3 to consider further steps for the sub-
committee's activities heard Dr. Dulberg read a letter he had
received from Churchill wherein[34]

acknowledging a letter of appreciation of his valuable
services, he stated that he was in hopes the Government
would see their way to accept some of the proposed
amendments.

On the same day Churchill put the resolution which he had moved at the Manchester meeting on record in *Hansard* by rising at question time and asking:[35]

> I beg to ask the First Lord of the Treasury whether his attention has been called to the resolution relating to the Aliens Bill passed on the 28th June at a meeting of citizens held in the Midland Hotel, Manchester, presided over by the Conservative candidate for North-West Manchester and supported by many gentlemen of both political Parties . . .

At this point Churchill read out the four basic demands as printed in the draft statement proposed by the *Jewish Chronicle* and concluded his question,

> whether, having regard to the fact that these resolutions were passed at a non-Party meeting not opposed to the general principle of excluding undesirable aliens by law, His Majesty's Government will endeavour to introduce the desired modifications into the Bill during its passage through the Committee stage.

The Speaker, however, ruled that this question was out of order.

While these efforts were being made, the Committee stage of the Bill was in full swing. It began on Tuesday, June 27, 1905, a day before the big meeting in Manchester, and lasted until July 10. The minutes of these deliberations read almost like a repetition of the debates in Grand Committee of the previous year. Again, as on the last occasion, a great number of amendments were moved and hours of heated debate devoted to such questions as whether or not to insert " passenger " instead of " immigrant ", and similar submissions which were of course mostly moved by the Opposition to improve the Bill. Churchill himself did not move any amendment during the Committee stage of the Bill, but he spoke in support of most of these amendments. His enormous energy and perseverance cannot be better illustrated than by stating that in the debate on the Bill on June 27 he spoke no less than thirteen times.[36]   On July 3 he intervened thirty-two times,[37] on July 10 once,[38] on July 11 six times,[39] on July 17 once[40] and also once on July 18,[41] altogether intervening fifty-four times. They were mostly brief remarks, very much to the point, which occasionally involved him in bitter and often heated exchanges with the government side. Only once during that period did he dwell at length on the importance of an amendment moved by A. Emmott, his successor at Oldham, since it seemed to him to elaborate a point of principle relating to the Bill and the Aliens question. He said in the debate:[42]

> The question of alien immigration divided itself absolutely into two sections—the exclusion of immigrants in volume and the improvement in the quality of immigration. It was as easy to reduce the quantity as it was hard to improve the quality. The Government had been asked to-night to which of these two courses they adhered. Did they want reduction in the body of alien immigration, or was it an improvement in the quality they were seeking? In regard to quality, the attitude which many on his side of the House has adopted was well known to the Committee. They wished to exclude the undesirable alien. If there was a practical plan, produce it by all means, and there would not be any great objection. Nothing else, on the other hand, would be more easy than to reduce the number of alien immigrants. But the necessity must be shown in statistics. Did right hon. Gentlemen opposite deny that there were fewer aliens in this country in proportion to the population than in any other country? It had been denied to-night by one of the most able Members on the Treasury Bench—the Parliamentary Secretary to the Board of Trade [Mr. A. Bonar Law]. The hon. Member stated that 75,000 aliens settled in this country last year. Did the Attorney General [Sir Robert B. Finlay] make himself responsible for that figure? Was the right hon. and learned Member a party to that assertion? He paused for a reply. He was sorry the Parliamentary Secretary to the Board of Trade was not in his place. There were very great disadvantages in the course of debate when members of the Government who occupied positions of importance came down to the House and made highly controversial speeches, and did not remain to hear the criticism, or to answer enquiries which might arise. If 75,000 immigrants came to this country

last year, and if the Parliamentary Secretary to the Board of Trade was right that in the last ten years the increase in the alien population of this country had been 750,000, that was a very serious number. An increase of 7,000 a year would not be a serious question, because the population was increasing at the rate of 400,000 a year, but 750,000 in ten years would indeed be a serious question and would justify some of the enthusiasm of the hon. Gentlemen opposite. If that number had landed in this country in the last ten years, where had they all been accommodated? It was only in particular districts in the country—in Stepney and in the East End of London, in parts of Glasgow and Leeds, that the alien question had produced a problem of a grave and complex character, but those were only particular districts, and so far as he knew they were the only localities in this country where the question could be said to be real. He admitted that it may be an acute question in these cases, but it was in no sense a national or racial, or an economic question . . .

The Royal Commission[43] said the nearest approach to accurate information about the number of alien immigrants who settled annually was to be found in the Census Returns, and these Returns stated that the number was between 6,000 and 7,000 and not between 70,000 and 80,000. If those figures were wrong the statement they had heard from the Treasury Bench was most misleading. If the Secretary to the Board of Trade believed that they were correct he could not have made himself thoroughly acquainted with the details of the question on which he professed to advise the House; and if the hon. Gentleman believed that they were not correct, then he would be drawn to a conclusion which the Chairman would not allow him to express in Parliamentary language. He wished to direct the attention of the Committee to the fact that when these grossly inaccurate figures were quoted, no one on the Treasury Bench got up and supported them; but, nevertheless, the Prime Minister [Mr. A. J. Balfour], the Minister in charge of the Bill [Mr. A. Akers-Douglas], the Under-Secretary for the Home Department [Mr. T. H. Cochrane], and the

right hon. and learned Attorney-General, instead of putting the Committee right on the matter, all sat there and
took full advantage of allowing the House to believe the
statements which they at least knew to be misleading.
He should regret to have to put an undue strain on the
indulgence of hon. Gentlemen opposite. He would support in the division the Amendment of his hon. friend
[Mr. A. Emmott], because it embodied the simple proposition, on the merits of which the country would have to
decide, that in the present state of alien immigration, and
in the present state of labour and trade in this country,
mere poverty, as such, should not be sufficient reason for
excluding aliens from our shores. That was a substantive
proposition which would induce him to support the hon.
Gentleman in the lobby. But he could not resist a passing expression of contempt at the spectacle of a great
Party trying to retrieve its shattered reputation by exploiting and aggravating the miseries of some of the weakest
and poorest of mankind.

The debates on the Bill in the House of Commons lasted
until July 20, when the third reading was carried by a majority
of 90.[44] Only one of the amendments framed by the Board of
Deputies, as mentioned below,[45] had been successful.[46] While
the amendments submitted by the Opposition were lost, some
alterations in the original text were finally made and incorporated in the Act.[47] These changes were the result of the
arguments advanced during the debate by the Opposition
speakers, who concentrated their attacks mainly on refuting
the principles upon which the Bill was based, contrasting them
with factual evidence derived from immigration statistics,
and bearing on the housing problem, the labour market and
other angles with the result that the ground was knocked
from under the proposed legislation. But the Government
was set on having its way and carried the Bill with the help
of its mechanical majority. The subsequent passage through
the House of Lords was then only a formality. And so, on
August 11, 1905, the 5 Edward VII, c.13, was added to the
Statute Book of the country in the form of the Aliens Act,
1905, to come into force on January 1, 1906. It was received
by the Jewish community in Britain with deep disappointment

for, as a contemporary chronicler pointed out,[48] " Great Britain bowed its neck to clamour nurtured and fostered by racial prejudice, and for the first time for centuries, yielded up its proud privilege of rendering free asylum to the oppressed of all the world ". But it was not only Anglo-Jewry that was disappointed. It was feared that this Act would also affect Jews in other lands, "for, every Jew hater and Jew persecutor will point to this Act as his justification, and argue with much plausibility that, if even England has had to legislate against the Jew, is it not proof that he is right in other circumstances to exercise towards him more violent methods?"[49]

The Act as finally adopted[50] left some important clauses open to interpretation and thus made their implementation and application dependent on the goodwill of the governments of the day. It was particularly regretted that the Board of Deputies' suggestion with regard to an unambiguous definition of refugees to be admitted on grounds of religious or political persecution was only partly accepted by the Prime Minister. Thus one of the most important provisions affecting Jewish immigrants, namely whether to take a broader or narrower view in individual cases was to be left entirely in the hands and to the discretion of immigration officials.[51]

The very vagueness of the Act provided of course further ammunition for the Opposition in its continuing fight against the Government and in its appeal to the country to demand improvements of a number of provisions. Churchill took the opportunity of a visit to Manchester on October 9, 1905, to tell a meeting:[52]

This Act is a sham. It contains absurdities which would make a deaf and blind mute roar with laughter. A poverty line is drawn for the first time, a few shillings make the difference between desirability and undesirability. The Act will not in any degree alter the situation in England. On the other hand, it may inflict hardships upon many deserving people, who seek a refuge of our shores, and it violates that tradition of British hospitality of which this nation has been proud, and for the practice of which it has at more than one period reaped marked and permanent advantage.

As the Balfour Government resigned at the beginning of December, i.e. before the date of the coming into effect of the Act, it is impossible to know how that Government, having fought so ardently for this legislation and having succeeded in pushing it through Parliament, would have carried it out in practice. The subsequent general elections of January 1906 brought about one of the worst defeats the Conservative Party has ever suffered. The Liberal Government, set up in December, was returned with a great majority. Churchill, who had been invited to join the new Government as Under-Secretary for the Colonies, considerably added to his stature by a resounding victory in North-West Manchester in the General Election. In an appraisal of the election from the Jewish viewpoint a correspondent in the *Jewish Chronicle*, after referring to Churchill's endeavours with regard to the Aliens Bills, pointed out: [53] " Mr. Churchill's inclusion in the Government is an additional guarantee, if any were needed, of the friendliness of the new ministry in the relations with Jews, whether the question be the treatment of aliens or the provisions of an asylum for the refugees from darkest Europe." [54]

By a strange irony of the situation the Liberal Party which had so consistently fought the Aliens Bills, was thus called upon to initiate the operation of the Aliens Act. This turn of events aroused new hopes in British and foreign Jewry of a liberal and more humane approach to the aliens problem, particularly when it became known that the administration of the Act was to rest with the Home Office, of which Herbert (now Viscount) Samuel had become Under-Secretary in the new Liberal Government. [55]

Yet the disappointment of the Jewish community at a great number of provisions in the Aliens Act, 1905, was not allowed to obscure in their eyes the services rendered in the struggle against the legislation by the foremost fighters on the Opposition side, Sir Charles Dilke, Major J. E. B. Seely, Charles P. Trevelyan and Winston Churchill, each of whom received a communication from D. L. Alexander, K.C., President of the Board of Deputies of British Jews, dated July 25, 1905, which read as follows: [56]

On behalf of this Board which is the Representative Body of the Jews of the United Kingdom, I beg to offer you the sincere thanks of the Jewish Community for the service which you have rendered it by your eloquent championship of its persecuted co-religionists throughout the discussions on the Aliens Bill.

On July 26, Churchill replied from his residence at 105, Mount Street, London, W.1,

Dear Sir,

I have to thank you for your kind letter and very much appreciate the sentiments you express therein on behalf of the London Committee of Deputies of the British Jews with reference to the action I have taken on the Aliens Bill.

Yours truly,

Winston S. Churchill.

*    *
*

At the beginning of the preparations of the Aliens Act, 1905, the Conservative Party celebrated with enthusiasm and fervour the centenary of their great Jewish leader Disraeli. Herbert (now Viscount) Samuel, who together with his brother Stuart almost alone of the twelve Jewish members of Parliament fought untiringly against the proposed legislation,[57] said during the second reading of the Bill with reference to the Disraeli celebrations:[58] " I wonder what Disraeli would have thought of this Bill. On April 19th you covered his statue with flowers, but the day before you introduced a Bill which might exclude from this country such families as his."

On the eve of the coming into force of the Aliens Act, 1905, Anglo-Jewry began its preparations for the solemn commemoration of the 250th anniversary of the re-admission of Jews into England which, without any specific legislation or an Aliens Act governing immigration, turned out to have initiated an era of great blessing for the country and for the Jewish community.

## CHAPTER III

## ANTISEMITISM

THIS chapter on Churchill's views on anti-Semitism and his stand with regard to anti-Semitic practices can most appropriately be opened with a quotation from a speech he made in Parliament which puts his approach to the matter in a nutshell: [1]

> I am against preventing Jews from doing anything which other people are allowed to do. I am against that, and I have the strongest abhorrence of the idea of anti-Semitic lines of prejudice.

In making this statement Churchill emphasised with regard to the Jews what he looked upon throughout his political career as his own philosophy of individual freedom. To him this is a sacred creed which does not admit any discrimination between peoples, nations, religions or races. In a broadcast address to the American people in October 1938 he gave a short historical review of the development of individual freedom among the Western peoples which is indicative of his thoughts on this subject: [2]

> Since the dawn of the Christian era a certain way of life has slowly been shaping itself among the Western peoples, and certain standards of conduct and government have come to be esteemed. After many miseries and prolonged confusion, there arose into broad light of day the conception of the right of the individual; his right to be consulted in the government of his country; his right to invoke the law even against the State itself. Independent Courts of Justice were created to affirm and enforce this hard-won custom. Thus was assured throughout the English-speaking world, and in France by

the stern lesson of the Revolution, what Kipling called,
" Leave to live by no man's leave underneath the law ".
Now in this resides all that makes existence precious to
man, and all that confers honour and health upon the
State.

In another place he describes in detail these precious
achievements, and formulates his basic approach to the liberty
and equality of the individual in a passage deserving to be
quoted in full: [3]

" The masses ", said Napoleon in one of his most pessi-
mistic pronouncements, " care little for liberty, but much
for equality ".   But more than a hundred years have
passed since then, and the world has moved on.   To-day
individual freedom, especially when combined with a
higher standard of living, makes a potent appeal to the
men and women of every country under every system.
Why should not an ordinary toiler have the chance to
keep a home together and rear a family, without being
vilely trodden in upon by well-paid uniformed officials
and professional party agents?   Why should the police
harry ordinary households in so many lands more than
they do in England?   Why should the ordinary wage-
earner not be allowed to express his opinion about the
government of his country, and say whether he thinks
it is being wisely or honestly conducted?   Why should
men's opinions be condemned as crimes, and buzzing
functionaries conduct an inquisition into the political or
party views of law-abiding folk?   Why should religion
be the subject of oppression?   Why should racial persecution endure?   Was it not Frederick the Great who
said, " In Prussia every man must get to Heaven in his
own way "?   Can anyone help being born with red hair
or a hook nose?

This is Churchill's conception of the liberty of human
beings as such and we have seen from the first quotation in
this chapter that he applies it unreservedly also to the Jews.
One could even say that he applies it especially to the Jews.
For it is particularly in the case of the Jews that this precious
possession of the Western Peoples is so often and so blatantly

betrayed. It is most painful to him to find that this twentieth century which, at the outset of his political career, was destined to be an era of enlightenment,[4] should have turned out to have denied the very ideals underlying the philosophy of individual freedom by working up to a climax of bestial persecution and annihilation. The Jewish problem, Theodor Herzl said in his *Judenstaat*,[5] is a " protracted piece of the Middle Ages ", and it is in almost the same terms that Churchill described the anti-Semitic theme of our days:[6]

> It is not a new theme; it leaps out upon us from the Dark Ages—racial persecution, religious intolerance, deprivation of free speech, the conception of the citizen as a mere soulless fraction of the State.

But this was not something to be approached in a theoretical manner, to be described as a literary theme in human or inhuman psychology: to Churchill anti-Semitism is a very concrete method of brutality, for thanks to his insight into the motive forces of history and his power of observation he understands its manifestations clearly. As he once told a Jewish gathering in London:[7]

> Your race, across the centuries in so many lands, driven from its own land, spreading into every land, and almost throughout the world, has experienced every vicissitude, suffering, persecution, martyrdom and oppression in every form, generation after generation, century after century.

Hence it is of great interest to investigate how Churchill re-acted to anti-Semitic manifestations and outbursts as they occurred during his half century and more of political activity. Since 1900, when he entered the political arena, a number of anti-Semitic outbursts have drawn public attention to the intolerable position of the Jews in various countries, and as a man who stood in the centre of political events Churchill could not remain indifferent to this vital problem.

UNBIASED BACKGROUND
Anti-Semitism played no rôle in his paternal home or in his early environment, both of which so often stamp ineradicable impressions on the youthful mind. Insofar as Jews

played a part in that era, he found nothing but respect and admiration for them in his father's home; as, for instance, with regard to Jews like Lord Rothschild,[8] or to men of Jewish descent like Lord Beaconsfield[9] or Sir Ernest Cassel,[10] the financier.

We have in a previous chapter[11] referred to Lord Randolph's great influence on Churchill, in particular posthumously. It might well have left an impression on him when, collecting the material for the biography of his father, Churchill learned of the interest which the former took in the first great anti-Semitic outbreaks in Russia in 1881. Lord Randolph, at the age of thirty-two, then asked in Parliament[12]

> whether Her Majesty's Government had received information as to a considerable massacre and plunder of Jewry which had taken place in a town, the name of which he was not able to pronounce, on the Galician frontier, and as to a large number of Jews being forced to cross the frontier? He also wished to ask whether a considerable massacre and plunder of Jews had taken place at the town of Odessa, and whether Her Majesty's Government had called for or intended to call upon Her Majesty's Charge d'Affaires at St. Petersburg, or the Consul General at Odessa, for reports on the subject.

*Sir C. Dilke,* Under-Secretary for Foreign Affairs, in his reply said:

> We have received no information as to massacres on the Austrian frontier, there being no representatives of Her Majesty in the frontier districts. With regard to Odessa, I have seen a paragraph in a paper, but we have heard nothing on the subject from Her Majesty's Consul at that place.
> *Lord Randolph Churchill*: Will the hon. baronet make formal enquiries into the matter?
> *Sir C. Dilke*: It is highly probable that we shall receive information in the course of a few days.

Thus, while the young Churchill was brought up in an atmosphere free from anti-Semitic bias, the mature man did not remain content with a negative and passive attitude, but almost from the outset of his public career took an active and positive stand in the face of this important problem.

## (A) CZARIST AND SOVIET RUSSIA

It is against this background then, that his stand in facing practical anti-Semitism can be assessed. For the first time in his mature life news about anti-Semitic outbreaks became generally current during the second wave of Russian pogroms between 1903 and 1905. In that period, the Russian defeat in the war against Japan and the subsequent peasants' revolt, led the Russian leaders to hit upon the age-old scapegoat—the Jews. The agitation against them was headed by reactionaries, among whom government officials played a very important rôle, and even Ministers of the Cabinet actively supported it. During the later period of these pogroms the wholesale butchery of the Jews was instigated by the " Black Hundreds ".[13] From October 31 to November 5, 1905, about three hundred towns and villages were laid waste, and nearly 25,000 persons were killed or wounded. The " Jewish Self-Defence " fought back heroically but was entirely crushed by overwhelming numbers. Noble-hearted Christians who tried to assist the Jews also fell victims to the blood-thirsty mob. " The cries of anguish from the millions of despondent and forlorn reverberated throughout the civilised world and in every land meetings of protest and indignation were held which were addressed by renowned diplomats, clergymen, authors and financiers."

When the news of these atrocities reached Britain, meetings of protest were organised throughout the country. One of the most impressive was that of December 10, 1905, held at the Palace Theatre, Manchester. At this Churchill, who had on the same day taken over the office of Under-Secretary for the Colonies, moved the principal resolution and accompanied it with a speech which, as a Churchillian classic, deserves to be recorded once again:[14]

Mr. Winston Churchill moved:

" That this meeting of Manchester and Salford of all denominations expresses its horror and indignation at the wholesale massacres of Jews in Russia, and condemns in the strongest terms, the bureaucracy which has instigated and connived at the unparalleled acts of brutality which have disgraced that country. And this meeting declares that Russia has thereby placed herself outside the pale of humanity and the comity of nations, and it calls upon the nations of the world to demand guarantees against the repetition of such outrages, together with reparation to the surviving victims."

We are gathered here this evening in unusual circumstances at a meeting into which there enters no party bitterness, and that is not divided by prejudices of race, creed or sex, to discharge a melancholy duty. This vast audience has met to record a solemn protest in the name of civilisation and in the name of all the elevated religions of the world against the appalling massacres and detestable atrocities recently committed in the Empire of Russia. The number of victims has been enormous, many thousands of weak and defenceless people have suffered terribly, old people alike with little children and feeble women who were incapable of offering resistance, and could not rely at all on the forces of law and the regulations of order. That these outrages were not spontaneous but rather in the nature of a deliberate plan combine to create a picture so terrible that one can hardly distinguish it in its grim reality, even amid the darkness of Russia.

We have met here to express, in no uncertain terms, how deeply moved the whole British nation is at such atrocious deeds. If one but contrasts the position of the Jews in Russia with that which they enjoy in this country—a position in which they have prospered greatly —living as peaceable, law-abiding citizens, who are an honour and a credit to any country, if they can compare the calm and tolerant method of their life in England with the violence and confusion that prevails in Russia, I think you will agree with me that there is a deep truth in the saying of Lord Beaconsfield that " The Lord deals with the nations as the nations dealt with the Jews ".

The wounded and the surviving victims have been aided to some extent by means of the large fund that has been raised, but what of the future? There comes home to us the melancholy and depressing feeling that for all that our numbers are strong and for all the immense influence we can exert in our own country, our power of protecting those whom we all wish to protect in that distant land is not a very great power.

We do not quite know what practical steps can be taken. We have sympathy in abundance, indignation and condemnation, but what practical measures could we adopt which would have the effect of preventing a renewal of these ghastly barbarities in the future? I am one of those who does not believe in intervention in the affairs of foreign States, as such intervention has the effect of goading to greater efforts the revolutionary party, and we have no assurance that remonstrance would be treated with respect. We do not know where to place responsibility or how to bring it home to those upon whom our indignation should descend the consequences of their actions.

Last session an Aliens Bill was passed, and I earnestly hope it might be found possible, at this period when so many distressed people are flying from persecution, to effect some relaxation in the severity of its provision, so that this country in the enlightened twentieth century should still remain, as ever, a refuge for those who are bowed down with affliction and in sore distress.

As to the possibilities of diplomatic action, I cannot speak, but so enormous an assembly and so important a meeting must strengthen the hands of any ministry in whatever course they might think proper to take. I hope that the expressions contained in the resolution will not be without effect, and that our efforts will be carried to such conclusions that such barbarities will cease, and that this meeting will discharge its duty of placing on record its strong protest and condemnation of atrocities that have shocked the whole civilised world.

Fourteen years later Churchill had another opportunity to concern himself with Russian anti-Semitism, though this time on a considerably larger scale as well as with great personal responsibility. When on January 19,1919, Churchill became

Secretary for War and Air in the re-shuffled Cabinet of Lloyd George, the campaigns of Gen. Denikin and Adm. Koltchak against the Bolsheviks in Russia were in full swing. The British Government had supported these campaigns, originally on a limited scale (from December 1917 onwards), but since the War Cabinet's decision of November 14, 1918, by a far-reaching aid programme.[15] Thus Churchill, as the new Minister for War,

> became an heir to the pledges and tragedies of this situation . . . Up to this moment I had taken no part of any kind in Russian affairs, nor had I been responsible for any commitment.[16]

He is obviously very anxious to make it clear that the Russian intervention was not initiated by him, for in another part of his book[17] he stresses this again and with more emphasis:

> I have explained the part I played in these events. I had no responsibility either for the original intervention or for the commitments and obligations which it entailed. Neither did it rest with me to decide whether intervention should be continued after the Armistice or brought to an end. It was my duty in a subordinate though important station to try to make good the undertakings which had been entered into by Great Britain, and to protect as far as possible those who had compromised themselves in the common cause of the Allies and of Russia herself. I am glad to think that our country was the last to ignore its obligations or to leave ill-starred comrades to their fate.

In his conviction that Bolshevism represented the very depth of evil, Churchill would have loved to elevate the campaigns of these Russian generals and their armies to a crusade of bearers of Western civilisation against Bolshevism. In this respect (as in many others) these campaigns met with complete failure. That period of 1918/1921 was for the Jews of Russia one of their most tragic. They were literally being ground between the millstones of the Bolsheviks and the interventionist anti-Bolsheviks. Wherever the troops of one party arrived, they proclaimed the Jews as the adherents of the other side, and the result was one of the most cruel slaughters that world history had seen until then. In that period 887

large and 349 lesser pogroms took place in 530 Jewish communities, particularly in the Ukraine, at a cost of some 60,000
dead and many more wounded Jewish victims.[18] Under these
circumstances Churchill felt that he had to intervene—where
he certainly could not escape responsibility—with the generals
whom he supported as Minister for War, in the name and on
the instructions of the British Government. The main British
assistance was given to the armies of General Denikin in
Southern Russia.[19] As mentioned above, Churchill's writings
on this subject do not leave us in doubt that these campaigns
were to him a kind of " holy crusade " in the name of Western
civilisation. He therefore found it irreconcilable with his
high principles to fight against the " barbaric Bolsheviks "
on the one hand and on the other to permit the soldiers of
those whom he supported to commit similar barbarities by
murdering Jews for the simple reason that they were Jews.

I used what influence I had to prevent excesses and
promote concerted action

he emphasizes,[20] and for his own justification this statement
is accompanied by quotations from official orders and telegrams. He records therein the efforts he made to stop or
prevent the pogroms, e.g.:

September 18.
It is of the very highest consequence that General
Denikin should not only do everything in his power to
prevent massacres of the Jews in liberated districts, but
should issue a proclamation against Anti-Semitism.

But this order did not fall on fruitful soil. The murders of
the Jews increased daily and the centre of anti-Semitic propaganda was established in Rostov, where the Department of
Propaganda of General Denikin's Army also had its headquarters.[21] Churchill therefore saw himself forced again to
wire to General Denikin on the subject of anti-Semitism. As
he records:[22]

On October 9 I telegraphed to Denikin urging him to
redouble efforts to restrain anti-Semitic feeling and to
vindicate the honour of the volunteer army (by such
restraint).

This effort of Churchill's shows how he personally tried to rid his protégés of anti-Semitic tendencies and to prevent their anti-Semitic excesses. In a newspaper article written a few months after these events Churchill reviewed the whole unfortunate period: [23]

Needless to say, the most intense passions of revenge have been excited in the breasts of the Russian people. Wherever General Denikin's authority could reach, protection was always accorded to the Jewish population, and strenuous efforts were made by his officers to prevent reprisals and punish those guilty of them. So much was this the case that the Petlurist propaganda against General Denikin denounced him as the Protector of the Jews. The Misses Healy, nieces of Mr. Tim Healy, in relating their personal experiences in Kieff, have declared that to their knowledge on more than one occasion officers who committed offences against Jews were reduced to the ranks and sent out of the city to the front. But the hordes of brigands by whom the whole vast expanse of the Russian Empire is becoming infested do not hesitate to gratify their lust for blood and for revenge at the expense of the innocent Jewish population whenever an opportunity occurs. The brigand Makhno, the hordes of Petlura and of Gregorieff, who signalised their every success by the most brutal massacres, everywhere found among the half-stupefied, half-infuriated population an eager response to anti-Semitism in its worst and foulest forms.

The fact that in many cases Jewish interests and Jewish places of worship are excepted by the Bolsheviks from their universal hostility has tended more and more to associate the Jewish race in Russia with the villainies which are now being perpetrated. This is an injustice on millions of helpless people, most of whom are themselves sufferers from the revolutionary regime. It becomes, therefore, specially important to foster and develop any strongly-marked Jewish movement which leads directly away from these fatal associations. And it is here that Zionism has such a deep significance for the whole world at the present time.

This description was obviously given in order to explain away the incredible inactivity on the part of the British authorities on the one hand, and on the other that of those generals, allies of Britain, who did not act in accordance with the instructions sent to them. But there is no doubt that on the basis of unimpeachable evidence the historian felt obliged to accuse both Petlura and Denikin for having been disinclined to suppress their troops' hatred of the Jews.[24] Churchill was told so at the time by no other than Israel Zangwill who attributed the War Secretary's failure regarding his Russian policy to a " perversity of vision ", created " in a brain that is seeing red and seeing falsely. To this ", Zangwill continued,[25] " and not to sheer bravado may charitably be accredited his acclamation of his instrument, Denikin, the destroyer and despiser of the Jewries along his path, as the protector of Israel." In support of his attack on Churchill, Zangwill quoted a statement by the head of Ukrainian Jewry, Vladimir Tiomkin, who described the terrible sufferings of the Jews in Russia, particularly in the Ukraine, and with regard to Denikin pointed out in conclusion that: " Throughout every spot that Denikin's armies touched, the same red line is to be traced, the same results found. Appeals were made to Denikin, appeals were forwarded to the European Powers which were maintaining his forces, but it was as an echo in the desert, no relief or protection came from anywhere."

Presumably at least one appeal to Britain was among those to the Powers referred to in Tiomkin's report, this perhaps explaining Churchill's intervention mentioned above. But it is obvious that the method which he employed to have his requests carried out was totally ineffectual. The chaotic conditions not only in Russia but also in the ranks of the " liberation armies " may account for the failure of his intervention. The Jewish tragedy in Russia moved dangerously towards the climax of extermination and abated only after the collapse of the " liberation armies ".[26] The one drastic measure that would have stopped these acts at once—the withholding of support to Denikin and his armies, Churchill could not bring himself to take. The war against the Bolsheviks was to him of much greater importance, and it was not to be abandoned or weakened by raising the question of trying to prevent barbaric murders. At that time, as also later in World War II, Churchill's dominating thought was first to defeat the enemy and only afterwards to reorganise the world.

For a number of years after the Revolution of October 1917 there were no reports of any anti-Jewish outbreaks in Russia.[26a] Though news could leak across the Soviet borders only on rare occasions, in all probability the Soviet law forbidding anti-Semitic activities brought these to a standstill. The famous purge trials in Moscow, in 1934-1937, of a number of " Old Guard " Communist leaders, many of whom were Jews or of Jewish origin, brought again a Jewish issue to the fore.[27] As will be remembered, they were charged with an underground counter-revolutionary conspiracy under Trotsky's auspices to which later was added the indictment of conspiracy with the Nazis to restore the capitalist regime in Russia. By then National Socialism, in power in Germany, had begun to show its hand with regard to the treatment of Jews and, comparing both, Churchill summarised their common denominator as follows:[28]

> The . . . point to notice is that these victims were nearly all Jews. Evidently the Nationalist elements represented by Stalin and the Soviet armies are developing the same prejudices against the Chosen People as are so painfully evident in Germany. Here again extremes meet, and meet on a common platform of hate and cruelty.

There is yet another aspect of Jewish significance, with regard to Soviet Russia, which fits perfectly into Churchill's formula of the common platform of the Bolshevik leaders and Nazi Germany. Maxim Litvinov, the Soviet Commissar, as a Jew, had to be dismissed from office in 1939 in order to make possible the official opening of negotiations which led to the Soviet-Nazi pact, the last stepping stone to World War II. In his *Memoirs* Churchill writes:[29]

> The eminent Jew, the target of German antagonism, was flung aside for the time being like a broken tool, and without being given a word of explanation, was bundled off the world stage to obscurity, a pittance and police supervision . . . The Jew Litvinov was gone, and Hitler's dominant prejudice placated.

By that time Nazi anti-Semitism had reached new and previously unsuspected depths of hatred against the Jews, and it is with these manifestations that the following section will deal.

## (B) GERMANY

In the first two decades of this century Russian anti-Semitism was regarded as the most brutal form of murder and loot. But it was left to Germany, where " scientific " anti-Semitism was born in the last century, to dwarf the brutalities, sadistic tortures, pillage and murders committed against the Jews in any age or by any people.

When Hitler assumed power in Germany in 1933, his anti-Semitic slogans were at first completely misunderstood. It was generally assumed indeed that the passages on Jews and Judaism in *Mein Kampf* and later preached in the Nazi propaganda were only meant to serve this propaganda and would fade out once the National Socialists were in power; for men then naively believed that brutalities could not long survive the test of responsible office. In the same way, almost all other demands contained in *Mein Kampf* and later propagated by the Nazis were similarly misinterpreted, and it was not least because of this lack of perspicacity that the world was inexorably plunged into World War II. Even when the *Judentag* of April 1, 1933, was proclaimed in Germany by the newly appointed National Socialist Government, and implemented by a general boycott against Jews, the civilised world condoned this outrage: for it was assumed that Hitler, having preached anti-Semitism for years, might feel he owed one such display to his adherents, and that with this single " day " the end of his anti-Semitic escapades had been reached.

Churchill was one of the first statesmen to draw conclusions for Europe and the world from Hitler's access to power, his aims and objects, his preparations for a war. To Churchill's mind the treatment of the Jews in Germany was one more factor reinforcing his conclusions. When in the course of the discussion of the " MacDonald Plan " of 1933 it became clear that the proposals would halve the French army and establish military parity between Germany and France, Churchill strongly attacked them in Parliament: [30]

When we read about Germany, when we watch with
surprise and distress the tumultuous insurgence of
ferocity and war spirit, the pitíless ill-treatment of
minorities, the denial of the normal protections of
civilised society, the persecution of large numbers of
individuals solely on the ground of race—when we see
all that occurring in one of the most gifted, learned and
scientific and formidable nations in the world, one cannot help feeling glad that the fierce passions that are
raging in Germany have not yet found any other outlet
but upon themselves.

Nevertheless, Churchill then regarded these and other manifestations as an internal affair of Germany (we know he
rejected interference in other countries' affairs almost from
the inception of his political activity).[31]   He stressed this when
discussing the problem of the relations between Britain and
the New Reich with German supporters of Hitler.  Referring
to these conversations he wrote:[32]

I have had from time to time conversations with eminent
German supporters of the present regime.  When they
say, as they so often do, " Will not England grasp the
extended friendly hand of Germany?" nearly everyone
in England will reply, " Certainly, yes.  We cannot pre-
tend to like your new institutions, and we have long freed
ourselves from racial and religious intolerance.  We
cannot say that we admire your treatment of the Jews
or of the Protestants and Catholics of Germany. We even
think our methods of dealing with Communism are better
than yours.  But, after all, these matters, so long as they
are confined inside Germany, are not our business.  It
is our duty and our sincere desire to live in a good
and neighbourly fashion with so great a nation united
to us by many ties of history and of race.  Indeed, we
will grasp the outstretched German hand."

As the quotation shows, Churchill at one time regarded
anti-Semitism as a domestic affair of Germany — in close
analogy to his attitude to Russian anti-Semitism in 1905[33]—
which did not justify intervention from outside.  But it was
not long before Churchill was to arrive at a correct appraisal

of the deeper implications of Hitler's and Nazi Germany's anti-Semitism.

While the events of April 1, 1933, were originally regarded as a gift to his adherents in satisfaction of their low instincts, the events of September 15, 1935, and November 9-11, 1938, could leave no doubt in the mind of any rational being that anti-Semitism constituted an integral part of the policy of the New Germany.

The first date opened the second phase of German official anti-Semitism. It marked the promulgation of the Nuremberg Laws, the aim of which was to " free Germany from the Jews " by splitting the German people into three categories: Germans and persons of kindred blood, those of mixed blood, and pure Jews; the last two categories were deprived of full citizenship and the right to hold office (apart from numerous other disabilities), and were thus condemned to a kind of Ghetto existence.[34]

On the second date the third chapter of official Nazi anti-Semitism opened. A few days earlier, on November 7, 1938, vom Rath, a member of the German Embassy in Paris, was shot by Herszel Grynszpan,[35] son of Polish Jewish parents who were among the victims of the gruesome expulsion of Polish Jews from Germany in the previous October.[36] On November 9 vom Rath died of his wounds.[37] This gave Hitler the long sought for and welcome excuse for drastic measures and further discriminatory legislation against German and Austrian Jewry.[38] These measures were preceded and accompanied by arrests of many thousands of Jews, by the destruction of Jewish business premises, the burning of Synagogues, and the loot of Jewish property by the German and Austrian population.[39] The culmination of this barbarism was reached on November 10—" A Black Day for Germany " as The Times headlined a leading article condemning these excesses.[40] This campaign against the Jews was let loose under the undisguised leadership of Germany's Minister of Propaganda, Dr. Josef Goebbels and his organ Der Angriff. Since the Nazis on every possible occasion spared a part of their hatred of the Jews for Churchill, it was quite natural that the Angriff should have announced vom Rath's shooting with the characteristic headline: " The work of the instigator-international. A straight line from Churchill to Grynszpan."[41] In the same issue the *Angriff* published a series of photographs, headed by pictures of Grynszpan and David Frankfurter (who shot the Nazi leader Wilhelm Gustloff in 1936) and followed by photographs of Churchill, Attlee, Duff-Cooper, Eden and others. The collection was surmounted by a headline, " Jewish murderers and the instigators ".[42]

As the news about the new wave of barbarities spread day after day, the civilised world was shocked. Britain protested in Berlin against the linking of Churchill and other British statesmen with the shooting of vom Rath,[43] and President Roosevelt recalled the U.S.A. Ambassador in Berlin, Hugh Wilson, to Washington, where he was to remain " indefinitely " as consultant on German affairs.[44]

Outstanding men in politics, religion, science, economics and the arts throughout the world expressed their horror at such inhuman treatment; in many countries meetings of protest were held. In fact, the days of November 9-11 at last drew the world's attention to the barbarism which had become inplanted in its midst and the menace of complete annihilation which overhung German and Austrian Jewry.

For Churchill this came as no surprise. For some time previously he had unmasked in articles and speeches the doctrine of destruction represented by National Socialism, which expressed itself not only in the treatment of the Jews but in all fields of Nazi activity. Churchill warned Britain of the approaching dangers and demanded preparation for the moment when the two worlds would unavoidably clash; but his warnings went unheeded.

When Churchill asked himself what it was that had given rise in the Nazis to their detestation of the Jews and to their desire to annihilate them, he turned to the one source from which he could expect to derive enlightenment, Hitler's *Mein Kampf*, the gospel of the Nazis.[45] In it he found at length the theory of the superiority of militant and aggressively nationalistic nations over the pacific and internationally minded ones. In his book Hitler tried to prove that the Jews were most prominent among the latter, and his conclusion was that only " superior races " had the right and duty to live, while the others must perish. But this racial theory could not alone explain the pathological fury characteristic of German anti-Semitism. Hitler's personal hatred gradually became the dominant theme in his party—and finally in Germany. Churchill traces[46] this hatred back to the personal make-up of Hitler who

> had mingled in Vienna with extreme German Nationalist groups, and here he had heard stories of sinister, undermining activities of another race, foes and exploiters of the Nordic world—the Jews. His patriotic anger fused with his envy of the rich and successful into one overpowering hate.

However, there is also another explanation for the prominence given in the Nazi conception to anti-Semitism. The Jews constituted an extremely suitable political and propaganda target within Germany, the proper use of which could help to reorganise the dissatisfied, disappointed, demoralised and desperate elements of the German people after the military disaster of World War I. It was simple to explain Germany's defeat by " Jewish betrayal " and thus single out the Jews as the real reason for Germany's misery. As so often in history—one need only read what has been said with regard to Russian anti-Semitism[47]—the Jews were once again the most convenient scapegoat.

In a broadcast to the people of the United States of America Churchill, dealing with this aspect, said:[48]

> In the German view, which Herr Hitler shares, a peaceful Germany and Austria were fallen upon in 1914 by a gang of wicked designing nations, headed by Belgium and Serbia, and would have defended herself sucessfully if only she had not been stabbed in the back by the Jews. Against such opinion it is vain to argue.

Later that year, in another address to the American people, Churchill reverted to this theme with brilliant satire:[49]

> Dr. Goebbels and his Propaganda Machine have their own version of what happened twenty-five years ago. To hear them talk, you would suppose that it was Belgium that invaded Germany! There they were, these peaceful Prussians, gathering in their harvests, when this wicked Belgium—set on by England and the Jews—fell upon them; and would no doubt have taken Berlin, if Cor-

poral Adolf Hitler had not come to the rescue and
turned the tables. Indeed, that tale goes further. After
four years of war by land and sea, when Germany was
about to win an overwhelming victory, the Jews got at
them again, this time from the rear. Armed with President Wilson's Fourteen Points they stabbed, we are told,
the German armies in the back, and induced them to ask
for an armistice, and even persuaded them, in an
unguarded moment, to sign a paper saying that it was
they and not the Belgians who had been the ones to
begin the War. Such is history as it is taught in topsy-
turvydom.

Hitler's propaganda borrowed another slogan from the
storehouse of pre-Nazi anti-Semitism, and elevated it to the
forefront of its fight against " the continued wickedness in
our midst "; thus another accusation was heaped upon the
ever-guilty Jew—Communism. In a full description of the
implications arising out of this propaganda, Churchill pointed
out: [50]

> The Jews, supposed to have contributed, by a disloyal
> and pacifist influence, to the collapse of Germany at the
> end of the Great War, were also deemed to be the main
> prop of communism and the authors of defeatist doc-
> trines in every form. Therefore, the Jews of Germany,
> a community numbered by many hundreds of thousands,
> were to be stripped of all power, driven from every posi-
> tion in public and social life, expelled from the profes-
> sions, silenced in the Press, and declared a foul and
> odious race. The twentieth century has witnessed with
> surprise, not merely the promulgation of these ferocious
> doctrines, but their enforcement with brutal vigour by
> the Government and by the populace. No past services,
> no proved patriotism, even wounds sustained in war,
> could procure immunity for persons whose only crime
> was that their parents had brought them into the world.
> Every kind of persecution, grave or petty, upon the
> world-famous scientists, writers, and composers at the
> top down to the wretched little Jewish children in the
> national schools, was practised, was glorified, and is
> still being practised and glorified.

The devilish brutalities of those years before World War II
which came to light surpassed the imagination even of the
fiercest opponents of Nazism.  At that time thinking people,
of whom Churchill was one, were of the opinion that the
persecution methods then applied by the Nazis could not
possibly be exceeded.  In an essay he once sketched in a few
lines some of the methods of Nazi persecution as they were
applied before World War II.  While in this particular case
they refer to Viennese Jewry, they are characteristic of the
Hitler method as a whole.  Churchill wrote: [51]

> It is easy to ruin and persecute Jews; to steal their private
> property; to drive them out of every profession and
> employment; to fling a Rothschild into prison or a
> sponging-house: [52] to compel Jewish ladies to scrub
> pavements; and to maroon clusters of helpless refugees
> on islands in the Danube; and these sports continue to
> give satisfaction.

It does not need to be emphasised that Churchill, when
describing these brutalities and investigating their causes, does
so for practical political purposes.  He felt obliged to find
an answer to the question of where all this hatred would lead
to, what purpose it pursued and how it affected or would
affect the world at large.  The idea which he held at one
time, and to which reference was made above,[53] that these
manifestations were local and internal German affairs, had
by then lost its validity in his view.  The issues at stake had
became much more serious.  Churchill came to the conclusion
that there were three important major problems involved in
this Jew-baiting policy which could not remain confined to
Germany alone, and thus ceased to remain an internal affair
of that country.[54]

First, it seemed to him a far from simple problem to
eliminate hundreds of thousands of Jews from the processes
of daily work, without causing serious damage and loss to
the economic life of the country

> when a busy, ingenious, industrious community, making
> themselves useful in a thousand ways, is reduced to a
> mass of helpless, miserable folk, who nevertheless cannot
> quite be allowed to starve wholesale.

The effects of such methods on the economic conditions of the State must necessarily make themselves felt, and as the economy of one country—particularly of a power like Germany—is closely interwoven with those of other countries, consequences on a large scale would inevitably set in.

The second problem raised by the methods of the Nazis in Germany was again one that could not remain confined to Germany herself. This was, in Churchill's opinion, the question of the refugees who, owing to Nazi persecution, were forced to emigrate to other countries, thereby creating difficult political, economic and social problems for those among whom they settled. In this connection Churchill refers to historical experience with regard to such migrations and says : [55]

> The persecution of the Jews in Germany, the exploitation of anti-Semitism as a means by which violent and reactionary forces seize, or attempt to seize despotic power, afflicted the civilised world with a refugee problem similar to that of the Huguenots in the seventeenth century.

Such complex problems arose in many European countries, particularly in Czechoslovakia, Poland and France, but the effects were also felt in Britain and America. Of all the countries thus affected Churchill took a particular interest in the question of the influx of Jewish refugees into Palestine. This created difficult problems for Britain as Mandatory Power both with the Arabs, who objected to this immigration, and the Jews, who welcomed it as the only salvation in a world otherwise closed to them. Churchill outlined this problem in a speech in the Commons : [56]

> Then the Hitler persecution of the Jews began. The cruel and forced exodus of the Jews from Nazidom began, and, from the best motives, under these cruel stresses, for which we were not in any way to blame, the immigration quota was increased, in my opinion, too suddenly and too rapidly.

With regard to Palestine, as will be seen in Part II of this study, these difficulties led to many complications. In connection with this migration, however, Churchill took a different view from the one he held about migration to other parts of the world, partly because of Britain's specific obligations in this area, and partly because of his sympathy with the Zionist conception of solving the Jewish problem. He therefore insisted on a positive approach to the problem of Jewish refugees pouring into Palestine: [57]

> I have been speaking of this matter in connection with Palestine, but of course there is in our minds an added emphasis upon this question of Jewish immigration, which comes from other quarters, at a time when the Jewish race in a great country is being subjected to most horrible, cold, scientific persecution, a cold " pogrom " as it has been called—people reduced from affluence to ruin, and then even in that position, denied the opportunity of earning their daily bread, and cut out even from relief by grants to tide the destitute through the winter; their little children pilloried in the schools to which they have to go; their blood and race declared defiling and accursed; every form of concentrated human wickedness cast upon these people by overwhelming power, by vile tyranny.  I say that, when that is the case, surely the House of Commons will not allow the one door which is open, the one door which allows some relief, some escape from these conditions, to be summarily closed, nor even allow it to be suggested that it may be obstructed by the course which we take now. [58]

The third inference which Churchill derived from the anti-Semitic complex of the Nazi system was again one of the widest possible importance, for it concerned the reaction of the world to these events. This, of course, presupposed Germany's desire not to antagonise the rest of the world though we know today that this was certainly not foremost in their thoughts at a time when they were preparing for World War II.  Churchill said in this connection: [59]

> The tale of their [refugees'] tribulation spreads widely through the world, and it is astonishing that the German rulers are not more concerned at the tides of abhorrence and anger which are rising ceaselessly against them throughout the heavily-arming United States.

On another occasion he returned to this theme, pointing out that[60]

> Of course, if any government in the twentieth century is engaged in persecuting people because of their race or of their religion, irrespective of their civic behaviour, and if these victims of ill-usage make feeble demonstrations of protest, the mere recording of these facts will be prejudicial to that government in the outer world.

However, the Nazi regime was not concerned with world opinion. Churchill, with his great instinct for the " things that will come ", was able also in this connection to predict that[61]

> it would almost seem as if the present German Government were resolved to isolate themselves morally as well as economically from the other great nations in the West. They seem to care nothing for world public opinion. Nothing matters but food and weapons—weapons first.

And so the world was plunged into World War II. The persecution of the Jews was only part of the all-embracing Nazi policy which prepared for and led up to the war. The many issues involved were dealt with by Churchill in his speeches and writings of that period. In the final analysis this was a clash of two worlds, for or against the supreme principles of individual freedom and liberty, Churchill's conception of which has been dealt with at the beginning of this chapter.[62] They were the principles which Churchill raised as a banner of hope for mankind when darkness descended upon the world in 1939, values worth while fighting and dying for. In his first speech on World War II he outlined the fundamental principles for which Britain stood in a noble passage : [63]

> We are fighting to save the whole world from the pestilence of Nazi tyranny and in defence of all that is most sacred to man. This is no war of domination or imperial aggrandisement or material gain; no war to shut any country out of its sunlight and means of progress. It is a war, viewed in its inherent quality, to establish, on impregnable rocks, the rights of the individual, and it is a war to establish and revive the stature of man.

## WORLD WAR II

### (a) PUBLIC STATEMENTS

THE outbreak of the War changed the picture. It was now not only the Jews who suffered under the Nazi oppression, but one by one the peoples of countries overrun by Hitler's armies in the first war years became automatic victims of brutal oppression and murder. The particular suffering of the Jews within this general ordeal was not given any special emphasis. Statesmen of the West then spoke primarily of the martyrdom of the peoples of Belgium, Czechoslovakia, Holland, Poland and Yugoslavia, also including in that collective word the Jews of these countries without specially mentioning them. In these first war years it was fatally overlooked that the Jews, as a collective body, and without exception, were selected for special Nazi torture far in excess of the general oppression of the various populations, from the day Hitler's forces entered a country. And only on a few rare occasions was this particular Jewish aspect of the great European tragedy mentioned.

There is no doubt that, right from the outset of the war, Nazi brutalities on the European continent became known and continued to become known to the civilised world as one country after the other was invaded by the Germans. Time and again Churchill, too, referred to them in Parliament and in other public addresses.[1] In a characteristic passage from a message broadcast to the Polish people on May 3, 1941, Churchill described the tortures of " those who are gripped at home in the merciless oppression of the Hun ":[2]

All over Europe, races and States whose culture and history made them a part of the general life of Christendom in centuries when the Prussians were not better than a barbarous tribe, and the German Empire no more than an agglomeration of pumpernickel principalities, are now prostrate under the dark, cruel yoke of Hitler and his Nazi gang. Every week his firing parties are busy in a dozen lands. Monday he shoots Dutchmen, Tuesday Norwegians; Wednesday, French or Belgians stand against the wall; Thursday it is Czechs who must suffer. And now there are the Serbs and the Greeks

to fill this repulsive bill of executions.  But always, all
the days, there are the Poles.

This and similar statements were only descriptive of the
barbarities; yet they did not contain any indication of the
remedy that was to come, and how the Nazis were to be
induced to stop this brutal slaughter.  It was only after the
shooting of French hostages as a reprisal for the assassination
of two German officers that President Roosevelt seized the
opportunity to condemn these atrocities and to proclaim the
policy of retribution after the end of hostilities as one of the
war aims.  In an official statement on October 25, 1941,
Churchill again listed all the European countries whose populations had become victims of Nazi atrocities and endorsed
the policy of retribution proclaimed by President Roosevelt:[3]

> The butcheries in France are an example of what Hitler's
> Nazis are doing in many other countries under their yoke.
> The atrocities in Poland, in Yugoslavia, in Norway, in
> Holland, in Belgium and above all behind the German
> fronts in Russia, surpass anything that has been known
> since the darkest and most bestial ages of mankind. They
> are but a foretaste of what Hitler would inflict upon
> the British and American peoples if only he could get
> the power.  Retribution for these crimes must hence-
> forward take its place among the major purposes of
> the war.

As can be seen from the above quotations as well as from
many other references to Nazi barbarities made at that time,
Jewish martyrdom as such remained anonymous.  " Either
because the reports of mass murders of innocent people by
a State that claimed to be civilized seemed incredible, or
because the reported numbers of victims seemed exaggerated,
the Governments of the United Nations long refrained from
taking cognizance of the outrages, and the press, with a few
honourable exceptions, maintained a studied silence."[4]  Also
in other respects Jews were not referred to in these first war
years.  Churchill's very first public mention of Jews in World
War II was in a passing reference some few months after
assuming the Premiership.  On August 20, 1940, in a speech
in the Commons dealing with the future conduct of the war,

he spoke of Germany's mistake in having driven out her Jewish scientists:[5]

> Since the Germans drove the Jews out and lowered their technical standards, our science is definitely ahead of theirs.

More than another year was to pass before Jews were again mentioned by Churchill in public in another passing reference, though this time he did not speak of them merely as victims, but qualified them, together with all the Nazi victims, as allies in a common cause. At the Lord Mayor's luncheon, held on November 10, 1941, he stated:[6]

> I would say generally that we must regard all these victims of the Nazi executioners in so many lands, who are labelled Communists and Jews — we must regard them just as if they were brave soldiers who die for their country on the field of battle. Nay, in a way their sacrifice may be more fruitful than that of the soldier who falls with his arms in his hands. A river of blood has flowed and is flowing between the German race and the people of nearly all Europe. It is not the hot blood of battle, where good blows are given and returned. It is the cold blood of the execution yard and the scaffold, which leaves a stain indelible for generations and for centuries.

By then the war had lasted over two years and it was gradually becoming obvious to serious observers that the sufferings of the Jews in Europe far exceeded those of other peoples. Churchill felt the moment opportune to give public recognition to their exceptional and tragic situation. His message to the *Jewish Chronicle* on the occasion of its centenary in November 1941, did not fail to make a deep impression:[7]

> On the occasion of the centenary of the *Jewish Chronicle*, a landmark in the history of British Jewry, I send a message of good cheer to Jewish people in this and other lands. None has suffered more cruelly than the Jew the unspeakable evils wrought on the bodies and spirits of men by Hitler and his vile regime. The Jew bore the brunt of the Nazis' first onslaught upon the citadels of

freedom and human dignity. He has borne and continued
to bear a burden that might have seemed to be beyond
endurance. He has not allowed it to break his spirit;
he has never lost the will to resist. Assuredly in the day
of victory the Jews' sufferings and his part in the struggle
will not be forgotten. Once again, at the appointed time,
he will see vindicated those principles of righteousness
which it was the glory of his fathers to proclaim to the
world. Once again it will be shown that, though the
mills of God grind slowly, yet they grind exceeding small.

Here, at long last, the anonymity was lifted and the Jews
the world over were told that Britain's Prime Minister was
fully aware, even in the darkest hours of the war, of the
Jewish tragedy and of the responsibility that such a situation
entailed.

But what was to be done before or until the arrival of
the " appointed time " of which he spoke in his message?
There was very little consolation for the Jews whose lives
were daily in danger, nor for those who trembled for the
fate of their brethren on the Continent, in the promise that
retribution woud be exacted, and punishment meted out after
the war to those guilty of murder and atrocities. Even so, the
announcements by President Roosevelt and Churchill, and
the subsequent endorsement of the policy of retribution by
the Inter-Allied Conference in London of January, 1942,[8]
were received with satisfaction by Jews and non-Jews. For
it came " not a moment too soon ", as the *Jewish Chronicle*
remarked in a leading article,[9] " having regard to the mount-
ing barbarities that have been perpetrated in contempt not
only of elementary human feelings but of public law ". But
for all its importance the proclamation of the policy of retribution was only a declaration of intent as far as the immediate possibility of saving the victims was concerned. No
plan for instantaneous help, no word of promise for prompt
relief followed upon these declarations. " Retribution after
the war " remained the only public answer given the Nazis
at the time. Churchill repeated it in a message, addressed
to Dr. Stephen S. Wise, which was read out to a mass demonstration against German atrocities which took place on July
21, 1942, in New York. While he again stressed[10] that

The Jews were Hitler's first victims, and ever since they have been in the forefront of resistance to Nazi aggression,

he failed also on this occasion to point to any practical relief for Jewish sufferings: [11]

You are meeting this evening to condemn Hitler's atrocities in Europe and to offer all assistance to the United Nations in the war on the Axis. You will recall that on October 25 last year President Roosevelt and I expressed the horror felt by all civilised people at Nazi butcheries and terrorism. Our resolve is to place retribution for those crimes among the major purposes of this war.

Yet when addressing New York Jewry for the first time since America's entry into the war, he emphasized in this same message the important part which Jewry the world over, and particularly the Palestine Yishuv, were playing in the great struggle:

All over the world Jewish communities have made their contribution to the United Nations' cause, and on behalf of His Majesty's Government in the United Kingdom I welcome your determination to help as gladly as I acknowledge the eager support which the Jews of Palestine above all are already giving. Over 10,000 are now serving with the British Forces in the Middle East; more than 20,000 are enrolled in the various police formations in Palestine, and, as in this country, great numbers are employed in the front line constituted by pursuits in industries essential for the prosecution of the war and in the various services for civil defence.

The first defences of Palestine are the armies fighting in the Western Desert in which Palestinians are playing their full part. Our efforts must primarily be concentrated on ensuring the success of these armies. His Majesty's Government in the United Kingdom took risks in the dark days in 1940 to discharge their obligations in the Middle East and have throughout been animated by the determination that the Jewish population in Palestine should in all practicable ways play its part in the resistance of the United Nations to the oppression and brutalities of Nazi Germany which is the purpose of your meeting this evening to condemn.

The policy implied in this message was: struggle until victory, and subsequent punishment of war criminals. It did not imply any change of attitude towards possible channels of rescue for Jews from Europe. Shortly after this message was sent, another opportunity presented itself to Churchill to refer to Nazi atrocities against Jews, this time with regard to the deportation of French Jewry. On this occasion Churchill again stipulated post-war retributions as one of the principal war aims of the Allies: [12]

In a dozen countries Hitler's firing-parties are at work every morning, and a dark stream of cold execution blood flows between the Germans and almost all their fellow men. The cruelties, the massacres of hostages, the brutal persecutions in which the Germans have indulged in every land into which their armies have broken have recently received an addition in the most bestial, the most squalid and the most senseless of all their offences, namely, the mass deportation of Jews from France, with the pitiful horrors attendant upon the calculated and final scattering of families. This tragedy fills one with astonishment as well as with indignation, and it illustrates as nothing else can the utter degradation of the Nazi nature and theme, and the degradation of all who lend themselves to its unnatural and perverted passions.

When the hour of liberation strikes in Europe, as strike it will, it will also be the hour of retribution. I wish most particularly to identify His Majesty's Government and the House of Commons with the solemn words which were used lately by the President of the United States, namely, that those who are guilty of the Nazi crimes will have to stand up before tribunals in every land where their artocities have been committed in order that an indelible warning may be given to future ages and that successive generations of men may say, " So perish all who do the like again ".

But day in, day out, news about the accelerating policy of

extermination of European Jewry leaked out from Axis held countries. It was regularly brought to the notice of the free world by various Jewish organisations in Britain and America, which had been able to establish occasional contact with groups or individual Jews through neutral channels, such as Geneva, Lisbon and Istanbul.

At that time German armies were victorious on all fronts and Hitler was at the zenith of his triumphs. Victory seemed assured and therefore it appeared to be safe to embark upon the " final solution " of the Jewish problem by a gigantic extermination programme, converting Europe, as Goebbels had once promised, into a " Jewish cemetery ". And so, a few months later, on September 20, 1942, a message was sent to the *Jewish Telegraphic Agency* from a point " on the border of Axis-held territory " which stated *inter alia*:[13] " Pogroms carried out according to plan and on an unprecedented scale are occurring throughout the Government General of Poland. The Pogroms are being organised in connection with mass deportations of Jews from Warsaw, Lwow, Przemysl, and a number of other towns . . . the Nazis have begun the extermination of Polish Jewry. Save us !" And from then onwards almost daily news about the atrocities against the Jews in all countries under the Nazi yoke burst upon the world like a hideous avalanche. As far back as March 1942 Dr. Goebbels had set the ball of the new policy rolling when the Nazi press prominently carried Dr. Goebbels' statement regretting Germany's past action in allowing tens of thousands of Jews to leave countries under her control to become " war agitators " in Britain and U.S.A. " But ", he stressed,[14] " the Jews, especially those locked up in the ghettoes, are entertaining false hopes if they believe that a defeat of Germany will bring them relief. Germany has the means of destroying the Jews whenever it may be found necessary and the last bullet and poison gas will be kept in reserve for the realisation of Hitler's prophecy that this war is to result in the destruction of the Jews so that they can never again celebrate a victory over Germany."

But even then the late Chief Rabbi of the British Empire, Dr. J. H. Hertz, felt obliged to protest[15] that the " appalling facts of the Jewish situation in Nazi-controlled lands had not been brought home sufficiently to the general public ". Anglo-

Jewry therefore called a representative mass meeting against the ruthless extermination methods applied by the Nazis against European Jews, an impressive demonstration which took place on October 29, 1942, at the London Albert Hall, under the auspices of the Board of Deputies and under the chairmanship of the Archbishop of Canterbury.[16]   Churchill sent the following message which was read to the vast audience by Dr. William Temple:[17]

> My dear Archbishop, I cannot refrain from sending, through you, to the audience which is assembling under your chairmanship at the Albert Hall today to protest against Nazi atrocities inflicted on the Jews, the assurance of my warm sympathy with the objects of your meeting.
> The systematic cruelty to which the Jewish people— men, women and children—have been exposed under the Nazi regime are among the most terrible events in history, and place an indelible stain upon all who perpetrate and instigate them.  Free men and women denounce these evil crimes and when this world's struggle ends with the enthronement of human rights, racial persecution will be ended.

In America also protest meetings were held.  In November of that year Dr. Stephen S. Wise announced that Sumner Welles at the State Department had confirmed the dreadful reports received by Rabbi Wise since August from Dr. Gerhart Riegner at the Geneva Office of the World Jewish Congress.  They emphasised that Hitler had ordered the extermination of all Jews in occupied territory before the end of 1942, and that some two millons had already perished or been deported.[18]  Shortly afterwards a day of mourning for Jewry was proclaimed by ecclesiastical as well as secular institutions and was observed during the month of December all over the world.[19]

On December 11, the Polish Government-in-exile sent a Note to the Allied Nations on the persecution of the Jews based on recent evidence that had come into its possession.[20] Eleven Allied Governments assembled in Conference at St. James's Palace in London[21] issued a declaration on December 17 condemning in strongest terms the atrocities against the

Jews. On the same day Anthony Eden, the Foreign Secretary, replying in the House of Commons to a private notice question by S. S. Silverman, read this Declaration which he prefaced with the words: [22] " I regret to have to inform the House that reliable reports have recently reached His Majesty's Government regarding the barbarous and inhuman treatment to which Jews are being subjected in German occupied Europe." The international declaration which he then read recorded and condemned the barbarities committed and concluded with an emphatic re-statement of Roosevelt's and Churchill's declarations a year previously: [23] " They [the Allied Governments] re-affirm their solemn resolution to ensure that those responsible for these crimes shall not escape retribution, and to press on with the necessary practical measures to this end." The House then stood in silence in solemn protest against German barbarism and in honour of the victims—an exceptional event in British Parliamentary history.[24]

## THE BERMUDA CONFERENCE

Expressions of hope for a better world after the war and the promise of retribution were in fact the only official public reactions while the extermination of European Jewry was steadily gaining strength and impetus. The " practical measures " referred to in the United Nations Declaration were confined to these strong condemnations, and to their being broadcast into enemy territory.[25] In vain did the Vaad Leumi, the National Council of Palestine Jewry, in its manifesto, express disappointment[26] that " no practical steps have so far been taken through international factors and neutral countries to enable Jews to leave Nazi Europe, and that no announcement has been made expressing readiness to open the gates of Allied and neutral countries and to grant shelter to persecuted Jews "; in vain it also declared in its concluding paragraph the readiness of Palestine Jewry to " receive as many Jews as can be saved and to share with them everything it possesses ". For a long time to come Eden's reply to McGovern's question arising from this Declaration, whether " any persons who can escape from any of these occupied territories will be welcomed and given every assistance in the territories of the United Nations?", remained the established policy of the Government.  Eden then said:[27] "Certainly we should do all we possibly can.  There are, obviously, certain security formalities which have to be considered.  It would clearly be the desire of the United Nations to do everything they could to provide wherever possible an asylum for these people, but the House will understand that there are immense geographical and other difficulties in the matter." Yet there was increasing pressure put upon the British Government from all sides following these protests—particularly with regard to the demand that the gates of Palestine be thrown open to refugees.  As a result, on January 20, 1943, the British Ambassador in Washington called attention[28] in a note to the American authorities, to "what may be unlimited demands for accommodation on the part of refugees threatened by Germany's extermination policy".  He added that in the event of the suggestion of international co-operation proving acceptable, the British Government and the Colonies would be glad to examine the situation with a view to establishing whether there were still possibilities of carrying food in ships for civilian internees in German camps and accepting more refugees in British territory.  It took over a month for the U.S.A. authorities to reply.  In their answer of February 25, 1943, they said:[29] "The refugee problem should not be considered as being confined to persons of any particular race or faith.  Inter-Governmental collaboration for the temporary asylum of refugees as near as possible to the areas in which these people find themselves at present is strongly supported."  What was later to become known as the Bermuda Conference was held between April 19 and 29, 1943.[30]  There, the representatives of both Governments met in secret and the report of the proceedings was kept confidential "for security and other reasons", as Lord Cranborne later explained in the House of Lords,[31] and "in the interest of the refugees themselves".  The subsequent statements on this conference by the Government's spokesmen in the Commons (Osbert Peake)[32] and in the Lords (Lord Cranborne)[33] show, however, that there was no justification for this secrecy. For even before these official disclosures of the proceedings, it had become quite clear that the practical results of the conference were nil.  Neither Britain nor the United States wanted to admit any large number of refugees.

During their statements in Parliament, both Osbert Peake and Lord Cranborne gave an outline of the scope of the deliberations, and enumerated the difficulties with which the participants were confronted. The various proposals mooted for (a) an exchange of refugees against internees or prisoners of war in Allied hands; or (b) for a release of potential refugees, were rejected in principle and the Conference denied " the possibility of any general negotiations with the German Government "[34] on any of these questions. " They did not think it was a practical proposal . . . It was most improbable in any case that the Germans would agree to such a proposal."[35] On the other hand, the serious shipping shortage facing the Allies contributed to the rejection of these proposals by the Conference " as such a scheme would involve a large diversion of shipping."[36] Thus, it was argued, it would not be possible to transport refugees, even if they were able to escape. As the Under-Secretary of State for the Home Department put it:[37] " Accepting the principle that winning the war in the shortest possible time was the best service which their respective Governments could render to the refugees and to all those who are suffering under German tyranny, they concluded that it would be a grave disadvantage not only to the Allies but to the refugee cause to divert shipping from essential war needs to the carriage of refugees." Arguments such as these were then frequently advanced, but they make strange reading in the light of an entry in Churchill's *Memoirs* of the previous year, when he wrote to Eden:[38]

> Mr. Hopkins suggested that the United States might gladly take these prisoners [German and Italian prisoners of war held in camps in Egypt and India] if asked. A start should certainly be made on the 8,000 Germans. There are many American ships returning empty from the Red Sea ports which might well carry them. No special escort would be necessary.

When, three months after the Bermuda Conference, S. S. Hammersley asked[39] the Secretary for Foreign Affairs whether " in view of the improved shipping position in the Mediterranean, and the release of shipping recently used for the transport of Moslem pilgrims to Jedda, progress is being

made with the admission to Palestine of Jewish refugees ",
Eden replied: " The transport of refugees for whom places
are offered in Palestine is not held up by shipping difficulties
which His Majesty's Government has made every possible
effort to overcome.  The reasons why the refugees have not
been moved is the withholding of exit permits by the enemy
Governments concerned."

As the one positive achievement of the Bermuda Conference the Government speakers hailed the establishment of
" an Inter-Governmental Committee, constituted on the
widest basis and with all possible means of action at its
disposal ".[40]  It was praised by Osbert Peake as " the most
effective way of planning the rescue and settlement of persons
who have had the opportunity of escaping the horrors of
deportation, and, it may be, death, in Europe ".[41]  In fact, this
was neither a new idea nor a new institution.  The Bermuda
decision merely revived the idea of the Inter-Governmental
Committee for Refugees brought forth by the Evian Conference held in 1938 by invitation of President Roosevelt and
attended by representatives of thirty-three nations.[42]  But this
Committee created in Evian " was nothing more than a
facade "[43] and never actually saw the light of life.  Also the
Inter-Governmental Committee that should have begun to
function immediately after the Bermuda Conference never
actually became operative.  Rightly, therefore, could Abba
Hillel Silver say with bitter irony in a " Review of the Political
Situation in Zionism ":[44] " The clamour of the Jews in the
world to help save their doomed brothers in Europe by opening the doors of Palestine was deftly detoured into a number
of inter-governmental refugee conferences."

In addition to the various arguments previously raised in
connection with practical measures to save refugees — the
danger of Nazi spies mingling among refugees freed from
Europe, the shortage of shipping space and the refusal of
the German authorities to issue exit permits—an entirely
new angle was now introduced by the British authorities,
namely that Britain and the Empire had already admitted
more refugees than conditions permitted.  A week before the
Bermuda Conference Churchill himself added the stamp of
his authority to this new argument.  He chose for that purpose the form of a written Parliamentary reply to S. S. Ham-

mersley who had asked the Prime Minister what help was given by the Government to the refugees.[45] Churchill's survey reviewed not only Jewish refugees but those of all countries overrun by the Nazis who were able to escape and to settle in Britain, in the Empire and in Palestine. The figures thus revealed show that some 682,700 had been received since the outbreak of war. This figure tended to prove that[46]

The resources of Great Britain have been strained to the utmost in maintaining her traditions of asylum and hospitality while subjected to intensive enemy attack and forming not only a base for offensive operations, but an armed camp to an extent far beyond anything in her previous history.

Here it should be noted, though, that these 682,700 were by no means only refugees (under which heading they were listed) but, as the statement reveals,[47] it referred to " refugees, evacuees, and additional population in the form of internees and prisoners of war maintained in British territory and Palestine ". In the particular case of Palestine which was then a Mandated Territory, the statistics were as follows:[48]

Over 18,000 legal immigrants reached Palestine between 1st April, 1939, and 30th September, 1942. The total number of Jewish immigrants who entered the country during that period, including illegal immigrants, was about 38,000 and the great majority of these came from countries in Central and Eastern Europe. The quota for the period ended 30th September, 1942, provided for the grant of 1,000 certificates, 800 of them being allocated to Polish-Jewish refugee children in Persia. Actually 858 children accompanied by 369 adults, reached Palestine from Persia on the 18th February last. The immigration quota for the three months' period ending 31st December, 1942, provides for 3,000 Jewish immigrants, and this includes 1,000 orphan children and 200 adults from former Vichy France. In addition arrangements have been made to admit Jewish children from Roumania and Hungary, and it has now been decided to admit further children from these countries up to a total of 500.
The Government of Palestine have agreed to admit

from Bulgaria 4,000 Jewish children and 500 adults, and the necessary negotiations for their release and transport are taking place through the Protecting Power. As the Secretary of State for the Colonies announced on 3rd February, His Majesty's Government are prepared, provided the necessary transport is available, to continue to admit into Palestine Jewish children with a proportion of accompanying adults, up to the limits of immigration permissible for the five-year period ending 31st March, 1944, that is up to approximately 29,000. In addition Palestine has provided a temporary refuge during the war for some 4,000 people from Central Europe and Greece.

In the subsequent debate in Parliament on the Bermuda Conference (May 19, 1943)[49] Osbert Peake made use of the Prime Minister's statement[50] to prove that the utmost had been done by Britain to give a refuge to Nazi victims within the Empire and in Palestine.

## SILENT SYMPATHY

This flood of expressions of sympathy on the one hand, and the absence of any practical steps towards relief on the other, came under strong attack from many quarters.[51] The few public statements on Jewish matters made at various periods during the war show that Churchill was fully aware of the brutal treatment of the Jews by the Nazis. Had he not up to the end spoken[52] to the world of the

exceptional brutality and horrible inflictions imposed upon the Jewish people?

The courageous fighting stand which he took up in the years preceding the war was frequently recalled when he not only condemned the Nazi persecution methods but also demanded that the doors of Palestine be kept open for those Jews who could escape.[53] In the Jewish press and in public meetings the demand was then often heard that, in response to the readiness of Palestine Jewry to receive those who could escape, the Prime Minister should issue a call to European Jews to try by all possible means to escape from certain death and to reach Palestine where open doors would welcome them.   This is not the place to deal with this problem, which not only involves the escape of Jews from Europe but the whole Palestine immigration policy, to which a special section is devoted in Part II of this Study.   Yet it must be stated in all fairness that these appeals and attacks never implied that the Jews doubted Churchill's friendly attitude; though this attitude often made it all the more difficult to understand his silence.   One event of those years (while out-side the problem of saving refugees, and dealt with in greater detail in Part II), is a perfect example of the confidence Churchill commanded among all sectors of the Jewish com-munity.   On November 6, 1944, the Minister of State, Lord Moyne, was assassinated in Cairo by two members of the Stern group.   For over thirty years he had been Churchill's " intimate friend "[54] and it is therefore easy to understand the Prime Minister's deep feelings when he rose to make his statement in Parliament:[55]

> This shameful crime has shocked the world.   It has affected none more strongly than those like myself who, in the past, have been consistent friends of the Jews and constant architects of their future.   If our dreams for Zionism are to end in the smoke of assassin's pistols, and our labours for its future to produce only a new set of gangsters worthy of Nazi Germany, many like myself will have to reconsider the position we have maintained so consistently and so long.

These were grave and bitter words addressed not to the Zionists, not even as a warning to the terrorists, but to the whole Jewish people.   " Had anyone but the Prime Minister made the statement ", wrote the London *Zionist Review*,[56] " it would have been resented as an unfriendly gesture towards the Yishuv which has given 30,000 volunteers to the British Forces, and has faithfully stood by this country." But because of his known friendship towards the Jews, the paper continued, " his warning was accepted by the Yishuv as bitter words but sound advice ".   The official organ of the Jewish Agency, *The New Judaea*, expressed these thoughts even more clearly when it pointed out:[57] " A powerless people, it is generally stressed, cannot be held responsible for the criminal acts of individual outlaws.   But it is felt that the warning came from a loyal and sincere friend." From these and many other similar statements in the Jewish press in connection with this and other events during the war, it is evident that the Jewish people had a deep-seated belief in Churchill's sincere friendship towards it. Hence the many appeals addressed to him to help save the remnants of the Jewish people martyred by the Nazis; hence also the many attacks on him inspired by and charging him with this friendship. Churchill, however, was not to be dragged into controversy. He remained unmoved and silent in face of both appeals and attacks. Throughout the war no public statement of his can be found in which he had tried to justify his stand or explain his attitude to what for European Jewry was a matter of life and death.[58]

But what went on behind closed doors?

## (b) BEHIND CLOSED DOORS

ONLY after the War, when an occasional reference in Churchill's *War Memoirs* brought certain facts to light, did it become possible to gain insight into what had been going on behind the closed doors of the Government. It appears from these references that controversies between Churchill and some of his colleagues took place both before the extent of the extermination of Jews became known as well as afterwards. They show unequivocally that Sir Winston, also during those difficult war years, was trying to live up to his sympathies for the Jewish people. And yet, at no time have these sympathies and endeavours sufficed to make him fight to a successful end or caused him to dismiss the one or other antagonist of his policy among his colleagues. For Churchill's dominant thought has been througout to avoid internal clashes or splits and to concentrate single-mindedly on prosecuting and winning the war.

One of the first references to a conflicting attitude with regard to Jewish matters at that time can be found in a correspondence between the Prime Minister and Lord Lloyd, the Colonial Secretary, whom Churchill calls " a convinced anti-Zionist and pro-Arab ".[59] In June 1940 Churchill was anxious to recall to Western Europe the eleven British regular battalions that had been sent to Palestine to suppress the Arab Rebellion (1936-1939),[60] and to have them replaced by

Indian troops as well as by Jewish volunteers. Leopold Amery, then Secretary of State for India, objected, since he was planning to create a large Indian army in India. Lord Lloyd objected for reasons of policy in Palestine as it was then pursued by the Colonial Office. The latter received the following outspoken note[61] from Churchill:

28.VI.40.

The failure of the policy which you favour is proved by the very large numbers of sorely-needed troops you [we] have to keep in Palestine: 6 battalions of infantry, 9 regiments of Yeomanry, 8 battalions of Australian infantry, the whole probably more than twenty thousand men.

This is the price we have to pay for the anti-Jewish policy which has been persisted in for some years. Should the war go heavily into Egypt, all these troops will have to be withdrawn, and the position of the Jewish colonists will be one of the greatest danger. Indeed I am sure that we shall be told we cannot withdraw these troops, though they include some of our best, and are vitally needed elsewhere. If the Jews were properly armed, our forces would become available, and there would be no danger of the Jews attacking the Arabs, because they are entirely dependent upon our command of the seas. I think it is little less than a scandal that at a time when we are fighting for our lives these very large forces should be immobilised in support of a policy which commends itself only to a section of the Conservative party.

I had hoped you would take a broad view of the Palestine situation, and would make it an earnest objective to set the British garrison free. I could certainly not associate myself with such an answer as you have drawn up for me. I do not at all admit that Arab feeling in the Near East and India would be prejudiced in the manner you suggest. Now that we have the Turks in such a friendly relationship the position is much more secure.

What makes this intervention remarkable is the fact that it was made less than six weeks after Churchill had become

Prime Minister in one of the darkest hours of World War II. Despite the superhuman task which absorbed him fully he took time off to write this long note. It was not written in vain. While the creation of a Jewish Army was not acceptable to Lloyd, Churchill's intervention bore some immediate fruit. For, six days after this letter was written, David Ben Gurion called on Lord Lloyd " who agreed to the establishment of large numbers of Palestine Jews into distinctive Jewish units for service with the British forces outside Palestine ".[62] This problem of the Jewish Army, however, is indicative neither of a favourable nor an unfavourable attitude towards the general Jewish problem, for it fell within the strict confines of military considerations on the one hand and of Zionist and Palestine politics on the other. The test to be applied are the events which occurred in the Jewish diaspora.

## THE SINKING OF THE " PATRIA "

Four months after Churchill's note was written, a very serious situation had arisen decisively affecting the fate of thousands of Jews trying to escape from Europe. The free world was then hermetically closed to any immigration and even denied asylum, while Palestine, the only remaining outlet, was still governed by the pre-war immigration restrictions. These had, for many years past, driven those whose lives were in danger to frantic efforts to reach by all possible means the haven of what they regarded as their National Home. In most cases they succeeded and landed in Palestine as " illegal immigrants ". Throughout that period " the search for boats carrying Jewish fugitives and the prevention of their landing became a major concern of the Palestine authorities "[63] It was particularly during the autumn of 1940 that " reports from the Balkans indicated a revival of illegal immigrants and the British Government decided that any Jewish illegal immigrants arriving in Palestine should not be allowed to remain, but should be provided with an alternative place of refuge in the Colonial Empire ".[64] Soon this new policy came under test. On November 1 and 3 respectively, two ships, the *Pacific* and the *Milos,* carrying 1,771 illegal immigrants were intercepted off the coast of Palestine and taken into Haifa harbour.[65] The Government's refusal to permit them to land led to a widespread protest by the entire Jewish community in Palestine, culminating in a Jewish general strike throughout the country on November 20.[66]   On that day a communique was broadcast stating that His Majesty's Government, while not lacking in sympathy for the refugees will not permit the landing in Palestine and will deport them to a colony for the duration of the war " but it is not proposed that they shall remain in the colony to which they are sent or that they should go to Palestine ".[67]   Arrangements were then made in Haifa harbour to transfer these refugees to Mauritius in the s.s. *Patria*.   But as a reaction to this decision the *Patria* was blown up on November 25 and sunk in the harbour. About 250 of its passengers were drowned and the survivors landed and interned.   A further 1,783 refugees, who at the same time arrived in Haifa on the *Atlantic* and who had been landed, were, with considerable use of violence, re-embarked and deported to Mauritius on December 9, 1940.[68]   Three days before the blowing up of the *Patria* and before the forced embarkation, Churchill in a communication to Lord Lloyd expressed an unwilling approval of the communique issued on November 20.   The tone of this note does not permit any doubt as to the writer's sentiments:[69]

22.XI.1940.

As the action has been announced, it must proceed, but the conditions in Mauritius must not involve these people being caged up for the duration of the war.   The Cabinet will require to be satisfied about this.   Pray make me your proposals.

The blowing up of the *Patria*, of course, altered the situation and it was expected that it might also alter the attitude of the Government.   With such hopes in mind Dr. Weizmann went to see Lord Lloyd to persuade him to allow the survivors to be landed.   " I was met with the usual arguments about the law being the law ", Dr. Weizmann writes,[70] " to which I retorted: ' A law is something which must have a moral basis, so that there is an inner compelling force for every citizen to obey.   But if the majority of citizens is convinced that the law is merely an infliction, it can only be enforced at the point of the bayonet against the consent of the community '."   But he was unable to obtain the minister's consent to the landing. "My arguments were wasted", Dr. Weizmann continues, "Lord Lloyd could not agree with me. He said so, and added: 'I must tell you that I've blocked all the approaches for you. I know you will go to Churchill and try to get him to overrule me. I have therefore warned the Prime Minister that I will not consent. So please don't try to get at him'." In making such a statement Lord Lloyd had probably Churchill's note of November 22 to him in mind in which the Prime Minister gave his reluctant consent to the transfer to Mauritius of the refugees in Haifa harbour. But since this note was written the catastrophe had taken place and public opinion been roused. Dr. Weizmann persisted in his efforts. While he accepted the approach to Churchill being blocked, "Lord Lloyd had not blocked the approach to the Foreign Office", writes Dr. Weizmann further, "so I went to see Lord Halifax". There he was more successful and to his full satisfaction "heard the next day that he [Lord Halifax] had sent a telegram to Palestine to permit the passengers to land ".[71] So far Dr. Weizmann's version. From Churchill's *Memoirs* we can conclude that he had a hand in this decision, notwithstanding Lord Lloyd's claim that he "had blocked the approach to the Prime Minister ". In fact, it was Churchill who overruled this opposition and sent the telegram to Palestine. He referred to this act of his a few months later when General Wavell opposed the creation of a Jewish Army to fight alongside the Allies against Nazism, using the argument of the serious reactions which such a step may arouse in the Arab world. Churchill wrote to Lord Moyne, who meanwhile had succeeded Lord Lloyd at the Colonial Office:[72]

1 March 41.

General Wavell, like most British military officers, is strongly pro-Arab. At the time of the licences to the shipwrecked illegal immigrants being permitted, he sent a telegram not less strong than this, predicting widespread disaster in the Arab world, together with the loss of the Basra-Baghdad-Haifa route. The telegram should be looked up, and also my answer, in which I overruled the General and explained to him the reason for the Cabinet decision. All went well, and not a dog barked.

## THE " STRUMA " TRAGEDY

Churchill's published works are silent about the *Patria* disaster and the other catastrophes which occurred under his Premiership during the war when refugees from Europe attempted to reach the safe haven of Palestine. One of the most tragic cases was the sinking, on February 24, 1942, of the *Struma* carrying 764 passengers. For nearly two months she had been lying at Istanbul waiting for Palestine visas. In the end the Palestine Government agreed to issue immigration permits for children under sixteen, but this permission arrived too late. For meanwhile the Turkish authorities had turned the vessel back into the Black Sea, where she sank, with only one survivor.[73] On all sides news of this disaster was received with profound shock. Palestine Jewry proclaimed a day of general protest strike on February 26.[74] All over the free world protest meetings were held and the blame for the catastrophe laid at the door of both the Turkish authorities and the British Government. Dr. Weizmann headed the attack from the platform of a Special Zionist Conference, called by the English Zionist Federation on March 8, 1942. In his speech about the *Struma* tragedy he blamed directly the Palestine Administration " and to some extent also those who were responsible for the conduct of Palestinian affairs in Whitehall ".[75] " One is horrified ", he continued, " to think what sort of people are those who rule the destinies of Palestine — people without understanding, without compassion, and without pity." In a subsequent debate in the Lords[76] Lord Davis and Lord Wedgwood, speaking of the disaster and of the general immigration policy into Palestine, branded the Palestine Administration as anti-Semitic. The Government speakers did not try to minimise the Government's responsibility. Harold Macmillan, Under-Secretary for the Colonies, frankly confessed in the Commons in connection with the *Struma* tragedy:[77] " While she was lying at Istanbul, the Turkish authorities intimated that the passengers could not be allowed to remain in Turkey. The Palestine Government also made it clear, with the support of His Majesty's Government, that they could not be admitted to Palestine."

The tragedy unavoidably followed.

Up to March/April 1942 the Government's policy with regard to "illegal" immigration into Palestine was laid down and adhered to in the various statements quoted and was repeated in Macmillan's speech in the Commons to which reference was made above. The Under-Secretary of State for the Colonies then said:[78] "His Majesty's Government earnestly hope that such a tragedy [*Struma*] will not occur again. It does not lie in their power, however, amid the dangers and uncertainties of war, to give any guarantee, nor can they be party to any measures which would undermine the existing policy regarding illegal immigration into Palestine, in view of the wider issues involved." It seems, however, that after the outcry which followed the *Struma* disaster this rigid administrative and legal principle could not be maintained. The official statement of the Jewish Agency reports with regard to the subsequent developments:[79] "After the *Struma* disaster the rules were relaxed. It was decided to admit and gradually release all refugees from Europe who got to Palestine on their own. At the same time it was made clear that nothing would be done to help them to get there. In a communication to the Jewish Agency in May 1942, the British Government said: 'In pursuance of the existing policy of taking practicable steps to discourage illegal immigration into Palestine, nothing whatever will be done to facilitate the arrival of Jewish refugees in Palestine.' It should be borne in mind that at that time no facilities existed in the Balkans for obtaining visas to Palestine. The only way for a refugee to seek legal admission to Palestine was to reach Istanbul and apply to the British Consul there. But at Istanbul he was already 'illegal'."

This "relaxation of the rules", as recorded by the Jewish Agency at the time, at first expressed itself only in declarations, while further steps towards more tangible relaxation of the rules were only gradually taken, not so much voluntarily as under growing international pressure. The protest wave against Nazi atrocities which became known to the outside world at the end of 1942, and to which reference has been made,[80] somewhat accelerated the pace. The two great demonstrations in Britain, that of the Board of Deputies and the subsequent solemn protest in Parliament, added weight to the demand now raised all over the free world, particularly

in America, that all those who might be able to escape
from Europe should be encouraged to do so and be helped
to enter countries in the free world, but particularly Palestine.
But the military situation too had by then, after the victories
of Stalingrad and Alamein, taken a definite turn for the better.
The latter victory particularly affected the Palestine issue and
Churchill was able to write to General Ismay on January 5,
1943: [81]

> Accounts must be taken of the complete change in con-
> ditions in the Middle East since August 1942.   The
> decisive victories in the Western Desert and the immense
> come-back of the Russians in South Russia and the
> Caucasus have removed for an indefinite period the
> principal dangers which we then faced.

All these facts contributed to a more serious consideration
of easing the immigration into Palestine.   But it still took
until the middle of 1943 that the Government " agreed to
facilitate the journey to Palestine of all refugees reaching
Istanbul ".[82]   However, even then some hidden forces seem
to have prevailed, for " this decision, of which the Jewish
Agency was informed confidentially, was not published, nor
was it, for a further nine months, communicated to the
Turkish Government.   This robbed it of much of its value ".[83]

* * *

This brings this part of our story up to 1944 or almost two
years after the sinking of the *Struma*. The two tragedies of
the *Patria* and *Struma* were described at length in this section,
although it may seem that these incidents should have been
dealt with in Part II of this Study, where Palestine and
Zionism are separately dealt with.   And yet, these tragedies
seem to me of far greater significance within the wider aspect
of rescuing Jews in the Diaspora from certain death, without
any regard to their final destination.   It is one of the tragic
facts of our generation that no other country could in those
years even be thought of as a potential haven for these
refugees.   It is for this reason that the story of the " coffin
boats [which] continued to wander over the Mediterranean,
unable to discharge their human cargoes ",[84] is given so pro-

minent a place in this section. This also explains why other migration problems, which in their narrower aspect also come under the heading of Palestine and Zionism, are nevertheless dealt with here, often in great detail.

That period of tragedies at sea was one of unbelievable inactivity and callousness where some aid might have altered the fate of many hundreds of thousands of Jews. It was a period, as a chronicler wrote,[85] when "all our cries and pleas for life-saving action were shattered against walls of indifference until we began to stifle in the black realization that we are helpless". One is accustomed in this connection to putting the blame on the British and Turkish Governments, but in all justice it must be said that all Governments and countries of the free world are equally guilty of not having helped or invited refugees to their shores — if only as an asylum as distinct from permanent settlement.

## THE WAR REFUGEE BOARD

This persisting inactivity accompanied by the barbarous extermination policy of Nazi Germany was causing deep grief within the Jewries of the free world. Many important non-Jews in the political, religious, cultural and other fields joined in expressions of great disappointment at the absence of any practical immediate help. A number of committees and organisations sprung up whose aim it was to devise some kind of rescue programme to be submitted for implementation by the Allies. In Britain, the most prominent of these was the National Committee for Rescue from Nazi Terror headed by the Archbishop of Canterbury, Lord Crewe, Miss Eleanor Rathbone, Col. Victor Cazalet and many others. The most impressive manifestations of such committees took place in the U.S.A., and as a result of these " a great number of suggestions were offered and discussed by government officials, political parties, labour groups, non-Jewish and Jewish organisations, and echoed by the press of the country ".[86] Important practical suggestions also emanated from the meetings of the " American Jewish Conference ", which consisted of 64 National Jewish organisations, and was headed by Henry Monsky, Dr. Stephen S. Wise and Dr. Israel Goldstein. These meetings took place in New York between August 29 and September 2, 1943.[87] Far-reaching proposals were adopted by the " Emergency Conference to Save the Jewish People of Europe ", organised by a group of young Palestinians and headed by Peter Bergson (Hillel Cook) and Shemuel Merlin. Upon recommendation of the " Emergency Conference " their two leading members, Will Rogers, Jr., and Guy M. Gillette, introduced identical resolutions in the House of Representatives and in the Senate respectively, providing for the President to establish a commission charged with effecting " the rescue of the Jewish people of Europe ".[88] During the hearings on the resolutions before the House Foreign Affairs Committee many important men in public life, such as Mayor Fiorello La Guardia of New York City, Dean Alfange, the American Labour Party leader, Wendell L. Willkie and others, gave them their support. After their approval by the Senate Foreign Relations Committee numerous messages were sent from all over the U.S.A. urging the government to rescue the Jews in Europe. These resolutions were withdrawn when on January 22, 1944, almost a year after the Bermuda Conference, President Roosevelt set up the War Refugee Board.[89]    Its object was " to take all measures within its powers to rescue the victims of enemy oppression who are in imminent danger of death and otherwise to afford such victims all possible relief and assistance consistent with the successful prosecution of the war ".[90] When three months later the representative of the War Refugee Board, Ira A. Hirschmann, arrived in Turkey to take up his post in Ankara, he carried out an inquiry into the reasons for the delay and obstructions of the escape of refugees. In a short paragraph in his book[91] he described the situation as he found it and which was characteristic of the " leisurely " methods used to save people caught in a hurricane of destruction: " The explanation varied with the nationality and position of the person consulted. The British placed responsibility for the tie-up on the Bulgarians. The Bulgarians blamed the Germans. The Turks said blandly that the British were causing the delay. In many quarters there seemed to be little doubt that it was the Turks themselves who were obstructing the work of rescue. It was a dismal and confusing state of affairs. As I made the rounds from embassy to embassy, I began to feel like a refugee myself."

As soon, however, as the War Refugee Board had started organised rescue work an intervention in London prompted an immediate instruction to the British Embassy in Ankara to render any possible assistance. " Suddenly ", writes Hirschmann,[92] " what can only be described as, at best, a desultory interest on the part of the British became productive. The visas were turned up in the British Embassy, where they had been on ice as the result of a technicality. They were quickly approved, and, within three weeks of my arrival in Ankara, the forty-five hundred children who had been approved for immigration into Palestine ever since 1942 began to arrive in Istanbul from Bulgaria, in groups of one hundred a week." It was then that the Turks raised new difficulties. They demanded a letter from the British Government guaranteeing that all Jewish refugees entering Turkey would be permitted by the British to leave Istanbul within twenty-four hours. " The bitter irony in the situation ", Hirschmann continues,[93] " lay in the fact that the British had not refused the required commitment. The British Government had, in fact, prepared the letter and sent it. The trouble was that *it had been mislaid somewhere.*[94] After persistent pursuits, I finally had this letter located, again in the British Embassy, and the movement of the refugees out of Axis lands was resumed immediately."

This lamentable and unsatisfactory state of affairs accelerated the efforts on the part of Jewish organisations to send or appoint their own representatives in various neutral places to organise some kind of rescue work, particularly after the refugees' escape from the Nazi grip. The most prominent of these places was Istanbul. Other Jewish groups were engaged in organising " illegal " escapes from Europe thereby opening one of the most glorious chapters in modern Jewish history. Jon and David Kimche describe one sector of these activities in their *Secret Roads*,[95] recording the efforts of a group of young men, known as " The Boys ", who organised the traffic of small ships to carry refugees to safety. " Although the Governments of the U.S.A. and Britain did not co-operate with these ' illegal groups ', high officials of the British and American intelligence services placed great value on their resourcefulness, they exchanged many services and favours. Allied intelligence profited by being able to interrogate the messengers in the pay of the Palestinians about conditions inside enemy territory, and used them as couriers to the Axis countries. The British, in turn, did not interfere with the work of 'the boys' in making deals with shipowners and captains."[96]

## THE TRAGEDY OF HUNGARIAN JEWRY

Just at that moment—March 19, 1944—Hitler had taken complete control of Hungary which up to then had been a tolerable haven of relative peace and humane treatment of Hungarian Jews as well as of the refugees who were able to escape there.[97]  One of the official German pretexts for the occupation was " the unrestricted presence of some one million Jews as a concrete menace to the safety of German arms on the Balkan peninsula ".[98]  Five days later President Roosevelt, sensing what such an occupation meant for the Jews there, issued a statement[99] warning that " all who knowingly take part in the deportation of Jews to their death " would be punished, and appealed to the Hungarian people to do all in their power to prevent the threatened extermination of the Jews. The President declared that he had consulted Churchill and Stalin before issuing the statement. The British Government associated themselves with this statement[100] in a declaration made by Eden in reply to a question by S. S. Silverman.  Soon afterwards matters took an extraordinary and surprising turn.

On May 19, 1944, two Nazi emissaries arrived in Istanbul with an offer to exchange human beings for coffee, tea and motor trucks;[101] " A million Jews for 10,000 trucks ".[102] These emissaries were taken by British intelligence officers from Turkey via Syria to Cairo, where Lord Moyne, Deputy Minister of State in the Middle East, had his headquarters. After great difficulties Ira Hirschmann was received by Lord Moyne, who conveyed to him Eden's invitation to visit London where the Jewish Agency representative Shertok (now Sharett), after passing through Cairo, had flown following a similar invitation.[103]  Hirschmann declined, however, to go to London and finally obtained permission to interrogate the emissaries on the spot.

During these conversations a question of principle arose, namely whether the Allies should enter into negotiations at all with the enemy. Lord Halifax, then British Ambassador in Washington, in a memorandum to the Americans outlined the British Government's negative attitude towards the proposed " humans for goods " exchange. Lord Moyne, opposing the deal, repeated the argument in his conversation with Hirschmann " that the British Government would not be put in a position of accepting bribes or being caught in a net of trick psychological warfare; that this could be one of the Nazis' many devious tricks. The very idea of exchanging money or material in the midst of a war was revolting. Of course they would not do it, as it was contrary to principle." In his testimony[104] in the Gruenwald-Kastner case, Joel Brand, one of the emissaries, replying to questions by his attorney, Shemuel Tamir, referred to another argument advanced by Lord Moyne. During his talk with the Deputy Minister of State for the Middle East Brand was clearly told " What shall I do with these million Jews? Where shall I put them?" On hearing this answer, Brand said, he became desperate and, losing all hope for the rescue of his brethren in Hungary, went on hunger strike in protest.[105]

The report on the interview between Hirschmann and Joel Brand (the other emissary, Gyoergy [Bandy] Gross, is said to have been a double agent)[106] a copy of which he handed by arrangement to Lord Moyne, was transmitted by the latter to London[107] and contained not only important information about conditions within Nazi occupied territories but also authentic information about the terrible plight of the Hungarian Jewry. It is probable that on the basis of this memorandum and of some other information that had meanwhile become available,[108] Churchill wrote on July 11, 1944, to Anthony Eden:[109]

> There is no doubt that (this persecution of Jews in Hungary and their expulsion from enemy territory) is probably the greatest and most horrible crime ever committed in the whole history of the world, and it has been done by scientific machinery by nominally civilised men in the name of a great State and one of the leading races of Europe. It is quite clear that all concerned in this crime who may fall into our hands, including the people who not only obeyed orders of carrying out the

butcheries, should be put to death after their association with the murders has been proved. I cannot therefore feel that this is the kind of ordinary case which is put through the Protecting Power, as, for instance, the lack of feeding or sanitary conditions in some particular prisoners' camp. There should therefore, in my opinion, be no negotiations of any kind on this subject. Declarations should be made in public, so that everyone connected with it will be hunted down and put to death.

Nine days later, on July 20, 1944, an official announcement was made through the B.B.C. in which the offer " Jews for trucks " was disclosed and emphatically rejected.[110]

It is difficult to judge today whether negotiations would have led to any practical results. The fact remains, though, that Churchill declined to sanction any negotiations. He may have had in mind previous experiences of the War Refugee Board when it had entered into negotiations with regard to organising legal emigration from Europe via Roumania. " All agreed ", the Report records,[111] " except the Germans. The Nazis were adamant in refusing to grant safe conduct despite repeated approaches made on behalf of the Board through the Governments of Sweden and Switzerland." Or he may have had in mind the statement of Goebbels in 1942 referred to above[112] in which Hitler's mouthpiece regretted Germany's past action in allowing Jews to leave countries under their control and proclaimed the decision to detain them until their complete destruction. In the light of such experiences Anthony Eden's reply to a question put to him by S. S. Silverman became and remained the official Government's policy:[113] " The reasons why the refugees have not been moved is the withholding of exit permits by the enemy Governments concerned."

Hirschmann, however, does not leave us in any doubt that Brand's mission, preceding as it did the German collapse, was of a different nature and when he met Brand in Jerusalem five months after the first interview, "the door was then still open ".[114] In reply to questions by Tamir, Joel Brand testified before the Jerusalem court that there never had been any doubt in his mind that an attempt to exchange " goods for people " should have been made, the more so as the release of 100,000 Jews " on account " had been promised him by Eichmann.[115]   Only such an experiment could have proved whether or not the Germans meant business.

Whatever the outcome of this by now purely academic dispute, the fact remains that other motives beside those of lofty principles or psychological warfare influenced the rejection of negotiations with Nazis or their emissaries. The *Jewish Chronicle*, after the B.B.C. announcement of the rejection of the offer, reported:[116] " The British Government immediately consulted Washington and Moscow regarding the proposed scheme, which official British circles regard as a foul and blatant attempt to divide the Allies." And in the *Final Summary Report* we read[117] that " the nature of the offer indicated that the Germans were attempting to use the Jews in their hands not only as pawns for possible economic and personal benefit but also as a means to create dissension between U.S.A., Great Britain and Russia. The offer was, of course, rejected and the Russian Government fully informed." From these statements it emerges that this was no longer a question of whether the Germans would or would not release refugees, but a much more involved issue of inter-Allied policy necessitating consultations between the three main Allied Nations.   This, because the Nazi offer of " a million Jews for war material " was accompanied by the promise that these materials would not be used against the Western Allies but " only " on the eastern front.[118]   Judging from various indications (in the absence of other documentary evidence), the Russians, apart from the particular anti-Soviet tendency of the scheme, also objected on principle to any negotiations with the Nazis.   At that time they were looking at Britain and the U.S.A. with some suspicion, and being already in Roumania and in the foothills of the Carpathian mountains, they could easily have blocked any escape route. Without their co-operation, therefore, any serious plans would have been doomed anyway.   Accusing as they did the Western Allies of seeking a separate peace with Germany, any contact or negotiations with the Germans (even if only for the release of refugees) would have been regarded by them as confirming their suspicions.

At that time the news leaked out from Hungary that, as a result of the warnings uttered by the leaders of the United Nations and of the storm of outraged protests against the deportation of Hungarian Jews to the death camps in Poland, an undertaking has been given by the Hungarian Government to the International Red Cross in Switzerland that no more Jews would be deported.[119]   As Professor Brodetsky informed a meeting of the Board of Deputies,[120] Eden had confirmed this to a deputation of the " National Committee for Rescue from Nazi Terror ". A few days later the Foreign Secretary repeated this confirmation in Parliament in a written answer to T. H. Hewlett.[121]   In fact, on July 18, 1944, an offer had been made by the Regent Nicholas Horthy to release Jewish children under ten as well as adult Jews possessing Palestine visas or visas to other countries.[122]   Meanwhile the rate of deportations of Hungarian Jews diminished, though they still continued; but their scale was far below the original massive transports.[123]   Even so, by July 1944 half of Hungary's Jews had already been deported to the extermination camps.[124]   Remained, therefore, the vital question of saving the surviving half.   On August 17, the State Department announced that the Governments of the United States and of the United Kingdom had " accepted the offer of the Hungarian Government for the release of Jews, and will make arrangements for the care of such Jews leaving Hungary who reach neutral or United Nations territory, and also that they will find temporary havens of refuge where such people may live in safety ".[125]   The acceptance of the offer (to which have to be added other factors such as the intervention of the Vatican, the King of Sweden, and Swiss organisations, all of which offered their assistance in carrying out Horthy's offer) contributed in no small measure to the slowing down of the deportations.[126]   No doubt the Russian onslaughts on Hungary's borders too deserve considerable credit for this turn of events, since the impetus of the Russian advance prevented a wholesale last-minute slaughter of Hungary's surviving Jewish population.[127]   But alas, Horthy's offer proved abortive:[128] the Germans deported him after he had on his own initiative requested an armistice of the Allies.

The Horthy offer enables us to understand the attitude of Britain and the United States in the case of the Brand " bargain ".   There, as we know, the offer was flatly refused. Here, on the other hand, Horthy having attached no strings whatever to his proposition such as a demand of " goods for Jews ", the Allies accepted. It was the Germans who prevented the carrying out of the agreement and thus of the escape of the refugees.

It seems, however, the Russians in this case too viewed the Horthy offer as reprehensible negotiations with the enemy and rejected it, as they had the Brand offer. In view of the entirely different nature of this second approach, Churchill felt that his negative attitude towards negotiations could not be justified. He sensed a possible chance of escape for the refugees and therefore, while the British and American Governments exchanged views on their reply to Horthy's offer, Churchill wrote to Eden[129] eleven days before its public announcement:

> This seems to be a rather doubtful business [the case of the Hungarian Jews]. These unhappy families, mainly women and children, have purchased their lives with probably nine-tenths of their wealth. I should not like England to seem to be wanting to hunt them down. By all means tell the Russians anything that is necessary, but please do not let us prevent them from escaping. I cannot see how any suspicion of peace negotiations could be fixed on this miserable affair.

*  *<br>*

Joel Brand's " bargain " offer and Horthy's scheme were only two of a number of similar overtures and negotiations which at one time or another were conducted by various organisations and individuals in Switzerland, Sweden, Portugal and other places. Some of these offers and the negotiations connected with them are described in the *Final Summary Report*.[130]  Others are referred to in the official *Political Report* (1946) of the Jewish Agency.[131]  Some particulars about the negotiations for the release of Jews from Hungary other than those referred to above, came to light in court in the Gruenwald-Kastner case.[132]. This pathetic literature allows us a glimpse at the way Jewish men, women and children were made the pawns of an unscrupulous trade in human beings, unparalleled in history in its magnitude.

The number of refugees who were able to escape, not only from Hungary but from other European countries as well, is insignificant compared with the staggering number of victims. The *Final Summary Report* gives some figures,[133] as does other literature.[134] The escape routes were, of course, limited but some few fortunate ones got out via Rumania, some via Tito's partisan territory, others via Bulgaria, others yet from Greece. Between January 1944 and February 1945,[135] 539 refugees succeeded in escaping from Greece in small fishing boats crossing the Ægean Sea to the Turkish coast. It is probably in connection with the escape of these refugees that some argument arose between Britain and the U.S.A. which prompted Churchill to intervene in a note to Eden of July 14, 1944:[136]

### ESCAPE OF JEWS FROM GREECE

This requires careful handling. It is quite possible that rich Jews will pay large sums of money to escape being murdered by the Huns. It is tiresome that this money should get into the hands of E.L.A.S.,[137] but why on earth we should go and argue with the United States about it I cannot conceive. We should take a great responsibility if we prevented the escape of Jews, even if they should be rich Jews. I know it is the modern view that all rich people should be put to death wherever found, but it is a pity that we should take up that attitude at the present time. After all, they have no doubt paid for their liberation so high that in future they will only be poor Jews, and therefore have the ordinary rights of human beings.

\*     \*
\*

Very little light is shed in his *Memoirs* and in other literature so far published on Churchill's direct intervention in the matters referred to in the preceding pages. It is quite possible and even probable that when the rest of the records will be made available, more and similar evidence of his positive and sympathetic attitude towards Jewish matters will come to light. Various statements were of course made at various times in the name and on behalf of His Majesty's Government,

for which Churchill and his colleagues in the Cabinet share
responsibility.   But these do not necessarily represent his
own viewpoint, for in most cases government pronouncements
are the result of a compromise of all individual views, good,
bad and indifferent ones being shared collectively.  It would,
therefore, be wrong to over-simplify matters by deducing that
all sympathetic declarations were the result of Churchill's
influence or vice versa.  He was a champion of the Jewish
cause, but not the only one nor an uncritical one.  He never
pressed his point to the extreme extent of imposing his view
on his colleagues if this might have led to a crisis.  He put
the winning of the war above any other consideration and
stubbornly stuck to this principle throughout the war.  Controversies there were, of course, and disagreements in Jewish
matters with his colleagues and with various departments.
Yet there can be no doubt in the mind of the objective student
as to his sympathy and friendliness towards all matters
Jewish.  Jewish leaders in touch with Churchill have often
expressed a similar viewpoint about his sentiments during
those fateful years.  It has been mentioned[138] that many
appeals were addressed to Churchill by people all over the
world who knew of his pro-Jewish leanings from before the
war, and who believed that he had not changed.  " Mr.
Churchill's blend of courage and realism is magnificent ",
wrote the official Zionist organ in a leading article.[139]  " His
supreme leadership is a blessing, if not a miracle, of democracy.  His leadership would only gain in stature, and reveal
its true qualities, if he were to overcome those prejudices and
misconceptions of the past which are causing the omission
of Jewish rights.  The Jewish people insist on their rights
and on their ideals.  They look to the British Government
under his leadership to maintain their cause."  This belief
in Churchill's friendship was the underlying motive of almost
every appeal made to him throughout the war, a belief which
was not only based on an instinct or a sentiment but on positive evidence.

It will be recalled[140] that Churchill's direct intervention in
1940 induced Lord Lloyd to change his " anti-Zionist and
pro-Arab " attitude with regard to Jewish armed units.  Even
more important is his overruling of General Wavell's objection to the landing of the *Patria* survivors in Palestine[141] and

his instructions that any deportees to Mauritius should not be caged up there for the duration of the war.[142] While we know that Dr. Weizmann visited Churchill two weeks after the *Struma* catastrophe,[143] it is not stated whether this tragedy was discussed. However, there is no doubt that subsequently some improvements in the admission of refugees into Palestine became operative,[144] which could hardly have been the case without directive from the Government in London. Also under the same heading fall Churchill's interventions in connection with the tragedy of Hungarian and Greek Jews[145] as does the sudden change of attitude towards the rescue work in Turkey upon the establishment of the War Refugee Board.[146]

Apart from these few concrete interventions, a number of others deserve to be recorded here. As we know, two weeks after the *Struma* disaster Dr. Weizmann saw Churchill and while, strangely enough, the Jewish leader does not record having discussed that event with the Prime Minister, his narrative reveals another very interesting and at the same time characteristic incident confirming Churchill's sympathy with the Jewish cause. Its timing at least leads one to believe that the *Struma* tragedy was responsible for the episode. Dr. Weizmann writes that on March 11, 1942, on the day of his departure to America to start work for the U.S. Government on the problem of synthetic rubber, he dropped in at 10, Downing Street, to say good-bye to Churchill's private secretary John Martin, who suddenly said:[147] "'The Prime Minister is in the other room. He has a few minutes' time, and I think I'll bring you in to him.' And then a strange brief colloquy took place—or I should say monologue, for I hardly did more than say good-bye to Mr. Churchill. He, however, packed a great deal into those few minutes which we passed together, standing on our feet. He first wished me luck on my American trip, on which he was, of course, fully informed. 'I am glad you are going', he said, 'and I am sure you will find a great deal of work to do there.' Then, without any questioning or prompting on my part, he went on: 'I want you to know that I have a plan which of course can only be carried into effect when the war is over. I would like to see Ibn Saud made lord of the Middle East—the boss of the bosses—provided he settles with you. It will be up to you to get the best possible conditions.  Of course we shall help you.  Keep this confidential, but you might talk it over with Roosevelt when you get to America.  There's nothing he and I cannot do if we set our minds to it.' "

From Churchill's *Memoirs* we know that he maintained this pro-Zionist line also in his confidential and personal correpsondence with President Roosevelt to whom he wrote from Cairo in August 1942, some two months after the conversation with Dr. Weizmann: [148]

> Here in the Middle East the Arabs might claim by majority that they could expel the Jews from Palestine, or at any rate forbid all further immigration.  I am strongly wedded to the Zionist policy, of which I was one of the authors.

And indeed, he was and remained throughout the war " an unrepentant Zionist ".[149]   In December 1939, Dr. Weizmann visited him at the Admiralty and, on leaving the First Lord, he recorded[150] that " it was particularly encouraging to find him at such a time, mindful of us and our problems ".  And when in September 1940 at a luncheon with the Prime Minister the question of a Jewish Army was discussed, Dr. Weizmann again recorded[151] that Churchill " was unreservedly co-operative.  I was, on the whole, satisfied with the results ".

We now know that during the war Churchill conceived the idea of a partition of Palestine as the solution to be suggested by him after the war, believing as he did that there was nothing that Roosevelt and he " cannot do if we set our minds to it ".[152]   Even the uncompromising leader of the *Irgun*, Menachem Begin, while dismissing a " good partition " as non-existent, could not reject out of hand the possibility that Churchill might be able to live up to his promise but posed the question: " Suppose he is no longer in power?"[153]   He probably himself did not suspect at the time that this question might become crucial in determining whether or not Churchill meant to fulfil his Zionist promise.  In fact. when the war ended Churchill was no longer in power.  But soon after conceiving of partition as a solution, he set to work—in the midst of the war — by appointing a Cabinet Committee[154] to elaborate in detail a partition plan which was to include the

Negev.[155] This Committee came to a sudden end after Lord Moyne's death in November 1944.[156]

But transcending all these expressions of sympathy, the sporadic interventions, the improvements in certain conditions and conceptions of future plans, the cardinal question, which was put time and again throughout the war period, remained: why does not Churchill do something immediately to lay the foundation for the future of Jewry in Palestine by enunciating a definite policy, thereby enabling countless thousands of Jews to be saved from the Nazi scourge? For it was then believed—and this belief persists to this day—that had a clear and definite policy as to the future of Jewry been announced, certain inevitable and immediate consequences would have altered the entire situation. Thus, if a partition of Palestine, which would have led to the establishment of an Arab and a Jewish State, had then been decided upon, there would have been no need to stop or limit immigration into the proposed Jewish sector of the country. This, in turn, would have justified an appeal to all Jews in Europe to save themselves by all possible means, as the gates of Palestine had been flung open to them. Hence all Jewish demands and the various rescue programmes centred on these two points: proclamation of a definite post-war plan for the future; and abolition of the restrictive measures governing the immigration into Palestine.

## THE WHITE PAPER OF 1939

The dominant instrument for the pursuit of the stringent immigration policy into Palestine by the British Administration was the *White Paper* of 1939 which is fully dealt with in Part II of this Study. When discussed in Parliament in 1939 it was condemned by Churchill in strongest possible terms in a speech which has since then been often re-printed and quoted in the Jewish press.[157] It fixed the total halt of Jewish immigration into Palestine for April 1944, and allowed an intake of no more than 75,000 immigrants up to that time. Repeated statements made during the war by Jewish organisations and leaders reveal that there was no doubt in their minds that the *White Paper* provisions were the guide for the Palestine policy of the Administration, as well as of the Government in London. In the light of the facts as they presented themselves there would in fact be no other conclusion.

Harry Sacher, in an illuminating paragraph, summed up the issue as follows: [158] " When war was imminent the Jewish Agency asked for the immediate admission, out of the 75,000, of 20,000 children from Poland and 10,000 young Jews from the Balkans. It was refused. They died in the gas chambers. When Hitler occupied the Continent no Jews were admitted from occupied countries on the pretext that Nazi agents might infiltrate. The Jews died, but with Arab assistance Nazi agents did infiltrate. When Jews managed to escape to Palestine all permits were suspended from October 1939 to March 1940 and from October 1940 to March 1941. The Government, with equal callousness and blindness, advised the Jewish Agency to save up permits for after the war, ' when they could be given to Jews from Germany, who were of a " better type " than those from the Balkans '. In November 1940 the Government declared that Jews coming from Europe without permits would be interned outside Palestine, and never be allowed into Palestine even after the war. Some 1,800 Jews were on the *Patria* in Haifa awaiting deportation; the ship blew up and 250 were killed. Another shipload of 1,700 were deported to Mauritius, where 100 died of disease. The coffin-ship *Salvador* sank in the Sea of Marmora and 230 refugees, many of them children, were drowned. The *Struma* lay off Istanbul for two months waiting for Palestine visas which did not come. She was sent to sea, and sank with 763 out of her complement of 764 pitiful souls. Istanbul was practically the only port of escape from Hitler, but it was not till the middle of July 1943, when the extermination of the Jews could no longer be discredited, that the Government agreed to admit Jewish refugees reaching Istanbul; but it delayed another nine months before so informing the Turkish Government. By that time there were not many left to be saved. Such was the Chamberlain White Paper in practice."

No wonder that the Government was attacked from all sides and that Churchill who had condemned the document and had voted against it in 1939 came under fire as well. Ben Gurion set the tone for these attacks when he stated the policy of the Jewish Agency[159] at the beginning of the war: " We shall fight the *White Paper* as if there were no war, and the war as if there were no *White Paper*." Innumerable meetings and conferences held in those years all over the world passed resolutions demanding the abolition of the *White Paper* and usually combined this demand with an appeal for help to Churchill. But as we know,[160] Churchill turned a deaf ear to both appeals and attacks, and no public defence or justification of his atttiude during the war is on record.

This silence could not but provoke comments. For Israel Cohen it indicated[161] that " during the war the Prime Minister (Mr. Winston Churchill) would not commit himself in support of that document ", while S. S. Silverman drew another conclusion. He said in the debate on the Refugee Problem in Parliament[162] that " it is very doubtful whether the White Paper of 1938[163] was not, itself, a breach of the Mandate with which His Majesty's Government was entrusted. The present Prime Minister said so at the time, and he has said nothing since to indicate that he does not think so still ". Some documents published after the war, which were not known or meant to be known to the public at that time, not only corroborate these negative conclusions but enable us to discern Churchill's attitude in respect of the *White Paper* in its true perspective. They all prove that he remained an uncompromising opponent of that document and of the policy it stood for.

In April 1943 Dr. Weizmann submitted to him a memorandum on the Jewish problem in which he pointed out that the *White Paper* of 1939 was " the firmly established policy of the Government ". Churchill, disagreeing completely with such a presumption, on April 18, 1943, sent the following note to Viscount Cranborne (Lord Privy Seal) and to Oliver Stanley (Colonial Secretary): [164]

> Please see the attached letter from Dr. Weizmann [about the Jewish problem]. I cannot agree that the White Paper of 1939 is " the firmly established policy " of His Majesty's present Government. I have always regarded it as a gross breach of faith committed by the Chamberlain Government in respect of obligations to which I was personally a party. Our position is that we have carried on for the time being in the exigencies of war

the policy of our predecessors and have made no new pronouncement upon the subject. My position remains strictly that set forth in the speech I made in the House of Commons in the debate on the White Paper. I am sure the majority of the present War Cabinet would never agree to any positive endorsement of the White Paper. It runs until it is superseded.

This was not merely Churchill's impulsive reaction upon reading Dr. Weizmann's letter. Even the official Jewish Agency report feels obliged to state[165] that " it was noticeable, however, that Mr. Churchill refused to commit himself to support of the White Paper which he had so unsparingly condemned when it was introduced ". Churchill's policy was then and remained: " It runs until it is superseded." It is noteworthy that the only Zionist leader who at the time foretold this fate of the *White Paper* was Vladimir Jabotinsky, who, analyzing the document in 1940, came to the conclusion[166] that " the life of a White Paper is very short ", though it " gives a precise and genuine indication of what a government wanted when it was published; but that is no indication of what the government may want a year later ". And he had no doubt that this Paper would eventually share the fate of the " series of contradictory [White] papers " of the Mandatory period.[167] In an evaluation of this policy as indicated in Churchill's communications, a historian of that period concluded[168] that " the constitutional features of the White Paper were allowed to languish under the Churchill Government ".

An official spokesman of the Jewish Agency and its Legal Adviser, Dr. Bernard Joseph, once during the war advanced the argument[169] that the British Government had created an important precedent when agreeing to " permit some forty thousand Jews from Hungary to enter Palestine, after the Hungarian Government had expressed its readiness to allow their emigration. The theatre of war that developed at the time in Hungary interfered with this plan. But the precedent of disregarding the restrictions of the White Paper has been established ".

It is worth mentioning in this connection that President Roosevelt too thought it important to create the kind of

precedent with regard to the *White Paper* as mentioned by
Dr. Joseph. Henry Morgenthau Jr. told us in his " Diaries "[170]
that in 1944 he had a talk with the President about the
ultimate destination of refugees who might be released or
escape from Europe. Roosevelt is quoted as saying: " What
I am trying to get the English to do is this . . . They don't
want to change the White Paper, but I want to get them to
say publicly, if I am successful through the Refugee Committee [War Refugee Board] in bringing Jews out of Europe,
(that) they will let them go to Palestine . . . I want them to
mention Palestine by name."

There is one more characteristic reference to the *White
Paper* in Churchill's *Memoirs*[171] which again confirms his
consistent stand in the matter. In January 1944 he wrote to
General Ismay on behalf of the Chief of Staff Committee:

> I have now read this paper about " British Strategic
> Needs in the Levant States ". The Chiefs of Staff seem
> to assume that partition [of Palestine] will arouse Jewish
> resentment. It is, on the contrary, the White Paper
> policy that arouses Jewish resentment . . . I therefore
> cannot accept in any way the requirements for internal
> security set out in the table, which proceeds upon the
> assumption that both the Jews and the Arabs would join
> together to fight us. Obviously we shall not proceed
> with any plan on partition which the Jews do not
> support.

Nothing of these sentiments or of his correspondence was
known to the public, who could only judge Churchill and
the Government by what had been done in practice. The
situation which had arisen owing to the absence of an
unequivocal official statement concerning the *White Paper* is
ably described in a short paragraph in Hurewitz's important
study: [172] " Meanwhile the 1939 White Paper was being
whittled down . . . the land laws were the one feature of the
White Paper to survive the war intact. The proposed constitutional innovations had become a dead issue by 1943, even
though the British did not openly admit it, the Zionists did
not believe it, and the Arabs would not accept it."

In the light of all this one cannot but agree with Churchill and feel that he was personally justified in stating in Parliament after the war: [173]

> I have never altered my opinion that the White Paper constituted a negation of Zionist policy which, the House must remember, was an integral and indispensable condition of the Mandate. That is the view which I hold today.

## THE JEWISH BRIGADE

It is worth mentioning at this point that the differences of opinion as they occurred within the Government or between Churchill and his collaborators, and which he tried hard to prevent from developing into a serious conflict, did not only relate to humanitarian problems such as the question of saving refugees, the proclamation of a definite Palestine policy or the abolition of the *White Paper*. Surprisingly they also applied to military matters. One such controversy with regard to recruiting Jews in Palestine has been mentioned.[174] In another connection,[175] General Wavell intervened against the admission of the *Patria* survivors to Palestine and Churchill overruled his objections. But in the same note to Lord Moyne in which he refers to this intervention Churchill also dealt with the problem of the Jewish Army. In this particular case he submitted to Wavell's opposition and postponed a decision for another six months, though his " consent to the programme for the creation of a Jewish army was given in September 1940 ".[176] (After the expiry of the six months new arguments against its formation were advanced and the decision again shelved until 1944.) Churchill gave in to Wavell's objections, because he feared that his insistence on the establishment of the Jewish Army would be resented by the General and thus adversely affect the conduct of the war, something Churchill was under no circumstances willing to permit. In the note to Lord Moyne of March 1941, he continued: [177]

> However, in view of the " Lustre " [Greek] policy I do not wish General Wavell to be worried now by lengthy arguments about matters of no military consequence to the immediate situation. Therefore Doctor Weizmann should be told that the Jewish Army project must be

put off for six months, but may be reconsidered again
in four months. The sole reason given should be lack
of equipment.

Churchill did not want to "worry" General Wavell or
others, and submitted against his better judgment, though he
was from the outset a staunch supporter of the idea of forming a Jewish Army. For he understood the desire of the Jews,
who were singled out for torture by Hitler, to take part in
the great struggle against Nazi barbarism. And he was, of
course, fully aware that it would not suffice to allow individual Jews to join the one or other national army. He
understood the necessity of an independent and specifically
Jewish fighting force, with its very own and clearly distinct
markings, its uniforms and its flag.

Without access to the relevant documentary evidence it is
difficult to ascertain what went on during the years between
1940 and 1944, when the creation of a distinct Jewish Brigade
was finally announced by the War Cabinet, though we know,
of course, of the untiring efforts of the Jewish Agency to
bring about the establishment of the Jewish fighting force.
Two chapters in the *Political Report* to the Zionist Congress in 1946[178] record these efforts from the outbreak of the
war until 1944. The Report makes it clear that, while correspondence and negotiations were being conducted between
the Government and the Agency on the one hand and the
War Office and Colonial Office on the other from 1940 until
1944, it became necessary in the end to appeal to Churchill
directly. In a letter to the Prime Minister of July 4, 1944,
Dr. Weizmann referred to the disappointment among Jews
at being denied their own fighting force and wrote:[179] "Now
I address to you a double appeal. First, that these men should
be gathered into a Division of their own, and that the Division
should be permitted to carry the flag with the Star of David
on to the European battlefield." Churchill's *War Memoirs*
at this point only reveal the difficulties he encountered with
some of his colleagues and the obstacles presented by
administrative technicalities. Thus in a note to Sir Edward
Bridges six days after receiving Dr. Weizmann's letter, the
Prime Minister wrote:[180]

July 10, 1944.

In your report [about the War Cabinet meeting on forming a Jewish fighting force] you say that it was decided that a brigade group would be carefully examined. I certainly understood and hold very strongly the view that a brigade group should be made. When the War Office say they will carefully examine a thing they mean they will do it in. The matter must therefor be set down for an early meeting of the War Cabinet only this week, and the Secretary of State for War should be warned of my objection. A copy of the further letter from Dr. Weizmann may also be forwarded to the War Office.

At long last Sir James Grigg, the Secretary of State for War, submitted to the Prime Minister the proposal for the establishment of a Jewish Brigade. On July 26, 1944, Churchill accepted the formula and confirmed his agreement in a note which reveals both his great eagerness to see the establishment of that fighting force and his warm understanding of the Jewish aspect of that creation: [181]

July 26, 1944.

I am in general agreement with your proposals [for a Jewish fighting force], but I think the brigade should be formed and sent to Italy as soon as convenient, and worked up to a brigade group there as time goes on by the attachment of the other units.

2. I like the idea of the Jews trying to get at the murderers of their fellow-countrymen in Central Europe, and I think it would give a great deal of satisfaction in the United States.

3. The points of detail which occur to me are:

I do not think this brigade should be any more liable to be split by serious military emergencies than any other unit in the Middle East. On the contrary, only a serious emergency should affect it, considering what it represents.

I believe it is the wish of the Jews themselves to fight the Germans anywhere. It is with the Germans they have their quarrel. There is no need to put the

conditions in such a form as to imply that the War
Office in its infinite wisdom might wish to send the
Jews to fight the Japanese, and that otherwise there
would be no use in having the brigade group.
Surely political as well as military considerations
govern the demobilisation or disposal of any of the
forces under British command. In the case of a
contingent of this kind there certainly might be
political reasons either for dispersing it or for maintaining it after the war . . .
I will consult the King about this [proposal that the
force shall have its own flag]. I cannot conceive
why this martyred race, scattered about the world
and suffering as no other race has done at this
juncture, should be denied the satisfaction of having
a flag. However, not only the King but the Cabinet
might have views on this.

4. Should I be able to visit Italy I will discuss the details
of this with General Wilson, and also very likely I shall
see General Paget. Meanwhile please go ahead within
the lines proposed and negotiate with the Jewish Agency.
Remember the object of this is to give pleasure and an
expression to rightful sentiments, and that it certainly
will be welcomed widely in the United States. Let me
see the form of any announcement that is made.

It was only after this intervention of Churchill's with the
Secretary of War that he replied to Dr. Weizmann's letter.
Unfortunately this reply is not published verbatim in the
*Political Report,* which merely records[182] that the " Prime
Minister replied on August 5 that he had given his personal
attention to the suggestion made, with which he had much
sympathy, and that the War Office should shortly be in
a position to discuss concrete proposals with the Jewish
Agency ".

Soon afterwards — on September 20, 1944 — the Jewish
Brigade was officially established, not least thanks to the
unceasing clamour for its formation by Palestine's Jewry and
the Jewish Agency, and also due to the intensive propaganda
of the Jewish Army Committees in America and Britain.[183]

Meanwhile from the first day of hostilities, Jewry all over

the world had contributed to the war effort in all fields of activities, not least in the military field. " About one million were fighting in the armies of the United Nations; over 30,000 Palestinian Jews alone volunteered for armed service in discharge of their national responsibility. Their units which served in many a campaign have remained scattered and anonymous ".[184] The formation of the Jewish Brigade group was, in the words of *The Times*,[185] " an acknowledgment of the fine response of the Jews of Palestine to the call of volunteers and to those multitudes of Jews in the armies of the United Nations ". It was Churchill himself who announced its formation in Parliament: [186]

> The British Army in Italy includes also Palestinian units . . . Here I would mention the announcement—which Members may have read and which, I think, will be appreciated and approved—that the Government have decided to accede to the request of the Jewish Agency for Palestine that a Jewish Brigade Group should be formed to take part in active operations. There are vast numbers of Jews serving with our forces and the American forces throughout all the armies, but it seems to me indeed appropriate that a special unit of that race which has suffered indescribable treatment from the Nazis, should be represented in a distinct formation among the forces gathered for their final overthrow, and I have no doubt that they will not only take an active part in the struggle but in the occupation which will follow.

There is no doubt that this was a military matter and one directly concerning the war effort. This makes it all the more difficult to understand all the delays that had so long prevented its establishment. If any proof of the military usefulness of the Jewish Brigade is required, Churchill himself supplies it in his letter of congratulations to Field-Marshal Alexander of April 29, 1945, after the complete destruction of the enemy south of the Alps: [187]

> Never, I suppose, have so many nations advanced and manœuvred in one line victoriously. The British, Americans, New Zealanders, South Africans, British-Indians, Poles, Jews, Brazilians, and strong forces of liberated

Italians have all marched together in that high comrade-
ship and unity of men fighting for freedom and for the
deliverance of mankind.

A week later he reported in Parliament on the surrender of
the German troops in Italy and enumerating all the military
units of the various nations who fought in those battles, he
made special mention[188] of

the Jewish Brigade, which we formed a year or so ago,
and which has fought in the front line with courage.

Thus the Jews having proved to be the equals of other
military units, their sevices to the war effort gained belated
military recognition. " The climax of a long effort came on
June 8, 1946, when the Jewish flag headed a contingent of
the Jewish Brigade through the streets of London in Victory
March."[189]

*      *
*

Churchill came up against similar difficulties and was
involved in similar controversies with regard to other issues
and nationalities. In dealing with the Greek issue,[190] his
Memoirs contain a very characteristic summary which could
equally be applied to his attitude in Jewish matters:[191]

Again the issue was in most cases not what ought to be
done—that would have been too easy—but what was
likely to be agreed to not only at home but between
the Allies.

On another occasion, he tried to ease the tension between
the Polish ₁Government in London, headed by General
Sikorsky, and the Soviet Union. The Poles had accused the
Russians of the wholesale murder of Polish officer prisoners
at Katyn. When Ivan M. Maisky, the Soviet Ambassador
in London, went to inform Churchill that because of these
Polish accusations, the Russo-Polish agreement of 1941
would be immemiately denounced, the Prime Minister tried
to persuade him to have his Government reconsider the
decision and, true to his attitude to avoid everything that
might impair the conduct of the war, he emphasised:[192]

We have got to beat Hitler and this is no time for quarrels and charges.

Though Churchill's efforts to compose the difficulties between the two Governments failed, this quotation shows his attitude on principle which he generally adopted during the war. For a long time to come the discussion about this attitude will continue to interest those defending unqualified expediency in time of war and those rejecting or qualifying it.

## NO PLEDGES WERE GIVEN

Referring to Churchill's refusal to agree to the exchange of "Jews for trucks" as offered by the Nazis through Brand,[193] J. and D. Kimche remark[194] that "reluctantly, and with heavy heart, Churchill had to refuse. Later in the changed atmosphere of post-war Palestine, only the refusal was remembered, not the reasons which led to it." I think that this comment also applies to many other measures and attitudes taken by Churchill during the war. So far only one aspect of his attitude has been elaborated and repeatedly stressed: his unshakable adherence, above any other consideration, to the primacy of conducting and winning the war. But there were other reasons, too. Thus for the historical record it deserves to be stated that there is no evidence that at any time during the war Churchill aroused any exaggerated hopes in the minds of the Jewish leaders, nor did he make any promises which he was later unwilling to honour. Even with regard to the creation of the Jewish Brigade—which he wholeheartedly welcomed, and in respect of which, at a meeting with Dr. Weizmann and others in September 1940, "he was unreservedly co-operative "[195]—no undertaking was given by him. While Dr. Weizmann and other Jewish leaders were disappointed at the protracted negotiations in the following years, Dr. Weizmann feels nevertheless obliged to state[196] that though satisfied with Churchill's co-operation, "the military authorities, unfortunately, were not so easy to handle. Mr. Churchill's consent to the above programme was given in September 1940. Exactly four years were to pass before, in September 1944, the Jewish Brigade was officially formed!"

Also in many other passages Dr. Weizmann bears witness to Churchill's consistently voiced proviso—that any decision about future policy would have to wait until after the war.

In this respect Churchill remained firmly unmoved by any appeal or tragic event. Soon after assuming the Premiership he laid down this policy in a statement in Parliament: [197]

I do not think it would be wise at this moment, while the battle rages and the war is still perhaps only in its earlier stage, to embark upon elaborate speculations about the future shape which should be given to Europe or the new securities which must be arranged to spare mankind the miseries of a third World War. The ground is not new, it has been frequently traversed and explored, and many ideas are held about it in common by all good men, and all free men. But before we can undertake the task of rebuilding we have not only to be convinced ourselves, but we have to convince all other countries that the Nazi tyranny is going to be finally broken. The right to guide the course of the world history is the noblest prize of victory. The task which lies before us immediately is at once more practical, more simple, more stern. I hope—indeed I pray—that we shall not be found unworthy of our victory if after toil and tribulation it is granted to us. For the rest, we have to gain victory. That is our task.

All subsequent discussions with Jewish leaders ended on the same note. Thus Dr. Weizmann reported to a Conference of British Zionists in September 1941: [198] " Here again, it would have been premature to assume that in the midst of war, when this country was fighting a life-and-death struggle, time and patience and disposition would be found to revise a policy which the Prime Minister himself has condemned in the strongest possible terms." As the war progressed, Jewish leaders believed that it might be possible to get Churchill to reverse his attitude, but in vain. On October 16, 1944, the Jewish Agency submitted a memorandum to the Government dealing with the future of Palestine.[199] Shortly afterwards Dr. Weizmann called on Churchill, who " indicated that, while it was impossible to decide on the future of Palestine at that time, it would be dealt with at the end of the war with Germany ".[200] When after the collapse of Germany another memorandum was submitted by the Jewish Agency on May 22, 1945,[201] to the Prime Minister, Churchill

in his reply of June 9, stated " that he saw no possibility of
the Palestine question ' being effectively considered until
the victorious Allies are definitely seated at the Peace
Table ' ".[202]

The sentiments expresesd by Dr. Weizmann in his *Memoirs*
and the *Policital Report* of the Jewish Agency in connection
with this disappointing trend, leave in the mind of the reader
the impression that, on this occasion, Churchill did not live
up to his promise to deal with the Palestine matter after the
end of the German war. " The European war ended in May
1945 ", wrote Dr. Weizmann,[203] " no action was taken."
Kimche's words that " only the refusal was remembered and
not the reasons " applies also in this context. The Agency
memorandum was submitted on May 22, 1945, four days
after Churchill had appealed to Attlee to extend the Coalition
Government until after the Japanese war was finished.[204] This
proposal was rejected on May 21[205] by the Leader of the
Labour Party, who suggested a General Election in October.
On June 4, Churchill made his first election broadcast,[206] and
the country was plunged into a bitter election campaign which
ended with Churchill's defeat. In the light of these facts it
seems less than fair to blame Churchill for not having prejudiced the policy of an as yet unelected future government
and for not having dealt with the important and difficult
problem of Palestine between May 22 and June 9.

## EXPEDIENCY AND DEFINITE SETTLEMENTS

It was often pointed out at that time that Churchill, notwithstanding his repeated emphasis on winning the war first
before finally settling future problems, found it possible, even
during the war, to take practical and concrete steps with
regard to the future of other peoples and States. " Does
anybody know whether there will ever be a Peace Conference?" asked Ben Gurion in March 1943,[207] adding that
" Churchill has been meeting Roosevelt in Casablanca. That
was part of the Peace Conference. So was the meeting of
Cordell Hull recently with Eden and friend Halifax in Washington." Similar disappointment was expressed by Jewish
leaders and in the press[208] at every stage—after Yalta, where
the future of Poland was discussed and decided upon and
after the proclamation of Syria's independence by de Gaulle's

Free French Forces and Britain. It was then pointed out that issues such as these were practical steps taken while actual fighting was still going on. Therefore, it was said, the principle of postponing any decision about the permanent settlement of vital problems until after the war had been violated.

In his statements on the developments leading up to the proclamation of Syria's independence and on the Yalta decisions regarding Poland Churchill makes it clear that they were not dictated by a desire to prejudge the future Peace Conference. They had been brought about by conditions created at a certain moment during the war and had to be tackled forthwith in the interest of the conduct of the war.

The proclamation of Syria's independence in 1941 preceded the occupation of her territory by Allied troops for the sake of preventing her from developing into an Axis stronghold in the Middle East. Churchill recollects: [209]

> With the Germans in control of Syria, Egypt, the vital Canal Zone, and the oil refineries at Abadan would come under the direct threat of continuous air attack. Our land communications between Palestine and Iraq would be in danger. There might well be political repercussions in Egypt, and our diplomatic position in Turkey and throughout the Middle East would be gravely weakened.

It was therefore decided to[210]

> enter Syria in some force tomorrow morning [June 8, 1941] in order to prevent further German penetration.

When General Wavell was informed by Churchill about the decision to occupy Syria he replied that he regarded " success as at least problematical, and dependent on the attitude of the French garrison and local population ".[211] This then was the reason why it was regarded necessary to win over the population by a promise and indeed a guarantee of independence to be given by the Free French Forces. Churchill in this connection wrote to de Gaulle: [212]

> I welcome therefore your decision to promise independence to Syria and the Lebanon, and, as you know, I think it essential that we should lend to this promise the full weight of our guarantee.

Churchill as well as the Cabinet and the war leaders thus regarded the occupation of Syria as a purely strategical and military effort for winning the war and in fact he stressed this aspect in his message to President Roosevelt: [213]

> We have no political interests at all in Syria except to win the war.

The promise of independence before the occupation of the country seemed to him and his advisers an unavoidable necessity if any hope of success was to be entertained. Hence the promise was given.

The settlement of the Eastern frontier of Poland at the Yalta Conference in 1945, on the other hand, was not only a matter of military necessity or of strategic importance, but one of administrative urgency arising out of newly created conditions. By that time the Russians had already occupied the territory of Poland and were penetrating deep into Germany proper. As Churchill explained in the House of Commons[214] it became imperative to act quickly:

> The Eastern frontier must be settled now, if the new Polish administration is to be able to carry on its own work in its own territory, and to do this in amity with the Russians and behind their fighting fronts.

While thus practical steps were taken by the Allies affecting the future of these countries at a time when fighting was still going on, the nature and background of these steps show that they lay outside the normal pattern of post-war settlements which were to be left over for the future Peace Conference.

In this respect, Churchill was almost dogmatic. In the very same speech in which he reported on the results of the Yalta Conference he streseed that[215]

> On the long-term measures, there are many points of great importance on which detailed plans have yet to be worked out between the Allies. It would be a great mistake to suppose that questions of this kind can be thrashed out, and solutions found for all the many intractable and complex problems involved, while the Armies are still on the march. To hurry and press

matters of this kind might well be to risk causing disunity between the Allies. Many of these matters must await the time when the leaders of the Allies, freed from the burden of direction of the war, can turn their whole or main attention to the making of a wise and far-seeing peace which will, I trust, become a foundation greatly facilitating the work of the World Organization.

This principle he applied to a whole range of intricate problems including the Middle East. On the other hand, it did not lead him to an absolute disinterested attitude towards the future. While avoiding any final commitment continuously throughout the war, he deeply pondered on plans for the future. Thus on his way back from Yalta he met Ibn Saud of Saudi Arabia, who had also met President Roosevelt.[216] Both leaders were impressed by " this most remarkable man ".[217] In connection with this meeting Churchill told the House[218] that Ibn Saud's

> aid will be needed at the close of the war in reaching a solution of the problem of the Arab world and of the Jewish people in Palestine. I have hopes that when the war is over good arrangements can be made for securing the peace and progress of the Arab world, and generally of the Midlde East, and that Great Britain and the United States, which is taking an increasing interest in these regions, will be able to play a valuable part in proving that well-known maxim of the old Free Trader, " All legitimate interests are in harmony ".

It will be remembered that as far back as 1942 Churchill informed Dr. Weizmann of his post-war plan with regard to the Middle East[219] and particularly concerning Ibn Saud's rôle.

Three years later Churchill revealed in the House of Commons, in the speech quoted above, that he still stood by that plan which he had devised almost immediately after assuming the Premiership and stored away in his mind until the appropriate moment. His plan, as we know, was a scheme of partition of Palestine[220] and the idea[221]

> of a wider union—an Arab-Jew federal system of four or five States in the Middle East, which would have been

one of the great Powers, with Jew and Arab combined together to share the glory and mutually protect and help each other.

Though this was his plan for post-war Palestine, he made no public or private promise as to its implementation. Nor did he feel irrevocably bound by this scheme. It was to be left to the Peace Conference for a final decision: [222]

> All these and many other matters affecting the Middle East are fitting and necessary subjects for the Peace Conference, at which we must resolutely strive for final settlements of lasting peace between all the States and races comprised in the Middle East, and in the Eastern basin of the Mediterranean.

As I explained before, Churchill applied this attitude to all problems which called for definite settlements but which, at the same time, could not be tackled immediately for reasons of military expediency or of the smooth progress of the war in a specific region. Some of the settlements hastily arrived at during the war, particularly the two mentioned, turned out to be sources of considerable trouble and new frictions. Thus the delays in the realisation of Syria's independence proclaimed in 1941 led to heavy clashes between French and Syrians in May 1945 and only came to an end with British armed intervention in favour of the Syrians, an intervention not forgotten to this day in France.

Also, the Yalta decisions with their tragic consequences for Poland continue to remain the unabated subject of heated controversies and will remain so for a long time to come.

These two events, quoted at the time as evidence that solutions could be reached even in the midst of war, have become almost classical examples of the unhappy consequences of improvisation. They strikingly confirm Churchill's *ceterum censeo* about the need to concentrate single-mindedly on conducting and winning the war, to make no binding promise as to the solution of any problem, and to leave its attainment to the Peace Conference. In addition to all the arguments advanced by Churchill for the justification of this attitude of his, he once listed some simple, practical considerations, which seemed to him no less plausible than the arguments of military expediency. In a note to Eden of January 4, 1945, he stated:[223]

> It is a mistake to try to write out on little pieces of paper what the vast emotions of an outraged and quivering world will be either immediately after the struggle is over or when the inevitable cold fit follows the hot. These awe-inspiring tides of feeling dominate most people's minds, and independent figures tend to become not only lonely but futile. Guidance in these mundane matters is granted to us only step by step, or at the utmost a step or two ahead. There is therefore wisdom in reserving one's decisions as long as possible and until all the facts and forces that will be potent at the moment are revealed.

Even so Churchill gave much thought to post-war problems and among these the Jewish question and its solution in Palestine had gradually assumed concrete shape in his mind. Already during the war his idea of a partition of Palestine into a Jewish and Arab sector became known to and was discussed among Jewish leaders.[224] Some voiced their doubts at the time and others wonder to this day whether Churchill would have lived up to his Zionist sympathies had he remained in power during the post-war period. This being a purely speculative approach, I do not see any reason why we should not accept unreservedly his statement in Parliament made a year after the conclusion of the war:[225]

> Had I had the opportunity of guiding the course of events after the war was won a year ago, I should have faithfully pursued the Zionist cause as I have defined it; and I have not abandoned it today, although this is not a very popular moment to espouse it.

He repeated this assertion when involved in an argument with Attlee, who had meanwhile assumed the Premiership, about the post-war settlement of the Palestine question. *Hansard* records[226] the following exchange:

> *Mr. Churchill*: I am sure we could have agreed immediately after the war upon a partition scheme which would have been more favourable to the Arabs.

*The Prime Minister*: May I ask the right hon. Gentleman if he thought that could have been done, why did he not do it after the war? He was in power.
*Mr. Churchill*: No. The world and the nation had the inestimable blessing of the right hon. Gentleman's guidance. I am sure that we could have agreed immediately after the war upon a partition scheme which would have been more favourable to the Arabs than that which will now follow their unsuccessful recourse to arms.

## " DEATH BY BUREAUCRACY "

In the foregoing pages I have tried to show that apart from public expressions of sympathy with the Jewish victims of Nazism, certain—though very limited and inadequate—steps were taken also towards easing their situation. But the absence of any practical steps and the failure to implement the urgently needed relaxation of immigration rules unavoidably heightened the tragedy. As regards Churchill's attitude, we have seen that it was dictated by three fundamental reasons: his desire to concentrate solely on winning the war; his insistence on not committing himself on any definite future policy; and the inability to deal adequately with post-war problems while the fighting was still on. While these principles were the result of Churchill's own reasoning and decisions, an additional, no less important, factor must be mentioned in this connection—the bureaucracy.

We know that " from 1940 to the end of the war, Winston Churchill worked a regular 120-hour week ",[227] and that the conduct of the war absorbed every minute of his time and every ounce of his energy. And while he was so " heavily preoccupied with the multitudinous labours of the war "[228] the carrying out in practice of the Government's directives rested entirely upon the administration. In the light of the documents referred to in this section it appears that on those rare occasions when some possibility of relief seemed practicable it was almost invariably reduced to nil by vacillation, protracted delays and rigid adherence to technicalities by the administrative machinery of the Civil Service. It is, of course, difficult, if not impossible, to ascertain the precise reasons for such an attitude. On a previous occasion Lord Davis and Lord Wedgwood were quoted[229] as having regarded the Palestine administration as anti-Semitic. Another time Lord Davis carefully hinted at some similarly negative sentiments in Whitehall when saying[230] that " in some quarters, at any rate, there is an uncomfortable feeling that the attitude of some Government Departments is not all that it might be ".

Why, for instance, the directive from the Government to facilitate the journey to Palestine of all refugees reaching Istanbul should neither have been published nor communicated to the Turkish authorities for nine months after it had been authorised[231] it is almost impossible to understand. Or why, on another occasion,[232] visas for Jewish refugees had been " on ice as the result of a technicality " before an intervention by the War Refugee Board in London caused them to turn up in the British Embassy in Ankara. Or again, when[233] requested by the Turkish authorities to give a guarantee that refugees would leave Turkey within twenty-four hours upon arrival en route to Palestine, the British Government sent such a letter but, as the official version has it, " it had been mislaid somewhere " and was finally located—again in the British Embassy in Ankara. Or, when visas were issued for the *Struma* children, but arrived unfortunately too late.[234]

It seemed almost impossible to overcome this insidious resistance, for how could its precise source be located? It was almost as difficult to understand its motives, which accounts for the profound bitterness with which Dr. Weizmann refers[235] to those responsible for delay or sabotage as " people without understanding, without compassion, without pity ".

The same attitude can be found with regard to the *White Paper* of 1939 which was one of the most formidable obstacles in the way of saving Jewish refugees from Europe to Palestine. Having been in operation for a number of years the *White Paper* became an integral part of the Administration's policy in Palestine. " Around it an official doctrine, an official practice, and official reputations and interests had grown. There were those who meant to fight for it, and, if possible, to perpetuate it."[236] Not even the fate of desperate victims from Nazi oppression could persuade them to abandon a pre-war document or at least to mitigate its stringent application. Having become wedded to it, the Palestine Administration remained unmoved, though it was well aware of the negative attitude towards the *White Paper* of Churchill and other, chiefly Labour, members of the Cabinet. "They did not disguise their contempt for the ignoramuses in London", remarks Harry Sacher in this connection.[237] It was this continuous and under-handed fight of the Administration's machinery against any attempt at relaxing rules governing Jewish immigration which to a considerable degree accounts for the innumerable Jewish victims of this policy.

The Prime Minister's pro-Zionist sentiments were, of course, well known to Jewish leaders who were in contac' with him or with his colleagues in the Cabinet. Some, a. we have seen,[238] blamed him because they expected positive proof of his friendship, others, even at that time, felt that his wishes and sentiments were being frustrated by the administrative machinery, a fact which now emerges from the documentary evidence, though it was then not generally accepted. Thus Louis Lipsky, American member of the Jewish Agency Executive, told a Zionist Conference in Columbus, Ohio, in September 1943:[239] " Is it not pertinent to ask, why do not the grand words of Churchill find response in the English administration which rules Palestine? Is the High Commissioner—who sits in Jerusalem and makes and executes laws—an authentic symbol of the fighting Empire reborn under Mr. Churchill's inspiration and guidance?"

If Churchill had tried to fight it out with these " realists " it would have meant a continuous internal struggle. In the same way as he avoided clashes with Lord Lloyd or General Wavell or Anthony Eden, so he also avoided becoming involved in a permanent controversy with the mighty machinery of the Administration. Only on very rare occasions did he feel compelled to intervene, as in the case of the establishment of the Jewish Brigade, when he wrote:[240]

> When the War Office say they will carefully examine a thing they mean they will do it in.

It was unfortunate — and considerably aggravated the Jewish tragedy during World War II — that, as post-war literature shows a similiar spirit prevailed also at the State Department in Washington. " Death by Bureaucracy " is the heading of a chapter in the *Memoirs* of Stephen Wise, in which he describes[241] his own and his colelagues' endeavours to enlist the assistance of the Washington Administration for

the rescue of Jewish Nazi victims. They failed utterly
because of the "realists in the Administration". Also Morgenthau, who during those fateful days was in charge of the
U.S. Treasury, confirms in his *Memoirs*[242] the incredible levity
and complacency with which the State Department treated
ways and methods of rescuing Nazi victims. "America has
no cause to be proud of its handling of the refugee problem"
he asserts.[243]   And it was only after long and protracted
efforts that "in the end we succeeded in getting the refugee
question out of the hands of the State Department, which had
kicked it around for so long, and into the hands of a special
Presidential commission—the War Refugee Board".[244]   A
similar attitude was encountered a year later by President
Truman when the problem of displaced persons became
acute. "I was sceptical", he wrote,[245] "about some views
and attitudes assumed by the 'striped pants boys' in the
State Department. It seemed to me that they didn't care
enough about what happened to the thousands of displaced
persons who were involved." Having investigated the reasons
for this lamentable situation Morgenthau concluded[246] that
"the basic trouble with the previous setup had been that the
State Department was simply not equipped, psychologically
or administratively, for the refugee job". A similar conclusion, not only with regard to the State Department but
also to Whitehall was reached by Dr. Nahum Goldmann when
he said in an address to the "American Jewish Conference"
in December 1944:[247] "I do not doubt that President Roosevelt would have been happy to have been able to save millions
of Jews. I do not doubt that Mr. Churchill would have been
happy to save millions of Jews. The tragedy was not lack
of good will, but, as I formulated it once in London, the
tragedy was that an emergency was met by routine methods."

\*    \*
\*

The tragic narrative in these pages is heavily overshadowed
by arguments of expediency in war time—the necessity of
winning victory first, of avoiding clashes with colleagues and
with the men on the spot. But also the Jewish tragedy in
World War II was not a routine matter that could be adjusted
to orthodox and well-tried patterns. It was in fact an attempt

to exterminate a whole people. Therefore, as Jews, as victims or relatives of victims, we do not feel inclined to listen when the failure through inactivity to save our brethren is being excused or explained away. Nor can we understand why in face of the catastrophe "practical" and "realistic" reasons were not simply brushed aside instead of those responsible putting their compassion into cold storage "for the duration". For we saw—to quote one mouthpiece of these sentiments[248] — "on the one hand the frightful and uninterrupted killing 'of Jews in Europe and on the other the lack of interest in high places, both in Britain and America, in providing the terrorized remnants of European Jewry with a means of escape or even with a ray of hope for survival". We believed then and believe now that this was "a tragedy of humiliation and betrayal. Much of the calamity was unavoidable; but a great part of it could have been mitigated, many thousands of lives could have been saved, both in the period preceding the war and during the war itself, had the democratic countries and their governments been sufficiently concerned ".[249] But above all this was true with regard to the doors of Palestine which "remained closed to the vast majority of those who wished to escape to their National Home. No other haven was offered them, and unable to flee from Europe, some five millions were slaughtered during the years of Nazi occupation ".[250]

None of the governments of the great nations can escape responsibility for indecision, inactivity and lack of help in the Jewish tragedy during World War II. It was possibly this sentiment which prompted Churchill to seize the first opportunity after the war to give public vent to the feeling which all human and enlightened statesmen of the West must have felt in their heart of hearts in the face of this great tragedy:[251]

> I must say that I had no idea, when the war came to an end, of the horrible massacres which had occurred; the millions and millions that have been slaughtered. That dawned on us gradually after the struggle was over.

This statement permits only one inference in the light of the innumerable statements made by Churchill on the sufferings of the Jews: while he knew them to be tragic and enormous and while he thought he knew the extent of Nazi barbarism, even he did not realise that the sum total of these atrocities had led to the all but complete destruction of a whole people.

## (C) GREAT BRITAIN

IN the course of his public activities Churchill encountered and reacted to anti-Semitic trends and manifestations not only in Germany, Russia and elsewhere—as has been shown in the preceding sections—but also to those in this country. Britain's anti-Semitism cannot be regarded as " original " in its motives or methods, nor has it made its mark by some particular form or technique, or by some linguistic innovation like, for instance, the German Jew-baiters who coined the very word " anti-Semitism ", or the Russian barbarians who added to the dictionaries of all modern languages the word " pogrom " for the organised massacre of Jews. In Britain only the " vibratory influences ", to use Lucien Wolf's phrase,[1] of anti-Semitism have been felt " when conditions favourable to its extension have presented themselves ".

### ALIENS

The first anti-Semitic elements with which Churchill was confronted in this country appeared during the struggle for and against the Aliens Bills.[2] As a matter of fact, throughout his fight against the restriction of immigration into Britain of Jewish refugees escaping from Europe, Churchill—apart from marshalling economic, statistical, political and other arguments—referred to anti-Semitism as a motive for the introduction of restrictive legislation. Thus in his first public utterance on the Bill, 1904, he wrote[3] that it

is expected to appeal to insular prejudice against foreigners, to racial prejudice against Jews, and to labour prejudice against competition.

But he warned the Government against using the danger of a Jewish influx into the labour market as an apology for the proposed legislation, stressing that the workers in this country

do not respond in any marked degree to the anti-Semitism which has darkened recent Continental history.

There is no doubt that anti-Jewish propaganda in the Press and at public meetings preceded the introduction of the Aliens Bills into Parliament and continued during the debates in the House of Commons. The incident in Grand Committee[4] when Churchill was accused of having been "bought by Rothschild" is one typical instance of this attitude. The attack on him by Captain Rawson is another.[5] He himself once complained[6] of having

> been subject to the foulest abuse and gross insults from all parts of the country for the hostile attitude he had thought fit to take against the Aliens Bill. Even charges of corruption had been made against him.

The situation assumed, however, more serious dimensions when important members of the Government ceased to mince words. There was, for instance, Joseph Chamberlain's speech at Limehouse in December, 1904;[7] or the remarks by the Attorney General, Sir Robert B. Finlay, which provoked this rebuke by Churchill in the House of Commons:[8]

> The right hon. gentleman [Sir Robert Finlay] seemed to be extremely anxious to make the ordeal of this unfortunate people as severe as possible, and apparently he came to the House with no other object than to put the screw on the most miserable members of the human family. If there was any means by which he could make their lot harder and their burden heavier, the right hon. gentleman did not hesitate to avail himself of it. It was obvious that whether before the immigration board or the immigration officer aliens were to have short shrift. The Prime Minister [A. J. Balfour] has stated that what was wanted was a rough-and-ready method of dealing with aliens, that it was a matter of administration and not of justice, and he certainly seemed to have got an Attorney-General [Sir Robert Finlay] who had thoroughly imbibed the principles of the Bill, and was ready to turn his legal talents to no better purpose than the finding of arguments to justify such a measure.

But the climax was reached in a statement by the Prime Minister himself, a passage of which was to shock the Jewish world. In his reply to Sir Charles Dilke during the Committee stage of the Aliens Bill, 1905, Balfour said: [9] " The right hon. Baronet [Sir Charles Dilke] had condemned the anti-Semitic spirit which disgraced a great deal of modern politics in other countries of Europe, and declared that the Jews of this country were a valuable element in the community. He was not prepared to deny either of these propositions. But he undoubtedly thought that a state of things could easily be imagined in which it would not be to the advantage of the civilisation of the country that there should be an immense body of persons who, however patriotic, able and industrious, however much they threw themselves into the national life, still, by their own action, remained a people apart, and not merely held a religion differing from the vast majority of their fellow-countrymen, but only inter-married among themselves." Stuart Samuel, M.P., immediately attacked this statement in an extremely outspoken speech,[10] and the *Jewish Chronicle* characterised it[11] as a " declaration which we hardly expected from the lips of an English Prime Minister ". Balfour —who twelve years later signed the famous Balfour Declaration of November 2, 1917, marking a historic Zionist victory —came under heavy attacks at the Seventh Zionist Congress by M. Shire, a delegate from England, who charged Balfour[12] with " open anti-Semitism against the whole Jewish people ". Neither subsequent denials by Balfour of any anti-Semitism, nor his insistence that he had a full understanding and feeling for the sufferings of the Jews and that therefore his Government had offered a territory in East Africa for a Jewish settlement,[13] could dispel the deep disappointment which his statement in Parliament had caused. In the light of all this, Churchill's attacks on the anti-Semitic motives of the Bills were turned against the Government and the Conservative party who were both openly accused of using anti-Semitism for their own partisan ends. In his speech on A. Emmott's amendment Churchill felt that[14]

We cannot resist a passing expression of contempt at the spectacle of a great Party trying to retrieve its shattered reputation by exploiting and aggravating the miseries of some of the weakest and poorest of mankind.

When Churchill, as Home Secretary, introduced some amendments to the Aliens Act in 1911 he recalled the reasons which had induced him to fight the legislation six years previously: [15]

It is quite true . . . that, when the 1904-1905 Acts were passing through Parliament I opposed them, not only because I disliked the electioneering rancour by which they were characterised, but also because of the cheap attempt, for party purposes, to exploit the misfortunes of a poor and wretched class of people . . .

And in contrast to the atmosphere which had existed six years previously Churchill could say that[16]

I was glad to hear the hon. Member for Worcester (E. A. Goulding) and those who followed him speak with an absence of prejudice—particularly of anti-Semitic prejudice and party rancour.

## ANTI-JEWISH RIOTS
### (a) IN SOUTH WALES

A serious anti-Jewish outbreak occurred in a number of places in South Wales during Churchill's tenure of office as Home Secretary. It started on Saturday, August 19, 1911, in Tredegar and by next evening " eighteen shops and houses, all of them owned by Jews, were looted and either entirely or partially wrecked ".[17] Two days later, rioting became general in the mining valleys. " Ebbw Vale, Rhymney, Tredegar, Cwm, Victoria, Brynmawr, Bargoed and Beaufort were all more or less seriously affected, and looting was carried out on a large scale."[18] It was estimated that the damage caused to Jewish property in that one week was as high as £100,000.[19] Hundreds of Jews overnight became refugees seeking refuge in Cardiff, Newport and other places, some as far as London. In many towns the outbreaks assumed such proportions that the Riot Act had to be read, and the military intervened.

The reason for these events was the growing unrest among the strikers affected by the months' old coal and rail strikes in South Wales. The Home Secretary, Winston Churchill, came under particularly heavy fire for having authorised the movement of troops into Tonypandy on November 9, 1910, where shops and houses had been attacked the previous day. During the rail strike in 1911, Churchill again authorised the despatch of troops to a number of rail centres in South Wales. The fatal, if accidental, shooting of two men at Llanelly in August of that year added to Churchill's unpopularity among the Trade Unions and Labour leaders.[20] At the same time he was being attacked by the Tories for not having made full use of the troops.[21] It was during the second strike wave that the riots against the Jews in South Wales broke out.

There was, however, no direct connexion between the strike and the riots, as is shown by the description of the events in Tredegar. " The trouble ", wrote the *Western Mail*,[22] " began shortly before midnight, when crowds of people were to be seen in the streets discussing the railway men's strike. There was, however, apparently nothing to provoke disorder. Suddenly a commotion was heard in a by-street, and there emerged into Castle Street a band of about 200 young men singing, shouting and making hideous noises. It soon transpired that this gang had attacked the residence of a Jew in Salisbury Street, smashing windows and greatly terrifying the occupants, although no personal violence was attempted. From Castle Street the mob marched into Commercial Street, and halting opposite a shop kept by a Jew, became very demonstrative and threatening. By this time the streets had become thronged with people attracted by the general pandemonium, the smashing of glass being frequently heard above the din. Only a small number of police were available, and they were quite unable to quell the riot."

The reports from every place where riots occurred following the trouble in Tredegar all show the same pattern: a sudden attack for no obvious reason and the failure of the local police to cope with the situation.

Only after newspaper correspondents had visited the affected places were accounts of the causes of these riots published. They were summarised and analysed in a leader in the *Jewish Chronicle*[23] and put into their proper perspective: " It is not difficult to understand the causes that have produced the recent outrages. The Jews of the South Wales towns have been largely engaged in business. Business in

Wales, especially, and with the Jews of Wales who have to adapt themselves to local demands and customs, means credit. Credit, unfortunatley, in the sort of trade followed, means too often legal pressure and process. That large numbers of native Welshmen should owe money to Jews (even for goods honestly sold), and that some of them should find themselves sued by these strangers (frequently not British-born) created a feeling of annoyance and irritation. Some of the Jews owned property, which meant the added annoyance of paying rent to them, or liability to ejection at their hands. The Jews, too, were seen, in many cases, to get on and prosper, as a result of keenness and assiduity; and that did not improve the popular feeling towards them. Occasionally one or two of them may have been harsh and tyrannical, or some, here and there, may have been over-reaching in business transactions, and so the animosity gathered strength. The next thing that happens is the strike. Passions are let loose, the law ceases to count, and the new development forms the match which ignites the inflammable anti-Jewish sentiments that pervade the Jewish area. Once the hillside is well alight, greed and the love of loot do the rest. And the ruin of the Jewish inhabitants—as we see it to-day—is the result."

Many newspapers compared these outbreaks with those in Czarist Russia, accounts of which were still filling the columns of the Press at that time. "The story reads", wrote the *Daily Mail*,[24] "like a chapter from the history of the dark ages. Men who imagined that they had found a refuge under the British flag are suddenly confronted with the horrors of a persecution that would disgrace a country in which anti-Semitism is a recognised policy." There was however one basic difference: while the local police force was inadequate for coping with the riots, the other authorities tried their utmost to suppress the unrest and to re-establish order. In contrast to the support officially given to anti-Semitic outbreaks by the authorities in Russia and later in Nazi Germany —not to mention the initiative frequently taken by them—no anti-Semitic manifestations were ever condoned by the British authorities.

As a contemporary writer emphasised,[25] the essential difference between the two forms of anti-Semitism lies in the

fact that " the protection of the law may always be counted
on by the Jews, if only they can invoke it in time. Hence
to compare the Welsh outbreak to a Russian pogrom is misleading in the extreme; the resemblance is superficial and
accidental, while the differences are profound and fundamental; and though the incident tarnishes the fair name of
England, it does not afford any palliation for the barbarities
of Russia." As Home Secretary Churchill was primarily
responsible for the preservation of order. Nor did he wait
for a request from Jewish leaders to translate his responsibility into action. On August 22, 1911, Stuart M. Samuel,
M.P., sent the following telegram to Churchill: [26] " Riots New
Tredegar Ebbw Vale directed specifically against Jewish
shops, renewal threatened New Tredegar this evening,
earnestly recommend you telegraph immediately affording
special police or military protection, definitely instructing
officers in command that life and property Jewish citizens
be exceptionally safeguarded throughout disturbed district."
On the same day Churchill replied: [27]

> Telegram received, instructions had already been tele-
> graphed to military and police authorities to take
> measures for protecting of Jews in the district named.

And indeed it appears from the reports from the various towns
affected that on the second day of the riots in Tredegar (Sunday, August 20) " fifty of the North Lancashire Regiment and
fifty of the Somersetshires arrived there from Cardiff ".[28] At
Ebbw Vale, where the riots started on Monday (August 21),
by midnight of that day military forces were sent in. " While
the looting was at its highest ", says one report,[29] " a few
minutes before midnight, the cry went round, ' The soldiers
are coming!' The effect was instantaneous. The looters fled
to their houses like rabbits to their holes." Similar reports
can be read about the arrival on Monday or Tuesday of the
military in the other places of the affected area. The instructions given by Churchill were carried out everywhere and
on Wednesday and Thursday no further outbreaks were
recorded.[30]

Churchill's swift action bore immediate fruit. He sent
troops to the Sirhowy Valleys notwithstanding the afore-

mentioned attacks on him by both Trade Unionists and Tories in connection with his despatch of troops during the strikes.[31]

Jewish leaders at the time did not fail to express their appreciation of Churchill's action. D. L. Alexander, K.C., President of the Board of Deputies, said in an interview:[32] " I have it on the authority of the Home Office that there is no further cause for alarm amongst the Jewish community in South Wales. There are now ample troops in the district, and until all is absolutely quiet again these will not be withdrawn." When the President reported to the meeting of the Board of Deputies on the outbreaks, he stated that[33] " he had come up to town on the following day (Monday, August 21) and had gone to the Home Office, where he had been most cordially received and invited to come as often as he had anything to communicate. He had received adequate assurances as to the protection of the Jews from further outrages in the affected parts."

Churchill once more showed his understanding of the necessity to stamp out anti-Jewish outrages in Britain on their first appearance. He felt that the South Wales riots should serve as a warning to anyone who might be tempted to repeat them — not only through the suppression of the riots but also through the subsequent punishment of the guilty persons. Thus many of the participants in the riots were arrested, brought before the courts and sentenced to up to three months' hard labour. After the passing of these sentences local populations called mass meetings and decided to collect signatures for a petition against the sentences. A deputation presented this petition to the Home Secretary, but Churchill replied[34]

> that, after giving the evidence in the case his careful and serious consideration, he cannot interfere with the decision of the local justices.

Soon afterwards Churchill relinquished his post as Home Secretary, having been appointed First Lord of the Admiralty. On the occasion of his departure from the Home Office the *Jewish Chronicle* in an editorial referred to his stand in the South Wales outbreaks and expressed thanks to him for his concern about Jewish interests:[35] " Mr. Churchill's resolute action in the South Wales anti-Jewish riots will be within the public recollection—action, of course, which would be taken by every Home Secretary in this country, whatever his politics, but none the less commendable in Mr. Churchill. Mr. Churchill's connection with Manchester[36] brought him into close touch with a constituency in which the Jewish element was considerable, if not decisive, and was the cause of a notable discussion on what was termed the Jewish vote. We would convey to Mr. Churchill our thanks for such consideration to Jewish interests during his tenure of the Home Secretaryship, which brought him so frequently into contact with Jews, and an expression of our good wishes in the equally important post with which he has now been entrusted."

### (b) IN THE EAST END OF LONDON

The year 1936 saw violent anti-Semitic activity in Britain, particularly in the East End of London. This was largely the result of the anti-Jewish propaganda perpetrated by Sir Oswald Mosley and his British Union of Fascists. Copying the methods used by the Nazis prior to their rise to power, Sir Oswald organised public meetings and parades in the course of which incidents usually took place; and as the Fascists deliberately chose their route through districts populated by Jews, the dangers and implications were obvious. Parliament debated Fascist activities in Britain on July 10, 1936,[37] and many Members expressed their abhorrence of these activities. They commented on the danger to the Jewish population which such propaganda might cause if allowed to continue unchecked. Sir John Simon, the Home Secretary, while defending the police, expressed grave concern at these developments.[38]

The situation grew rapidly worse. The Jewish population, following the lead of the Board of Deputies, got prepared to defend itself,[39] and indeed this was none too soon. In reply to a question by James H. Hall, M.P., the Labour Member for Whitechapel, " What measures he [the Secretary of State for the Home Department] contemplates taking to prevent members of the British Union of Fascists from intimidating persons attempting to purchase goods at Jewish shops or stalls ", Sir John Simon replied[40] " that the police are paying special attention to this matter ". On the same day the

Attorney General, Sir Donald Bradley Somervell, wrote in reply to a question by Commander Oliver Locker-Lampson who had asked what steps he intended to take relative to the charges of ritual murder in a recent copy of the *Fascist*:[41] " I have given instructions for proceedings to be instituted in this matter."

The climax of the Fascists' efforts was reached on October 4, 1936, after Mosley had announced a march of his followers through London's East End. Some 250,000 persons, Jews and non-Jews, had turned out, determined that " He shall not pass ", and were barring the route of the announced march. Popular feeling was running so high that the police, so as to avoid disorder, were forced to ban the Fascist march. But it was too late to prevent a number of clashes between Mosley's followers and counter-demonstrators during which many persons were injured and 53 arrests made.[42] There was no doubt that this counter-demonstration was skilfully organised by the Communists who expected to profit from their rôle as " protectors of the Jews ". This design became obvious when, on October 11, the Communists celebrated their " victory " of October 4 by mass parades in the East Fnd of London.[43] Fascists attacked the participants in this demonstration, and fourteen persons were arrested, subsequently fined and imprisoned.

It was in consequence of these events that Churchill felt it necessary to warn both Fascists and Communists against introducing riots into Britain's streets, and also to advise British Jewry not to fall into the trap of Communist " protection " but to rely on the rule of law upheld by the Government. This advice, given in 1936, was a reflection of his own actions during the South Wales riots in 1911.[44] On October 16, five days after the Communist " victory march ", he wrote:[45]

> An eddy of this Continental whirlpool has had its ebullition in the East End of London. An attempt has been made, joined in with equal zest by both factions, to reproduce before our decent, kindly English audience the dark passions which torment Europe. The proper course for British Communists and Nazis, if they feel so strongly their reciprocal hatreds, is to go over to the Continent

and fight out their quarrels there. We do not want to have any of these displays over here. We do not mean to have them. The impartial hand of the law should fall with heavy weight upon all disturbers of the King's peace. The Government will be supported by Parliament in measures which may be judged apt and necessary to prevent our streets being used as a cockpit. Everything should be done to isolate these factionaries, and thus reveal how small their numbers are. The great steady masses of British Conservatives and Labour men have many real conflicts to fight out, and we have a free Parliament to fight them out in. We neither fear the malice of one side, nor do we require the aid of the other.

It is especially important that British Jewry should keep itself absolutely clear from this brawling. In Great Britain the law-abiding Jew need not look to the Communist for protection. He will get that as his right from the Constable.

Less than a month later, on November 10, the Public Order Bill was introduced in Parliament,[46] which gave comprehensive powers to the authorities for suppressing semi-military organisations; it gave the police the right to search their premises on suspicion of an offence by members of such organisations; it empowered the police to prohibit parades that might cause disorder; and it listed penalties both for the possession of weapons by persons attending public meetings, and for threatening or abusive words or behaviour with intent to provoke a breach of the peace. The Bill was read a third time and passed by the House of Lords on December 16, 1936.[47] Two weeks previously there had been launched at a mass meeting a new movement to be known as the " Defence of Freedom and Peace ". The meeting, held on December 3, 1936, at the Royal Albert Hall under the chairmanship of Sir Walter Citrine, was arranged by the League of Nations Union, and attended by members of all political parties. In a rousing speech Churchill, the principal speaker, referred to the latest developments in Britain — as outlined shortly above—saying: [48]

There is another cleavage in the world to-day. It is the

war between the Nazis and the Communists; the war of
the non-God religions, waged with the weapons of the
twentieth century. The most striking fact about the new
religions is their similarity. They substitute the devil
for God and hatred for love. They are at each other's
throats wherever they exist all over the world, and have
even appeared in the East End of London.

Denouncing Fascism, Communism and persecution, he made
a passionate plea for tolerance and for

> stamping out the disgusting Jew-baiting which some
> people are trying to import across the North Sea.

In 1937 the Fascists split into two factions, the seceding
one organised and headed by William Joyce ("Lord Haw
Haw"), who after World War II was hanged as a traitor.
Following all these events disorders became less frequent,
though they did not altogether cease. Only the outbreak of
the war put a final stop to them.

## THE CASE AGAINST LORD DOUGLAS

In the summer of 1920 a newspaper made its appearance
in England which excelled in its scurrilous accusations against
Churchill and other leading British statesmen. *Plain English*
was edited by Lord Alfred Douglas, a man in his early fifties,
poet and one time friend of Oscar Wilde. The allegations
which Lord Douglas published against Churchill were centred
round the Battle of Jutland which took place on the night of
May 31 — June 1, 1916, between the British and German
fleets. In spite of heavy losses to the British, it resulted in
the German ships being driven into port, not to emerge again
till the war was over.[49]   Lord Douglas accused Churchill of
having plotted with Sir Ernest Cassel, the well-known financier and friend of Churchill's,[50] for him (Churchill) to publish
a false report of the battle, stating that the British Fleet had
been defeated. Such a report would cause a panic on the
stock exchanges in Britain and America, stocks would fall
rapidly, and Sir Ernest and his friends would enrich themselves by buying in a falling market. This "plot", so Lord
Douglas maintained, had in fact been carried out; Churchill
had published a report after the Battle of Jutland as planned

and Sir Ernest Cassel had made a profit of eighteen million pounds. As part of the plot Churchill was alleged to have been given seven thousand pounds' worth of furniture by way of payment. Later Lord Douglas altered this figure to £40,000.[51]

When these statements were first published in *Plain English*, a disreputable and almost unknown " paper ", Churchill had taken no action against Lord Douglas who, subsequently, felt so sure of himself that he continued in his campaign of abuse. Once launched, the attacks were of course not confined to the strategic problems of the Jutland Battle, but from the outset showed a distinct anti-Jewish bias. In the years 1920-1921 a number of papers had published anti-Semitic articles, foremost among them the London *Morning Post*, which between July 12 and 30, 1920, ran a series of seventeen articles : " The Cause of World Unrest." It contended — as anti-Semitic writers had done before — that every unrest was artificially provoked and that therefore the hidden hand behind all the revolutions was a sect of Freemasons now unmasked as the Jews.[52] From there it was only a short step to the *Protocols of the Elders of Zion* which were supposed to have contained the Jewish plan for world domination by violent means. It was sufficient for the *Morning Post* to reprint uncritically statements from *The Jewish Peril*, a pamphlet published in London in 1920, which was in fact another title for the *Protocols*. In three now famous articles, *The Times* proved the *Protocols* to be a literary forgery and presented " for the first time conclusive proof that the document is in the main a clumsy plagiarism ".[53]

Such were the sources from which Lord Douglas culled his teachings and on the basis of which he launched his attacks against Churchill and the Jews. Admittedly, he was encouraged to persist in his abuse when no steps were taken against him after the publication of his articles. Again, when during the Genoa Conference in March 1922 the German-Russian friendship treaty of Rapallo was concluded, the circumstances surrounding the agreement lent themselves to more anti-Semitic slogans. Rathenau, who acted for the Germans, was a Jew, while Bolshevik Russia had in any case been identified by anti-Semitic writers with the fulfilment of the Jewish dream of world domination. It was not difficult, therefore, for the *Morning Post* to exploit this treaty to the full. "The Joy Ride to Genoa ", was the title of an article which appeared in that paper on March 31, 1922. Laurie Magnus, the editor of the London *Jewish Guardian,* wrote a protest under the heading " The Call of the East " which was published on April 21, 1922. He wrote therein *inter alia*: " It must no longer be a paying proposition to men like Mr. Crosland and Lord Douglas to invent vile insults against the Jews." The *Morning Post* answered in a leading article " Whose the Blame?" which induced the *Guardian*'s editor to send a communication to the *Morning Post* emphasising that the words complained of were not meant against the *Morning Post* but against both Mr. Crosland and Lord Douglas.

This correspondence gave Lord Douglas the chance to raise his voice again. He instituted proceedings against the *Morning Post* for " damages for an alleged libel published in the *Morning Post* on April 26, 1922 ".[54]

The action was heard on July 17, 1923, and attracted wide attention.[55] A. S. Comyns Carr, for Lord Douglas, defended his client by pointing out with justification that the *Morning Post* " was in the habit of making bitter and virulent statements about the Jews ", while this paper was now suggesting " that the plaintiff invented vile slanders against them to make money ". Carr however accepted the challenge on behalf of his client and pointed out that Lord Douglas was justified in his statements in *Plain English* for which he accepted responsibility, particularly in " dealing with the alleged influence of the Jews in various events, such as the report issued in connexion with the Battle of Jutland, the assistance alleged to have been given to Mr. Churchill by Jewish financiers, the death of Lord Kitchener, and other matters . . ." By this gambit Churchill was brought into the front line of the controversy. When Lord Douglas was later cross-examined by Patrick Hastings, K.C., the following " charges " against Churchill, which were elicited with the help of quotations from *Plain English,* emerged:

HASTINGS: Your article says: ' It may also be said that the Cabinet Minister who drew up and issued the false report about the Battle of Jutland which produced this fall in stock had spent the week-end with one of the most powerful members of the financial group, Sir Ernest Cassel.' Who was the Cabinet Minister?

DOUGLAS: Mr. Churchill.

HASTINGS: Do you happen to know that Mr. Churchill had not been a Cabinet Minister for twelve months before the Battle of Jutland?

DOUGLAS: That has been explained as being a slip of the pen.

HASTINGS: Do you know that Lord Balfour has stated in his evidence taken on commission that the only person who drew up the so-called false report was himself?

DOUGLAS: I know, but I don't believe it.

HASTINGS: You suggest he has committed perjury?

DOUGLAS: He has either committed perjury or his memory has failed.

HASTINGS: Do you suggest now that Mr. Churchill drew up that report?

DOUGLAS: Certainly.

The cross-examination continued and, in the course of his questions, Hastings returned to a significant paragraph in *Plain English* which he quoted:

HASTINGS: You say later on [in your article]: ' It is true that by most subtle means and by never allowing him more than a pony ahead, this ambitious and brilliant man, short of money and eager for power, was trapped by the Jews. After the Jutland business his house was furnished for him by Sir Ernest Cassel.' Do you mean to say that Mr. Churchill was financially indebted to the Jews?

DOUGLAS: Yes, certainly.

HASTINGS: Do you want to persist in that now?

DOUGLAS: Of course, I do.

HASTINGS: Who were the Jews in whose clutches he was?

DOUGLAS: Chiefly Cassel.

HASTINGS: What justification had you in your own mind for making that charge against Mr. Churchill?

DOUGLAS: I had the evidence of what was told me by men at the Admiralty, and Sir Alfred Fripp told me that Cassel had given Mr. Churchill £40,000 in one cheque . . .

HASTINGS: Was it after the Battle of Jutland that he got a cheque for £40,000?

DOUGLAS: Certainly.

HASTINGS: You say in your article: 'The Jewish Jutland plotters never paid him properly.'

DOUGLAS: Well, they made £48,000,000.

In view of such grave accusations it was natural that Lord Balfour's evidence was called for. He made it on commission and it was read in Court by William A. Jowitt (now Earl Jowitt), also appearing for the defendant. Lord Balfour stated that in May and June, 1916, he held the office of First Lord of the Admiralty. On May 31, 1916, the Battle of Jutland took place. The course of the battle was reported to the Commander-in-Chief. On June 2, he drew up a *communiqué* dealing with the battle and then took it into Admiral Oliver's room, and some quite trifling alterations were made in it. The document produced to him was the one which he drew up in his own handwriting. The *communiqué* was sent to the Press through the ordinary official channels. Churchill had nothing to do with the drafting, the preparation, or the issuing of the *communiqué*. Churchill called on the following day and was shown the telegrams which had been received from the Fleet. He (Lord Balfour) invited him to issue an appreciation of the situation. He consented to do so, the object being to inform neutral governments of material and relevant facts of which they had no knowledge, to counteract the misleading statements issued by the German Admiralty. That was issued on June 4.

Then Churchill went into the box. He was examined by Patrick Hastings, who immediately came to the point:

HASTINGS: I want to ask one question and apologise for asking it. Is there a single word of truth in the suggestion that you were ever in the hands of any man,

Sir Ernest Cassel or anyone else, Jew or Gentile?

CHURCHILL: No, never at any time.

HASTINGS: Is there any truth in the suggestion that you entered into a plot with Jews or anybody else in relation to reports of the Jutland battle?

CHURCHILL: There is no truth in it.

HASTINGS: Is there any truth in the statement that after the battle Sir Ernest Cassel or anybody else paid you a farthing in any shape or form in regard to anything you had done in connexion with the Jutland Battle?

CHURCHILL: It is an absolute lie.

HASTINGS: When you first saw the articles, did you consider the advisability of prosecuting the man who wrote them?

CHURCHILL: I sent the article to the Law Officers, and the Attorney General (now Lord Hewart) gave a great deal of attention to the matter, and he most strongly advised me against instituting a prosecution either personally or through the Director of Public Prosecutions. His view was that the status of the paper was so obscure and contemptible that it would only give it a needless advertisement and notoriety if a State prosecution or an action for libel were started. Lastly, he considered that the character of Lord Alfred Douglas made it unnecessary for me to take any notice at that stage of these very gross and cruel libels; but he assured me that if at any time the question was raised and I was asked why I had not taken action to clear my honour, he would himself testify to the advice he had given me and the reason for doing so. That was the reason why I abstained from prosecuting.

There were a number of other small points which had come out in the cross-examination of Lord Douglas or in his articles, and they were all gradually raised by Hastings in his questioning of Churchill. "Is there a word of truth in the suggestion", asked Hastings, "that you drew it [the report] up yourself?"

CHURCHILL: Not a word.

HASTINGS: Or that you came straight from the house of

Sir Ernest Cassel to draw it up at his instigation?
CHURCHILL : Not a word of truth . . .
HASTINGS : Is there a word of truth in the suggestion that
you wrote the second report at the instigation of Sir
Ernest Cassel or any Jew?
CHURCHILL : I never saw Sir Ernest Cassel at that time.
I wrote it at the request of the First Lord of the
Admiralty [Lord Balfour].
HASTINGS : Had it anything to do with any manipulation
of stocks in any market in the world?
CHURCHILL : Such an idea never entered my mind.
HASTINGS : Did you make a penny piece of money in any
way out of it?
CHURCHILL : No.
HASTINGS : I think Sir Ernest Cassel was a close friend
of your father and mother?
CHURCHILL : Yes.
HASTINGS : And you have known him since you were a
small boy?
CHURCHILL : Since I was a young man of 19.

No cross-examination of Churchill by counsel for the plaintiff followed. Carr in his summing up only said that the
question of truth or lie had never arisen, but that the Court
was called upon to decide whether Lord Douglas made his
statements honestly believing that they were true. The case
only ended so unfortunately because, as the *Jewish Chronicle*
emphasised,[56] the sentence for which action was taken by
Lord Douglas employed the single word " inventing " vile
slanders against Jews.[57]  The Jury awarded one farthing
damages and each party had to pay their own costs.

Encouraged by the outcome of this action, Lord Douglas
continued his defamations, and finally summarised them in
a brochure *The Murder of Lord Kitchener and the Truth
about the Battle of Jutland and the Jews.*  There was thus
nothing left to Churchill but to fall back on the Attorney
General's promise to him that, if it should become necessary,
proceedings would be instituted.  The case was heard on
December 11 and 12, 1923, and Lord Douglas was accused
" of publishing a malicious and defamatory libel of and concerning Mr. Winston L. S. Churchill ".[58]

In fact the proceedings, as far as the statements against Churchill were concerned, were almost an exact repetition of Lord Douglas's action against the *Morning Post*. The same arguments were made by the Attorney General, Sir Douglas Hogg, K.C. [later Lord Hailsham], and Churchill's denial of all of them elaborated. On this occasion Lord Balfour appeared personally and repeated the gist of what he had stated on the previous occasion on commission, namely, that it was he who drew up the report. His testimony about the events at the Admiralty was corroborated by witnesses who served at the Admiralty at the time. Churchill again went into the witness box, but on this occasion was also cross-examined by Cecil Hayes who appeared for Lord Douglas. Some new facts came to light during the cross-examination which deserve to be recorded here:

Churchill denied that Sir Ernest Cassel had made him a gift of furniture or anything else after the Battle of Jutland, but to a question put to him by the Attorney General he replied:

> In 1905 I took a small house in South Molton Street and Sir Ernest Cassel asked Lady Randolph whether he could furnish a library for me. She consented.

And he added:

> When I was married, in 1908, instead of making me a wedding present, Sir Ernest sent me £500, which I spent.

In the subsequent cross-examination by counsel for the defence this matter was again raised:

> HAYES: Was Sir Ernest Cassel alive when the articles appeared in *Plain English*? Why was no action taken then?
>
> CHURCHILL: Sir Ernest was alive then. He died in September 1920. No action was taken. I was advised not to institute any because the paper was so obscure, and Lord Douglas so well known, that proceedings were needless.
>
> HAYES: Who suggested these proceedings?
>
> CHURCHILL: I certainly sent the libels to the Public Prosecutor; if the Crown had not taken action I should

have done so. I have been persistently pursued by these libels, and after the *Morning Post* case these matters were continually repeated, and retailed at the street-corners; therefore I appealed to the Crown.

HAYES: Haven't you delayed taking proceedings because Sir Ernest was still alive and it would be more difficult for the defendant to prove his case?

CHURCHILL: Definitely not.

HAYES: Do you know that Sir Ernest Cassel was born in Germany, of German parents?

CHURCHILL: I know that.

HAYES: And he came to England a German subject?

CHURCHILL: He did.

HAYES: And in due course was made a knight and a Privy Councillor?

CHURCHILL: Yes.

HAYES: You know he started in the City of London as a clerk at £2 a week?

CHURCHILL: Is that very much against him?

On the following day Hayes continued his cross-examination. The greater part of it bore on Sir Ernest Cassel and Churchill's relations with him. When in the course of the questioning Churchill mentioned that Sir Ernest would have been appointed Master of the Quorn Hounds, Hayes exclaimed:

A naturalised German! You remember how he used to speak. A full-blown German naturalised in England. Do you remember what he looked like when sitting on a horse? Do you think for a moment he could have been Master of the Quorn?

CHURCHILL: I have said so already.

HIS LORDSHIP: What was the matter with his voice? (Laughter.)

HAYES: I suggest his German accent.—I put it to you as a well known hunting man who has hunted with the Quorn that this suggestion is grotesque?

CHURCHILL: No.

HAYES: It requires a man born and bred in the saddle for that position?

CHURCHILL: The Master is not the same as a huntsman. I am talking of Sir Ernest Cassel nearly 30 years ago, when he was received everywhere with the greatest respect and regard.

HAYES: In 1907 you were on close terms of friendship with Sir Ernest Cassel?

CHURCHILL: Yes, on terms of honourable friendship.

HAYES: You were grateful to him in 1907?

CHURCHILL: He was a very great friend of mine.

Hayes then reverted to the presents received by Churchill from Sir Ernest and asked whether any more gifts were obtained. Churchill replied:

After Sir Ernest's death the family sent me his watch and chain, because they thought he would like me to have them.

Sir Ernest Cassel's private secretary and financial advisers also appeared as witnesses. They, as the people most intimately informed about all his transactions, confirmed that no share deals had been transacted by Sir Ernest Cassel at the time of the Jutland Battle.

Lord Douglas was found guilty and sentenced by Mr. Justice Avory to six months imprisonment.[59]

# CHAPTER IV

## THE SOLUTION

HIS long acquaintance with Jewish problems must inevitably have led Churchill to ask himself what could be done to solve them and to alleviate the tragic sufferings of so large a part of the Jewish people. It is indeed noteworthy that that great statesman was one of the very first men in British public life to try to understand the problem, to express some contributory thoughts to its clarification, and finally to endorse a solution to which he had adhered with unshakeable confidence.

He first became aware of the brutal treatment of the Jews in Russia in the early years of the present century,[1] thanks to the publicity given it by the Press. As the horrifying evidence mounted he became more and more convinced that the Jews of Central and Eastern Europe had no share in that liberty, tolerance and equality of opportunity which were his ideals for mankind as a whole. His immediate reaction to Russian anti-Jewish manifestations was the hope that " strong protest and condemnation of atrocities put solemnly on record might suffice to stop the barbarities ",[2] but he was soon driven to the conclusion that the victims of oppression could not be allowed to remain in territories where they would be subject to persecution. He therefore whole-heartedly supported the endeavours of those who were hoping to find a refuge for them elsewhere. It was on this assumption that he fought the Aliens Bills, for in his opinion Britain should have remained an open haven of refuge—though not, of course, the only one—for people fleeing from persecution.

These thoughts were dictated by the needs of the hour which never ceased to confront him and his generation. It seemed then that by healing a wound, or by rendering aid in a few individual unhappy cases, the situation might be eased.

185

This, however, was only a superficial method of approach. Theodor Herzl had a few years before unfolded his penetrating analysis of the Jewish situation and had proposed a solution in the creation of a national sovereign State. Seven years after his first visit to London in the Zionist cause, Herzl was able to convince the Balfour Government of the necessity of this territorial and national solution. Joseph Chamberlain, the great " Empire Builder ", was the prime mover within the Government in favour of the Zionist solution. He received Herzl in October 1902 and arranged for the latter's subsequent discussions with Lord Lansdowne, the Foreign Secretary, Lord Cromer, Britain's Agent and Consul General in Egypt, and others,[3] on the possibility of creating an autonomous Jewish settlement in the Sinai Peninsula. Under the prevailing circumstances however, the scheme could not be carried through. Chamberlain then suggested a Jewish settlement in the East Africa Protectorate[4] to Herzl's representative in London, Leopold J. Greenberg. The negotiations which followed led to the greatest political success attained by Herzl. An official letter, signed by Sir Clement Hill, Under-Secretary for Foreign Affairs, dated August 14, 1903, and addressed to Leopold J. Greenberg, stated that " if a site can be found which the Trust and His Majesty's Commissioner consider suitable and which commends itself to His Majesty's Government, Lord Lansdowne will be prepared to entertain favourably proposals for the establishment of a Jewish colony or settlement, on conditions which will enable the members to observe their National customs ". This was indeed a great triumph for political Zionism, as even Dr. Weizmann, Herzl's great opponent, conceded,[5] for " this was the first time in the exilic history of Jewry that a great government had officially negotiated with the elected representatives of the Jewish people. The identity, the legal personality of the Jewish people, had been re-established ".

The announcement caused a stir among Jews and non-Jews. Articles and letters appeared in the press and focused wide public attention on the Jewish problem. After the House of Commons had debated the matter on June 20, 1904,[6] a Commission was sent out in December 1904, in accordance with the decision of the Sixth Zionist Congress,[7] to the East African Protectorate, consisting of Major A. St. Hill Gibbons, Professor Alfred Kaiser and Dr. N. Wilbusch, to examine the territory offered for a settlement.[8]

Shortly before the Commission left, Churchill, whose pro-Jewish sentiments had by then become well known by his courageous stand over the Aliens Bill, 1904, was asked by a correspondent for his opinion about a Jewish settlement in that territory. He replied that[9]

> the proposal to form a colony of refugees in some part of the British Empire not less healthy but less crowded than these islands, deserves fair and patient consideration.

The Commission spent a few months in the Protectorate and published its Report in May 1905,[10] shortly after the second reading of the Aliens Bill, 1905.[11] Its conclusions being unfavourable, the Seventh Zionist Congress decided not to proceed with the scheme, and to concentrate all Zionist efforts on Palestine.[12] But those who refused to be discouraged by the Report and to accept the decision of the Zionist Congress decided to persist in the efforts to find a refuge elsewhere and seceded from the Zionist movement. Their leader became Israel Zangwill who, some three weeks after the conclusion of the Congress, issued a " Manifesto " in which he outlined his views and announced the establishment of the Jewish Territorial Organisation (I.T.O.). Its object was two-fold:[13] " I. To procure a territory upon an autonomous basis for those Jews who cannot, or will not, remain in the lands in which they at present live. II. To achieve this end the Organisation proposes (a) to unite all Jews who are in agreement with this object; (b) to enter into relations with Governments and public and private institutions; (c) to create financial institutions, labour-bureaus, and other instruments that may be found necessary."

A number of prominent Jews in Britain—among them Lord Rothschild, Leopold de Rothschild, Lucien Wolf and R. M. Sebag-Montefiore — joined the Organisation which started a lively propaganda campaign throughout the country. The Manchester I.T.O. branch was particularly active and the Committee which had only recently been formed to organise the struggle against the Aliens Bill, 1905, in that city,[14] consisting of B. I. Belisha, Nathan Laski, Dr. J. Dulberg, J. Besso, S. Finburgh and H. B. Morris, now also became the nucleus of the new organisation. The branch was formed in September 1905,[15] and selected as its Hon. Secretary Dr. J. Dulberg. These were the same men who had all along favoured the British offer of a settlement in East Africa and who had participated in a Conference called by Nathan Laski on April 3, 1905, in Manchester,[16] to resolve upon organizing "a special conference at which the provinces might be worthily represented to consider the offer of the British Government".

It will be remembered that the above-mentioned Committee had called a mass meeting in Manchester to protest against the Aliens Bill, 1905, at which Churchill delivered the principal address.[17]   These same men, as has been shown,[18] became the principal workers and propagandists among Manchester Jews for the candidature of Churchill at the general election in January 1906.   It was therefore natural that they should have approached their candidate to ascertain his opinion on the issue.   When he was thus approached he was, of course, fully aware of the problem, not only from press reports but also from frequent reference, particularly during the debates on the Aliens Bill, 1905, to the British offer by the members of Balfour's Government and by the Prime Minister himself.   Joseph Chamberlain's statement to that effect[19] has already been quoted, and, during the Committee stage of the Bill, Balfour, having been charged by a speaker with indifference towards Jewish sufferings in Russia, said in defence[20] that "he would remind the Committee that at all events they who sat on that bench could not be regarded as indifferent to the interests of the race on behalf of whom the hon. member for Whitechapel [Stuart Samuel] spoke. So far as he knew, alone among the nations of the world, and certainly among the Governments of this country, they had offered the Jewish race a great tract of fertile land in a British possession in order that they might, if they so desired it, find an asylum from the persecutors at home".

By then it had also become clear to Churchill that no palliatives would meet the grave problem of Jewish homelessness, but only a fundamental approach to it on a national and world wide basis.   Recalling these events some 25 years later he stressed[21] that

in 1903 the British Government had offered Jewish colonists a national home in East Africa.

The phrase "national home" in this statement shows that he had fully grasped the national and political implications of the problem.

Though they were initiated and promoted by a Government which he had strongly opposed, Churchill welcomed these efforts from the start. For this issue seemed to him sufficiently important to be elevated above party interests. When he was asked by Dr. Dulberg, the Hon. Secretary, on behalf of the Manchester I.T.O. group, to voice his views on the issue, he showed some reluctance, as in the meantime a change of Government had taken place and he had for the first time assumed ministerial office. When he did reply, his statement was no longer merely the personal view of a great friend of the Jewish people, but the utterance of a member of H.M. Government. Clearly conscious of this fact, Churchill wrote to Dr. Dulberg:[22]

Downing Street,

1st January, 1906.

My Dear Sir, I have delayed to answer your letter of the 26th of December until I have had an opportunity of studying the documents in this office which relate to the subject.[23] You are no doubt aware of the numerous and serious difficulties which present themselves to a scheme of establishing a self-governing Jewish Colony in British East Africa, of the differences of opinion among the Jews themselves, of the doubtful suitability of the territory in question, of the rapidly extending settlements by British colonists in and about the areas, and of the large issues of general state policy which the scheme affects. Those difficulties had powerfully impressed themselves upon Mr. Lyttleton;[24] and although Lord Elgin[25] will approach the consideration of this subject in a spirit of profound sympathy both for the aspirations of the Jewish race, and for their recent terrible sufferings, I cannot believe that those difficulties will be absent from his mind.

But I will own that I hope that they may be surmounted. I agree most heartily with the spirit of Mr. Zangwill's letter to *The Times* of December 12, 1905. I recognise the supreme attraction to a scattered and perse-

cuted people of a safe and settled home under the flag
of tolerance and freedom. Such a plan contains a soul,
and enlists in its support energies, enthusiasms and a
driving power which no scheme of individual colonisa-
tion can ever command. And although Lord Rothschild's contention that the immediate needs of Jewish
refugees are best met by affording them opportunities
of settling in Canada and the Argentine may be powerfully urged, I do not feel that the noble vision you behold
so vividly ought to be allowed to fade, and I will do
what I can to preserve it and fulfil it. There should be
room within the world-wide limits of the British Empire,
and within the generous scope of Liberal institutions,
for the self-development and peculiar growth of many
races, and of many traditions, and of many creeds. And
from an Imperial point of view it is on the varied excel-
lence of its parts, that there is most surely to be founded
the wealth, the happiness and the higher unity of the
whole.

Yours very truly,

WINSTON S. CHURCHILL.

In connection with this letter, Israel Zangwill wired his
thanks to Churchill, and in a communication to Dr. Dulberg
referred to Churchill's statement as follows:[26] " A batch
of letters from Jews in various parts of the continent, all full
of enthusiastic gratitude for the magnanimous attitude of
Winston Churchill towards the Jewish people, remind me that
I have not yet acknowledged your letter. I trust you will
convey to Mr. Churchill my personal appreciation of his
inspiring words. I am particularly glad that he recognizes
that a scheme of colonization needs a soul. In fact, history
shows that none of our colonies succeeded without a soul to
start with, or until a soul was introduced. Those parts of our
vast Empire that are given over to profit-hunting syndicates
are just the ones that have no real being.

" Mr. Churchill's statesmanlike vision is of the happiest
augury for our plans. He has certainly earned the good will
of the Jews of the world. By the bye, all my continental
correspondents call him Lord Churchill, but I suppose he
won't mind that."

Churchill's letter expressing sympathy with the efforts of the Territorial Organisation was soon followed by similar expressions by other prominent members of the new Government. Herbert Gladstone, the Home Secretary, wrote to Isaac Carmel, Hon. Secretary of the Leeds I.T.O. branch on January 9, 1906:[27] " I have your letter of the 5th inst. I take much interest in the proposal of Mr. Zangwill for the establishment of a Jewish settlement under British protection. I shall receive the details of such proposals with the hope that they may be of such a nature as to secure the support of the Government. I wish sucess to Mr. Zangwill's enterprize." And the Colonial Secretary, Lord Elgin, authorized his secretary, Bernard Holland, to send the following reply, dated January 29, 1906,[28] to an enquiry by Israel Zangwill. This answer is couched in very similar terms to those which Churchill employed in his letter to Dr. Dulberg: " Lord Elgin desires me to reply as follows to your letter of the 23rd inst. He feels very deep sympathy with the people of your race in their recent afflictions, and fully understands their desire to inhabit some land in which they would enjoy safety and freedom, and would be glad if it should prove possible to find some unoccupied or undeveloped part of the British Empire where, as you desire, a Jewish Colony might be planted with fair prospects of success. Lord Elgin appreciates the practical difficulties of many kinds which stand in the way of a realization of this fine aspiration, but he will give his most careful and sympathetic attention to any schemes which may be brought before him."

Meanwhile Churchill, during a visit to Manchester, seized the opportunity of a meeting there on January 7, 1906, to point out again[29] that

He believed in the idea of creating an autonomous Jewish colony in East Africa under the flag of toleration and freedom, and recently, when he received a letter from Mr. Zangwill, he obtained the assent of the Earl of Elgin, the Secretary of State for the Colonies, before replying, so that such reply might carry the weight of having been approved by a Cabinet minister.

This happened just at the time of the general election and Churchill's friends and supporters in Manchester made ample use of his efforts in connection with the Aliens Bills and of his openly proclaimed sympathies with a solution of the Jewish problem by means of territorial settlement on a national basis. Since the Prime Minister, Arthur Balfour, also had his headquarters there, the attention of the whole country was particularly focused on Manchester. Owing to the large Jewish vote, Jewish support for a candidate was of especial importance. It was then that Dr. Dreyfus, Chairman of the Manchester Conservatives and President of the local Zionist Organisation, a strong supporter of Balfour's candidature, introduced Dr. Weizmann, Vice-President of the Manchester Zionist branch, to Balfour, and a conversation took place which was to become of historic significance.[30] Thus it came about that the issue of Territorialism versus Zionism played a certain rôle in these elections with the territorialists, Laski, Belisha and Dulberg, backing Churchill, while the Zionist Dr. Dreyfus and some others worked hard for Balfour's victory. Even so the latter was heavily defeated in Manchester E. by Thomas Horridge, a Liberal, while Churchill won his seat in Manchester N.W. convincingly against Joynson-Hicks. This success, as an editorial in the *Jewish Chronicle* stressed,[31] " was in considerable measure due to the support of Jews, who approved of his gallant fight against " the Aliens Bills.

Churchill, as his letter to Dr. Dulberg shows, was fully aware of the difficulties which confronted the establishment of a self-governing Jewish settlement. He therefore laid down some fundamental principles which he considered the prerequisite for a successful implementation of a colonization scheme. From the above-quoted communications one can deduce his definition: the territory must be " not less healthy but less crowded than these islands ", it must therefore be climatically suitable for European settlers and have sufficient space for colonization on a larger scale. Furthermore, it must offer to settlers the possibility for " self-development " in the frame of their own peculiar racial, religious and traditional characteristics. Therefore it must be the result of a national effort, and not rest on a temporary or individual basis. It must also have " a soul and enlist in its support energies, enthusiasms and a driving power ". It is interesting to note in this connection that these fundamental conditions set out by Churchill for a Jewish colonization scheme are almost identical with those which Theodor Herzl set out in a letter to Sir Francis Montefiore, President of the English Zionist Federation, dated December 14, 1903:[32] " To my mind four elements are necessary for our deeming within the range of practical politics the suggestion of the British Government: (1) The territory has to be sufficiently extensive to admit of an immigration of such a character as should be eventually a material relief to the pressure which to-day exists in Eastern Jewry; (2) it follows that the territory has to be one colonizable by such people of ours; (3) the concession has to be invested with such autonomous rights as would ensure the Jewish character of the settlement; and (4) perhaps governing all, the enthusiasm of our own people in respect to the offer has to be of such a nature as will overcome all the obvious difficulties which under most favourable conditions will be bound to arise in the creation of the settlement."

It was for such a territory, either within the Empire or elsewhere, that Zangwill and his friends marshalled all their resources with boundless enthusiasm and energy. And yet they failed. When asked in the House of Commons by Sir William E. Evans-Gordon almost a year after the establishment of the I.T.O. whether " in view of the renewed outrages upon the Jews in Russia, any steps can be taken to give effect to the colonization scheme of the Territorial Society ", Churchill could only reply:[33]

> The Society are in communication with the Secretary of State [Earl of Elgin] on the subject, but no practical scheme has yet been submitted.

The Organisation continued to look out for territories and concentrated its interest mainly on Western Australia,[34] Canada,[35] and elsewhere, especially Cyrenaica.[36] But nothing came of these efforts.

In order to co-ordinate the search for territory the I.T.O. set up a Geographical Commission[37] consisting of such prominent men concerned with migration problems as Dr. Max Mandelstamm (Russia), Dr. Paul Nathan and James Simon (Germany), Lord Rothschild (England) and the Hon. Oscar Strauss (America). But, beyond establishing a re-distribution centre for immigrants at Galveston[38] in the U.S.A., no tangible results were achieved. Thus Zangwill had to confess at a conference in Manchester:[39] " Two years ago, when the I.T.O. was founded, we probably most of us thought—foolishly enough—that by this time we should be organizing a definite Jewish territory. We thought this, even without knowing what these two years were to bring."

Throughout that period Churchill's name is not mentioned again in connection with the colonization scheme. Only once, in the speech just quoted, did Zangwill refer to him as one of the advocates of the idea which seemed to the speaker of particular interest to Manchester, part of which Churchill then represented in Parliament. Zangwill exclaimed:[40] " Do you remember the noble words written by Mr. Winston Churchill to your Dr. Dulberg in support of I.T.O., pointing out that national colonization, unlike individual, contains a soul, a driving spirit?"

At the time these words were spoken, Churchill was on a journey in East Africa.[41] On his return he described the impressions gained there in his book *African Journey*.[42] In a special chapter[43] describing the area where the proposed Jewish settlement was originally contemplated, he came to the conclusion[44] that it

> can never be a white man's country, in the sense that Canada, or, indeed the United Kingdom, are white men's countries.

This conclusion, however, and the failures of the I.T.O. to find any other suitable territory for a Jewish settlement,[45] did not cause Churchill to abandon his belief in the solution of the Jewish problem on a national and territorial basis. It was therefore natural that he should find his way to the Zionist movement which, though unable at that moment to attain its geographical goal in Palestine, nevertheless comprized in its conception all those vital elements which made it even before attaining the territory, " the Jewish nation on its way ", to use Herzl's phrase.[46] It was imbued with those ideals which Churchill regarded as the paramount prerequisites of a nation. When on the occasion of the Annual Conference of the English Zionist Federation, at Manchester on February 2, 1908, a public meeting was held, the chairman,

Jacob Moser, J.P., read to the audience packing the Palace Theatre the following letter from Churchill: [47]

I am in full sympathy with the historical aspirations of the Jews. The restoration to them of a centre of racial and political integrity would be a tremendous event in the history of the world. Whether the whole effort of the Jewish race should be concentrated upon Palestine to the exclusion of all other temporary solutions, or whether, in the meanwhile, some other outlet of relief and place of unification should be provided for the bitter need of those who suffer from day to day—are questions on which I could scarcely presume to express an opinion. But my visit to East Africa has made me acquainted with the many difficulties which seem to be in the path of that country, and this fact necessarily increased my sympathy with your efforts to reach what must be your ultimate goal.

This letter is of historic significance, not only because it displays Churchill's full grasp of the Herzlian Zionist conception long before other statesmen in this and other countries, but also because it refers to the " sympathy with the historical aspirations of the Jews " a phrase which nine years later was to appear in the preamble to the Balfour Declaration of November 2, 1917, conveying on behalf of His Majesty's Government a " declaration of sympathy with Jewish Zionist aspirations ". But above all this letter of Churchill's to the Manchester Zionists initiated a period of close co-operation with the movement of which Sir Winston spoke with pride in 1921 when, as Colonial Secretary, he addressed a Jewish gathering on Mount Scopus in Jerusalem, and said inter alia: [48]

Personally my heart has throbbed with Zionism since twelve years ago,[49] when I made the acquaintance of Manchester Jewry.

He has remained true to the Zionist cause ever since 1908, unshaken in his resolve to assist its implementation, and faithful to the noble ideal which inspires it.

END OF PART I

# NOTES AND REFERENCES
## CHAPTER I

1. Speech at a dinner of the London Jewish Education Board on January 18, 1926. See *Daily Telegraph*, January 19, 1926, p. 7, col. 3.
2. "Churchill the Philosopher", in *Churchill by his Contemporaries*, p. 477.
3. "Zionism versus Bolshevism".
4. *My Early Life*, pp. 26-28.
5. In his essay "Personal Contacts" (*Thoughts and Adventures*, p. 52) Churchill writes that after his father's death "I read industriously almost every word he had ever spoken and learnt by heart large portions of his speeches."
6. *Lord Randolph Churchill*, p. 215.
7. *Ibid.*, pp. 100-106, 169, 203-206, 208, 241, 269-270.
8. "Personal Contacts", in *Thoughts and Adventures*, pp. 55-56, also for the following.
9. *My Early Life*, p. 124.
10. *Ibid.*, p. 128.
11. *Ibid.*, pp. 129-130.
12. "Churchill the Master of Words", in *Churchill by His Contemporaries*, p. 458.
13. *The Great War I*, 40.
14. "Fifty Years Hence", in *Thoughts and Adventures*, p. 272.
15. *Ibid.*, pp. 272-273.
16. *My Early Life*, p. 130.
17. *Ibid.*
18. In *Thoughts and Adventures*, pp. 283-294.
19. *J.C.*, May 27, 1921, p. 21.
20. "Zionism versus Bolshevism". In this passage as well as in others quoted in this chapter and referring to the impact of Judaism on Christianity, one can easily discern Disraeli's influence on Churchill. See, for instance, Disraeli's *Lord George Bentinck* (1851), *Tancred* (1847), or his speech on the removal of Jewish disabilities on May 25, 1854, when he said: "I have, Sir, always upheld that opinion because I believed that the Jewish race was that one to which the human family in general has been under the greatest obligation." (*Hansard*, May 25, 1854, Vol. 133, col. 961.)
21. "Moses", in *Thoughts and Adventures*, pp. 293-294.
22. Churchill's attitude towards Nazi anti-Semitism is dealt with on pp. 94-163.
23. "Hitler and his Choice", in *Great Contemporaries*, p. 202.
24. *Daily Telegraph*, January 19, 1926, p. 7, col. 3.
25. *Second World War V*, 470-471.
26. *Thoughts and Adventures*, p. 292.
27. Message to the 25th Anniversary of the Hebrew University in Jerusalem, June 3, 1950. (*Friends News Sheet*, London, No. 1, July 1950, p. 2.)
28. *Daily Telegraph*, September 27, 1941, p. 3, col. 1.
29. *Hansard*, August 20, 1940, Vol. 364, col. 1160.
30. *J.C.*, November 26, 1954, p. 6. See also *Illustrated Technion News*, London, Vol. 1, No. 1, February 1955, Supplement II and III.

31. This meeting was held in the Palace Theatre in support of the Jewish Hospital Fund, on October 21, 1906. (*Times*, October 22, 1906, p. 12, col. 5.)
32. This aspect is dealt with in Part II of this Study.
33. See pp. 27-28, 60.
34. *Second World War V*, 470.
35. *Daily Telegraph*, January 19, 1926, p. 7, col. 3.
36. *Times*, October 22, 1906, p. 12, col. 5.
37. " Zionism versus Bolshevism ".
38. *Ibid.*
39. *Marlborough IV*, 483, 525-526.
40. " Zionism versus Bolshevism ".
41. *My Early Life*, p. 22. In a broadcast he once said: " I was brought up on the maxim of Lord Beaconsfield which my father was always repeating: ' Health and the laws of health '." (*Onwards to Victory*, p. 40)—See also pp. 43-44, 196, footnote 20; p. 198, footnote 90.
42. *Lord Randolph Churchill I*, 222-223.
43. *My Early Life*, p. 376.
44. *Ibid.*
45. Churchill's evidence in the libel case, see *Times*, December 11, 1923, p. 7, col. 6.
46. See pp. 175-184.
47. *Times, l.c.*
48. *Ibid.*, December 12, 1923, p. 7, col. 2.
49. *Second World War I*, 220.
50. *Ibid.*, p. 455.
51. " France Faces a New Crisis ", in *Step by Step*, pp. 99-100.
52. *Second World War VI*, 645-646.
53. *Times*, March 22, 1955, p. 7, col. 4.
54. *Hansard*, January 26, 1949, Vol. 460, No. 46, col. 956.
55. See pp. 86-88.
56. Dr. Weizmann's letter to me of May 17, 1944.—It was during Churchill's term of office as Home Secretary (1910) that he signed Dr. Weizmann's naturalisation certificate. (*Ibid.*)
57. " Zionism versus Bolshevism ".
58. *Hansard*, August 1, 1946, Vol. 426, No. 189, col. 1260.
59. *Stemming the Tide*, p. 364.
60. *J.C.*, March 19, 1954, p. 1.—A message in similar terms, sent by Churchill to a Weizmann Memorial Gathering in Rehovot, was read by Lord Jowitt, and is reproduced in *J.C.*, November 5, 1954, p. 28.
61. Broad, *Churchill*, p. 160.
62. In *Churchill, Servant of Crown and Commonwealth*, pp. 162-170.
63. See pp. 50-54.
64. *J.C.*, June 24, 1904, p. 28.

65. *J.C.*, January 19, 1906, p. 9.—In addition to the assistance rendered by Nathan Laski during the Manchester election period, another Jew and prominent Liberal in the area, Barrow I. Belisha, an uncle of Lord Hore-Belisha, was partly instrumental in Churchill being nominated as candidate, and subsequently established friendly relations with him. (See also Leslie Hore-Belisha, "How Churchill Influences and Persuades", in *Churchill by his Contemporaries*, p. 393.)
66. Reproduced in Martin, *Laski*, p. 12.
67. *Ibid.*
68. *Ibid.*
69. This whole matter is dealt with *Ibid.*, p. 168, and in "Threat to Freedom", in *Victory*, p. 203-204, and "The Voter's Choice", *Ibid.*, pp. 209-210.
70. Martin, *Laski*, p. 173.
71. *Victory*, p. 209.
72. *Ibid.*
73. Martin, *Laski*, p. 12.
74. *Ibid.*, p. 153.
75. *Rufus Isaacs*, p. 206.
76. Speech at a banquet of the English Speaking Union on February 12, 1921, at a farewell party to Lord Reading on his assuming the post of Viceroy of India. (*Times*, February 14, 1921, p. 14, col. 3.)
77. *Ibid.*
78. *Hansard*, January 31, 1947, Vol. 432, No. 38, col. 1347.
79. *Ibid.*
80. "Zionism versus Bolshevism".
81. *Great Contemporaries*, pp. 201-205.
82. See p. 93.
83. See p. 30 and *Times*, October 22, 1906, p. 12, col. 5; and *J.C.*, October 26, 1906, p. 31.
84. "Zionism versus Bolshevism".
85. *Ibid.*
86. See p. 99.
87. "Zionism versus Bolshevism".
88. See above p. 30.
89. *J.C.*, October 16, 1908, p. 29.
90. This is Churchill's quotation in the speeches referred to below. They express Disraeli's sentiments, but I cannot trace them anywhere as a verbatim quotation. The nearest formulation to it seems to me Disraeli's sentence in *Lord George Bentinck*: "It may be observed that the decline and disasters of modern communities have generally been relative to their degree of sedition against the Semitic principle." He expressed this same thought in the debate on the Oaths Bill of 1854: "I cannot conceal from myself that there is no country in which the Hebrew race has been persecuted which has not suffered, whose energies have not been withered, whose political power has not decayed, and where there have not been evident proofs that the Divine favour has been withdrawn from the land." (*Hansard*, May 25, 1854, Vol. 133, col. 962.) And the last sentence in this speech reads: "So

far as the Jews are concerned, I have faith in that Almighty Being who has never deserted them." (*Ibid.*, cols. 969-970.)
91. See p. 87.
92. "Zionism versus Bolshevism".
93. *Ibid.*
94. See p. 195 and Part II.
95. "Zionism versus Bolshevism".
96. *Ibid.*
97. Speech to a Jewish delegation in Jerusalem on March 29, 1921. (*J.C.*, May 27, 1921, p. 21.)

CHAPTER II
The Aliens Question

1. *Report of the Royal Commission on Alien Immigration*, 1902-1903. (*Cmd.* 1741; *Minutes of Evidence, Cmd.* 1742.)
2. L. J. Greenberg, " Alien Immigration (1902-1903) ', in *The Jewish Year Book*, 1903-4, p. 434.
3. *Hansard*, April 25, 1904, Vol. 133, col. 1106.
4. May 6, 1904, p. 7.
5. For full text of these speeches and the Under-Secretary's reply, see *J.C.*, May 27, 1904, p. 10f.
6. *The Times*, May 31, 1904, p. 10, reprinted in *J.C.*, June 3, 1904, p. 9.
7. See pp. 55-56.
8. Made as head of the Board of Deputies' delegation which waited upon the Hon. T. H. Cochrane. See *J.C.*, May 27, 1904, p. 10; also p. 50.
9. See his letter in *The Times*, May 31, 1904, reprinted in *J.C.*, June 3, 1904, p. 9. Sir Kenelm Digby was one of the two members who had dissented from the recommendations of the Royal Commission on Alien Immigration. (See p. 48.)
10. See pp. 55-56.
11. June 3, 1904, p. 7.
12. Who also published a letter in *The Times* on the same day. See also footnote 9.
13. Sir George Arthur, *Concerning Winston Spencer Churchill*, London (William Heinemann Ltd.), 1940, p. 85.
14. *Hansard*, June 8, 1904, Vol. 135, col. 1109-1110.
15. This deputation is referred to on p. 50.
16. Sir Howard Vincent.
17. June 10, 1904, p. 7.
18. *J.C.*, June 17, 1904, p. 9.
19. June 24, 1904, pp. 9-10 (first meeting); July 1, 1904, pp. 14-17 (second, third and fourth meetings); July 8, 1904, pp. 28-31 (fifth and sixth meetings); July 15, 1904, pp. 20-22 (last meeting).
20. *J.C.*, June 24, 1904, p. 9.
21. *Ibid.*, July 1, 1904, p. 16.
22. *Ibid.*, July 8, 1904, p. 30.
23. Churchill then sat in Parliament for Oldham.
24. *J.C.*, July, 1904, p. 17.
25. *J.C.*, July 15, 1904, p. 20.

26. The misunderstanding with regard to the Churchill-Rothschild incident may have arisen from a news item in the *J.C.* of July 1, 1904, p. 17, reporting a meeting in Manchester at which " Mr. Nathan Laski said that he had interviewed Mr. Winston Churchill, who had seen Lord Rothschild with reference to the Bill. The result of the interview was that Mr. Churchill was practically leading the attack on the Bill in Grand Committee."
27. *J.C.*, July 15, 1904, p. 21.
28. *Ibid.*, p. 20.
29. *Ibid.*, p. 21.
30. *Ibid.*, July 1, 1904, p. 15.
31. *Ibid.*, July 15, 1904, p. 21.—Sir Harry Samuel was no relation to Stuart M. and Herbert (later Lord) Samuel.
32. *J.C.*, July 15, 1904, p. 21.
33. Major W. Evans-Gordon.
34. See pp. 27-28, 30.
35. *J.C.*, July 1, 1904, p. 17.
36. *Ibid.*, July 15, 1904, p. 21.
37. *Ibid.*, p. 20.
38. *Ibid.*, July 8, 1904, p. 31.
39. *Ibid.*, July 15, 1904, p. 22.
40. *Ibid.*, p. 7.
41. Major W. Evans-Gordon.
42. *J.C.*, July 15, 1904, p. 23.
43. *Hansard*, August 2, 1904, Vol. 139, col. 571.
44. *J.C.*, July 15, 1904, p. 11.

## The Aliens Act, 1905

1. *J.C.*, January 6, 1905, p. 7.
2. The speech in full in *J.C.*, December 23, 1904, p. 13.
3. See p. 186.
4. Herzl's *Diaries* (German ed., Berlin, 1923), III, 414. Quoted in Herzl's own English.
5. *J.C.*, January 6, 1905, p. 12.
6. *Ibid.*
7. *Ibid.*, January 20, 1905, pp. 8 and 21.
8. See for instance, *J.C.*, January 20, 1905, p. 22; February 10, 1905, pp. 10, 11.
9. *J.C.*, December 23, 1904, p. 14.
10. *Hansard*, May 2, 1905, Vol. 145, col. 688.
11. See p. 80.
12. of December 19, 1904, reprinted in *J.C.*, December 23, 1904, p. 14.
13. A demonstration against unemployment was held on December 18, 1904, in Trafalgar Square, London, and passed resolutions demanding the provision of work by the local authorities and a special session of Parliament. (See *Annual Register*, 1904 (Longmans, Green & Co.), London, 1905, p. 233.)
14. *J.C.*, April 21, 1905, p. 9, where Balfour's letter to the Hon. W. F. D. Smith is quoted.
15. *Hansard*, April 18, 1905, Vol. 145, col. 464.

16. *Ibid.,* col. 473.
17. *Ibid.*
18. *Ibid.,* April 14, 1905, Vol. 145, col. 466-468.
19. *J.C.,* April 28, 1905, p. 8.
20. *Ibid.,* p. 7.
21. *Hansard,* May 2, 1905, Vol. 145, col. 689-699.
22. *Ibid.,* col. 768.
23. *Ibid.,* col. 808.
24. *Ibid.,* col. 806-808.
25. *J.C.,* May 12, 1905, p. 7.—This refers to a resolution passed at a meeting of East End Liberal members and candidates on April 27, believing the present Bill to be satisfactory and expressing the hope that " the second reading of the Bill will not be opposed by the Liberal Party ". (*J.C.,* May 5, 1905, p. 25.)
26. *Ibid.,* pp. 13-15, where the full report about the meeting and the memorandum are recorded.
27. *Ibid.,* p. 14.
28. *Ibid.,* June 16, 1905, p. 25, where a specimen of such an address is reproduced.
29. *Ibid.,* June 9, 1905, p. 7.
30. *Ibid.,* June 30, 1905, p. 28.
31. *Ibid.,* July 7, 1905, p. 28.
32. See about him p. 198, Note 65.
33. See about him p. 37.
34. *J.C.,* July 7, 1905, p. 28.
35. *Hansard,* July 3, 1905, Vol. 148, col. 790/791.
36. *Hansard,* June 27, 1905, Vol. 148, col. 270, 272, 277, 280, 295/296, 306, 312, 313, 320/321.
37. *Ibid.,* July 3, 1905, col. 790, 796, 797, 805, 806, 811, 856-860, 861, 875, 878, 882, 884, 885, 886, 891, 892, 894, 903, 907, 909, 910, 916, 917, 918.
38. *Ibid.,* July 10, 1905, Vol. 149, col. 119.
39. *Ibid.,* July 11, 1905, Vol. 149, col. 286, 292, 300/301, 353, 355.
40. *Ibid.,* July 17, 1905, Vol. 149, col. 990.
41. *Ibid.,* July 18, 1905, Vol. 149, col. 1152.
42. *Ibid.,* July 3, 1905, Vol. 148, col. 856-860.
43. See pp. 46-49.
44. *Hansard,* July 20, 1905, Vol. 149, col. 1294.—Churchill's vote is recorded *Ibid.,* col. 1295.
45. See p. 79.
46. Statement by D. L. Alexander at the annual meeting of the Board of Deputies, held on July 16, 1905. (*J.C.,* December 8, 1905, p. 11.)
47. A list of those improvements and changes are enumerated in *J.C.,* July 28, 1905, p. 12.
48. L. J. Greenberg, " Alien Immigration (1904/1905) ", in *Jewish Year Book,* 1905-1906, p. 464.
49. *Ibid.,* 465.
50. For full text of the Aliens Act, 1905, see *Jewish Year Book,* 1905-1906, pp. 472-477.
51. See *J.C.,* July 21, 1905, p. 7.
52. *J.C.,* October 13, 1905, p. 20.

NOTES & REFERENCES TO pp. 80-92

53. S. Gelberg, "The New Government and the Jews", in *J.C.*, December 15, 1905, p. 11.
54. This last sentence refers to Churchill's support of the aims of the Jewish Territorial Organization, headed by Israel Zangwill. (See pp. 189-190.)
55. *J.C.*, December 15, 1905, p. 9.
56. I should like to thank Mr. A. G. Brotman, Secretary to the Board of Deputies, for supplying me with copies of the communications quoted above.—Churchill's reply is also reprinted in *J.C.*, November 24, 1905, p. 15.
57. *J.C.*, December 15, 1905, p. 9.
58. *Hansard*, May 2, 1905, Vol. 145, col. 731.

CHAPTER III
Unbiased background, Czarist and Soviet Russia, Germany

1. *Hansard*, August 1, 1946, Vol. 426, No. 189, col. 1258.
2. "The Defence of Freedom and Peace", in *Into Battle*, pp. 55-56.
3. "It's Not All Over Yet", in *Step by Step*, pp. 206-207.
4. See p. 88.
5. Introduction.
6. "The Defence of Freedom and Peace" *l.c.*
7. *Daily Telegraph*, January 19, 1926, p. 7, col. 3.
8. *My Early Life*, pp. 46, 60.
9. *Ibid.*, p. 22.
10. *Ibid.*, pp. 247, 376.
11. See pp. 20-21.
12. *Hansard*, May 19, 1881, Vol. 261, col. 825. Lord Randolph here probably referred to a news item which appeared on that day in *The Times* (May 19, 1881, p. 5, col. 6) that Jews were attacked at Woloscza near the Russian frontier, half their houses had been destroyed and 330 families had fled into Galicia.
13. See Julius Greenstone, "The Year 5666", in *The American Jewish Year Book*, 1906/07, p. 237/242, also for the following. See also Roth, *Short History*, p. 390; Greenberg, *Jews in Russia*, II, 50f; Mark Vishniak, "Antisemitism in Tsarist Russia. A Study in Government-Fostered Antisemitism", in *Essays on Antisemitism*, ed. by Koppel S. Pinson (Conference on Jewish Relations), New York, 1946, pp. 136-141.
14. *J.C.*, December 15, 1905, p. 31, where the speech is quoted in *oratio obliqua*. I feel, however, justified in changing it to *oratio recta*.
15. *Aftermath*, p. 164-166.
16. *Ibid.*, p. 169₁
17. *Ibid.*, p. 274.
18. Dubnow X, 530. See also Roth, *Short History*, p. 402/403.
19. *Aftermath*, p. 250.
20. *Ibid.*, p. 255.
21. *American Jewish Year Book*, Vol. 24, 1922/23, p. 340.
22. *Aftermath*, p. 255.
23. *Illustrated Sunday Herald*.
24. Dubnow X, 528-529.

202

25. *The Voice of Jerusalem,* pp. 215 and 216.
26. Dubnow *l.c.*
26a. See Dr. A. Steinberg, " The Fight Against Anti-Semitism in Soviet Russia ", in *The Future of the Jews.* A symposium edited by J. J. Lynx (Lyndsay Drummond Ltd.), London, 1945, pp.101-109.
27. For a full description of these trials see *Survey of International Affairs,* 1934, pp. 367-368; 1936, pp. 376-378; 1937, pp. 12-22.
28. " Enemies to the Left ", in *Step by Step* (1939 ed.), p. 60.
29. *The Second World War, I,* pp. 285, 287.
30. *Hansard,* March 23, 1933, Vol. 276, col. 542-3.
31. See p. 88. It was only recently that he said at Woodford: " But this, i.e. communism, is an internal issue for the Russian people to settle for themselves." (*Manchester Guardian,* May 17, 1955, p. 3, col. 3.)
32. " Friendship with Germany ", in *Step by Step,* p. 161. In his *Second World War, I,* p. 65, he relates a somewhat different version of this conversation.
33. See p. 88.
34. For a full description and evaluation of these laws see *J.C.,* September 20, 1935, pp. 9, 16-19.
35. *The Times,* November 8, 1938, p. 14, col. 2.
36. *Ibid.,* November 9, 1938, p. 13, col. 1.
37. *Ibid.,* November 10, 1938, p. 16, col. 2.
38. *Ibid.,* November 14, 1938, p. 12, col. 1.
39. *Ibid.,* November 11, 1938, p. 14, col 1.
40. *Ibid.,* p. 15, col. 4.
41. *Ibid.,* November 9, 1938, p. 13, col 1.—Grynszpan's name is here misspelled.
42. *Ibid.*
43. *Ibid.,* November 15, 1938, p. 14, col. 3.
44. *Ibid.,* November 16, 1938, p. 14, col. 4, and November 28, p. 14, col. 4.
45. *Second World War, I,* pp. 43-46.
46. *Ibid.,* pp. 41-42.
47. See p. 86.
48. " Hitler Speaks ", in *Into Battle,* p. 103. (The speech was delivered on April 28, 1939.)
49. " Europe in Suspense ", *Ibid.,* pp. 125-126.
50. " Hitler and his Choice ", in *Great Contemporaries,* p. 209.
51. " Rape of Austria ", in *Step by Step,* pp. 251-254.
52. *Ibid.,* p. 252.—Baron Rothschild was arrested after the occupation of Austria and confined to the Metropole Hotel, Vienna, where he was kept until his release in 1942.
53. See p. 95.
54. " Rape of Austria ", in *Step by Step,* p. 252.
55. " A Plain Word to the Nazis ", *Ibid.,* pp. 151-154.
56. *Hansard,* November 24, 1938, Vol. 341, col. 2035-6.
57. *Ibid.,* March 24, 1936, Vol. 310, col. 1115-1116.
58. At the time the establishment of a Legislative Council in Palestine was under discussion, which Churchill opposed.

59. "The Rape of Austria", in *Step by Step*, p. 252.
60. "A Plain Word to the Nazis", *Ibid.*, p. 151.
61. *Ibid.*
62. See pp. 82-83.
63. *Hansard*, September 3, 1939, Vol. 351, col. 295.

## World War II

1. See for instance Churchill's Broadcast Address, October 1, 1939 (*Into Battle*, p. 134); Broadcast Address, November 12, 1939 (*Ibid.*, p. 144/145); Address in the Free Trade Hall, Manchester, January 27, 1940 (*Ibid.*, p. 168/169); Broadcast Address, March 30, 1940 (*Ibid.*, p. 182); Broadcast Address on assuming the office of Prime Minister, May 19, 1940 (*Ibid.*, p. 212); Speech in Glasgow, January 17, 1941 (*Unrelenting Struggle*, p. 37); Message to the Polish people, May 3, 1941 (*Ibid.*, p. 117); Speech to the Conference of Dominion High Commissioners and Allied Countries in London, June 12, 1941 (*Ibid.*, p. 169/170); Broadcast Address on German invasion of Russia, June 22, 1941 (*Ibid.*, p. 177); Broadcast Address after the meeting with President Roosevelt in the Atlantic, August 24, 1941 (*Ibid.*, pp. 231, 234); and many others in subsequent years.
2. "A Message to the Polish People", in *Unrelenting Struggle*, p. 117.
3. *Ibid.*, p. 272.
4. Israel Cohen, "The Doom of European Jewry", in *The Contemporary Review*, February, 1943.
5. *Hansard*, August 20, 1940, Vol. 364, col. 1160. See also p. 29.
6. *Unrelenting Struggle*, p. 283.
7. *J.C.*, November 14, 1941, p. 1.
8. *Ibid.*, January 16, 1942, p. 1.
9. *Ibid.*, p. 12.
10. *Ibid.*, July 24, 1942, p. 1; *J.T.A.*, July 23, 1942, Vol. 23, No. 170, p. 1.
11. *Ibid.*
12. *Hansard*, September 8, 1942, Vol. 383, col. 96/97. — On the tragedy of French Jewry see the comprehensive study by Henri Monneray, *La Persécution des Juifs en France* (Ed. du Centre de Documentation Juive Contemporaine), Paris, 1947.
13. *J.C.*, September 25, 1942, p. 1.
14. *Ibid.*, March 13, 1942, p. 1.
15. *Ibid.*, November 6, 1942, p. 5.
16. For full report see *Ibid.*, p. 5; and *The Times*, October 30, 1942, p. 2.
17. *J.C.*, November 6, 1942, p. 5.
18. Wise, *Challenging Years*, p. 274-276; *The Times*, December 21, 1942, p. 2; *Survey of International Affairs*, 1939-1946, p. 248; Henry Morgenthau Jr., "The Morgenthau Diaries", in *Collier's*, November 1, 1947, p. 23; see also p. 125f.
19. *The Times*, December 4, 1942, p. 3 (mourning in Palestine); *Ibid.*, December 14, 1942, p. 2 (mourning in Britain).
20. *Ibid.*, December 11, 1942, p. 3.

21. *Ibid.*, December 14, 1942, p. 2.
22. *Hansard*, December 17, 1942, Vol. 385, col. 2082.
23. *Ibid.*, col. 2083, where the Declaration is reproduced in full.
24. *Ibid.*, col. 2086/7.—This great demonstration is fully described in *The Times*, December 18, 1942, p. 4, and in a leader on p. 5; also in a communication by A. L. Easterman in the *J.C.*, December 25, 1942, p. 5.
25. Eden's statement in the House of Commons. See *Hansard*, July 1, 1942, Vol. 381, col. 184.
26. *The Jewish Standard*, London, January 1, 1943, p. 3.
27. *Hansard*, December 17, 1942, Vol. 385, col. 2086.
28. *J.C.*, March 12, 1943, p. 1; *Hansard* (Lords), July 28, 1943, Vol. 128, col. 347.
29. *Ibid.*
30. *Ibid.*, col. 848.
31. *Ibid.*, col. 861.
32. *Hansard*, May 19, 1943, Vol. 389, col. 1129 ff.
33. *Ibid.* (Lords), July 28, 1942, Vol. 128, col. 858 ff.
34. *Ibid.*, col. 861.
35. *Ibid.*
36. *Ibid.*
37. *Hansard*, May 19, 1943, Vol. 389, col. 1130.
38. *Second World War*, IV, 763.
39. *Hansard*, July 28, 1943, Vol. 391, col. 1603.
40. *Ibid.*, May 19, 1943, Vol. 389, col. 1131.
41. *Ibid.*
42. *Survey of International Affairs*, 1938, Vol. 1, 596.
43. Hirschmann, *Life Line*, p. 14.
44. *Palestine Year Book*, 1945/1946, Vol. 2, p. 4.
45. *Hansard*, April 7, 1943, Vol. 388, col. 637-640.
46. *Ibid.*, col. 640.
47. *Ibid.*, col. 639.
48. *Ibid.*, col. 638/639.
49. *Ibid.*, May 19, 1943, Vol. 389, col. 1117 ff.
50. *Ibid.*, col. 1119.
51. The Jewish press of those years is full of appeals to Churchill accompanied by quotations from his pre- and war speeches in which he expressed his sympathy with the Jewish Nazi victims. No one, however, has put the case more eloquently than van Paasen in his book, *The Forgotten Ally*.
52. *Hansard*, May 15, 1945, Vol. 410, col. 2267.
53. See p. 102.
54. *Hansard*, November 7, 1944, Vol. 404, col. 1269.
55. *Ibid.*, November 17, 1944, Vol. 404, col. 2242.
56. November 24, 1944, p. 1.
57. October-November, 1944, Vol XXI, No. 1-2, p. 6.
58. See in this connection pp. 136-139, 142, 152.
59. *Second World War*, II, 153.—In comparison with this outspoken characterization by Churchill, written in June 1940, one is tempted to point to an official statement by the Jewish Agency in their

*Political Report*, 1946 (p. 32) to the XXII. Zionist Congress that " But until the late Lord Lloyd became Colonial Secretary in May 1940 Dr. Weizmann's proposals met with little response ".

60. *Survey of International Affairs*, 1939-1946, *The Middle East*, p. 237.

61. *Second World War*, II, 154.

62. *Political Report*, 1946, p. 33.—In contrast to this official statement (published by the Jewish Agency Executive under Ben Gurion's chairmanship in 1946), Ben Gurion's biography (ed. 1954) records an entirely negative result of the meeting as well as Ben Gurion's awareness of Lord Lloyd's anti-Zionist attitude. (Litvinoff, *Ben Gurion*, p. 136/137.)

63. *The Jewish Case*, p. 295. — A description of some of these attempts throughout the Nazi period is given in *Sefer Hama'apilim*, 1933-1946. (Publications of the Zionist Organisation), Jerusalem, 1947.—See also Jon and David Kimche, *Secret Roads*.

64. *Survey of International Affairs*, 1939-1946, p. 239/240; *Survey of Palestine*, I, 60.

65. *Ibid.*

66. *Survey of International Affairs*, 1939-1946, p. 239/240.

67. *Ibid.*

68. *The Jewish Case*, p. 295.—*Survey of Palestine*, I, 61.

69. *World War*, II, 614.—The conditions in Mauritius turned out to be much worse than Churchill in this note anticipated. The internees were held there until 1945 when they were repatriated to Palestine. All in all, 150 of the refugees died of disease during the five years' internment, and hardly one among the repatriated ones was not suffering from some disease or other. (*Jewish Observer & Middle East Review*, London, August 19, 1955, p. 5).—See also *American Jewish Year Book*, 1945/1946, Vol. 47, p. 450.

70. *Trial and Error*, p. 495.

71. *Ibid.*, p. 496.—The official announcement regarding the permission to land the *Patria* survivors was made by the Palestine Government on December 4, 1940. (*Survey of Palestine*, I, 61.)

72. *Second World War*, III, 658.

73. *The Jewish Case*, p. 295/296; see also *Survey of Palestine*, I. 63/64.

74. *J.C.*, March 13, 1942, p. 6.

75. *Ibid.*, p. 10.

76. *Hansard* (Lords), March 10, 1942, Vol. 122, cols. 200-223.

77. *Hansard*, March 12, 1942, Vol. 378, col. 1048.

78. *Ibid.*, col. 1049.

79. *The Jewish Case*, p. 296.

80. See pp. 110-112.

81. *Second World War*, IV, p. 823.

82. *The Jewish Case*, p. 296.

83. *Ibid.*

84. Dr. Weizmann, *Trial and Error*, p. 512.

85. *Congress Weekly*, New York, September 24, 1943, Vol. 10, No. 27, p. 3.
86. Martha Jelenko, " Reaction to Overseas Events ", in *American Jewish Year Book*, 1944/1945, Vol. 46, p. 148.
87. *Ibid.*
88. *Ibid.*, p. 151.
89. *Ibid.* and p. 152.
90. *Final Summary Report*, Introduction.
91. Hirschmann, *Life Line*, p. 33.
92. *Ibid.*, p. 43.
93. *Ibid.*, p. 44.
94. The author's italics.
95. London, 1954.
96. Hirschmann, *Life Line*, p. 79.
97. Hevesy, " Hungary ", in *American Jewish Year Book*, 1944/1945, Vol. 46, p. 254-256. About the conditions prevailing then in Hungary and the subsequent ordeal of Jewry there see *Ibid.*, pp. 257-261; 1945/1946, Vol. 47, pp. 292-296; János Kovács, " Neo-Antisemitism in Hungary ", in *Jewish Social Studies*, New York, Vol. VIII, pp. 147-160; Shalom Rosenfeld, *Criminal File 124, The Case of Gruenwald-Kastner* (Karni Publishers Ltd.), Tel-Aviv (in Hebrew), 1955.
98. Hevesi, " Hungary ", in *American Jewish Year Book*, 1944/1945, Vol. 46, p. 257.
99. The statement in full in *Final Summary Report*, pp. 49-51.
100. *Hansard*, July 5, 1944, Vol. 401, col. 1160-2.
101. Hirschmann, *Life Line*, pp. 104-132, where the incident is described in full. See also *J.C.*, July 21, 1944, p. 1. *Political Report* (1946), p. 47/48. *The Times*, July 20, 1944, p. 2, col. 3.
102. Joel Brand's testimony, in *Court Protocol*, Jerusalem, *Criminal File* 124/53, p. 648.
103. Moshe Sharett in a statement on this matter does not refer to any visit of his in this connection to Cairo pointing out that he flew on his own initiative to London. (*Haaretz*, July 13, 1955, p. 2.)
104. *Court Protocol*, Jerusalem, *Criminal File* 124/53, p. 648ff.
105. *Ibid.*
106. Hirschmann, *Life Line*, p. 115.—The interview is fully described *Ibid.*, pp. 117-127.
107. *Ibid.*, p. 127.
108. On May 30, reports from London based on news from the Polish underground stated that 62 railway cars packed with Jewish children aged between two and eight had arrived in Poland from Hungary, and that six railway trains loaded with Jewish adults had run daily between 15th and 27th May en route to the Oswieczim (Auschwitz) " extermination camp " in Silesia (*J.C.*, June 30, 1944, p. 1). By the end of June 1944, some 400,000 to 450,000 Jews had already been deported to the notorious extermination area in Polish Silesia. (*American Jewish Year Book*, 1944/1945, Vol. 46, p. 258/9.) —The Kimche brothers report (*Secret Roads*, p. 13) that Dr. Weizmann had intervened in the matter with Churchill personally, though I cannot find any corroboration for this. On the other hand we know

from the *Political Report* (1946, p. 47) that with regard to the "exchange" offer Dr. Weizmann saw the Foreign Secretary on June 7. "Three weeks later", the *Report* continues, "Mr. Shertok arrived in London and called at the Foreign Office to discuss the question of the rescue of Jews from Hungary. It was agreed to keep the matter going, so as to gain time and postpone further deportations. On July 10, Dr. Weizmann, accompanied by Mr. Shertok, again saw the Foreign Secretary."
109. *Second World War*, VI, p. 597.
110. The full announcement is reproduced in Rosenfeld, *Criminal File* 124, p. 67.
111. *Final Summary Report*, p. 22.
112. See p. 110.
113. *Hansard*, July 28, 1943, Vol. 391, col. 1603.—See also p. 115.
114. Hirschmann, *Life Line*, p. 127.
115. *Court Protocol*, Jerusalem, *Criminal File* 124/53, p. 648.
116. July 21, 1944, p. 1.
117. p. 40.
118. Hirschmann, *Life Line*, p. 120.
119. *J.C.*, July 21, 1944, p. 1.
120. *Ibid.*, July 28, 1944, p. 1.
121. *Hansard*, August 2, 1944, Vol. 402, col. 1410.
122. *Ibid.*; *Final Summary Report*, p. 25/26; *J.C.*, August 4, 1944, p. 1; *Political Report* (1946), p. 48; Eugene Hevesi, "Hungary", in *American Jewish Year Book*, 1945/1946, Vol. 47, p. 423.
123. *Ibid.*, p. 426.
124. *The Trial of German Major War Criminals* (His Majesty's Stationery Office), London, 1946, Part II, 365, 366; Part XI (1947), p. 359.
125. Hevesi, "Hungary", in *American Jewish Year Book*, 1945/1946, Vol. 47, p. 424.
126. *Ibid.*, p. 425.
127. *Ibid.*, p. 428.
128. *Final Summary Report*, p. 26.
129. *Second World War*, VI, 603.
130. pp. 40-45.
131. pp. 40-51.
132. In addition to the book by Rosenfeld, referred to frequently above, see also Porat-Pirotinsky, *The Big Trial: The Kastner Affair* (Publishing House Or), Tel-Aviv, 1955. (In Hebrew.)
133. pp. 21-26.
134. As for instance *Political Report* (1946), Kimche. *Secret Roads*, and Hirschmann's *Life Line.*—For a small but significant effort in this respect see Jon Kimche, "The War's Unpaid Debt of Honour", in *Jewish Observer and Middle East Review*, October 14, 1955, pp. 10-12.
135. *Final Summary Report*, p. 22/23.—About the ordeal of Greek Jewry see Eugen Hevesi, "Greece", in *American Jewish Year Book*, 1944/1945, Vol. 46, pp. 268/269; and 1945/1946, Vol. 47, pp. 443/444.
136. *Second World War*, VI, 598.—See also Jon and David Kimche, *Secret Roads*, p. 68.

137. E.L.A.S., the Greek "People's National Army of Liberation", a Communist controlled guerilla formation assisted at one time Jews to escape from Athens. (*American Jewish Year Book*, 1945/1946, Vol. 47, p. 444). For the reasons for Churchill's attitude towards E.L.A.S. see *Second World War*, VI, 92-103.
138. See pp. 117-119.
139. *Zionist Review*, September 9, 1941, p. 3.
140. See pp. 120-121.
141. See p. 123.
142. See p. 122.
143. *Trial and Error*, p. 525.
144. See p. 125.
145. See pp. 131, 135 and p. 136 respectively.
146. See p. 129.
147. *Trial and Error*, pp. 525/6.
148. *Second World War*, IV, 786.
149. Harry Sacher, *Israel*, p. 26.
150. *Trial and Error*, p. 514.
151. *Ibid.*, pp. 521/522.
152. See above.
153. Menachem Begin, *The Revolt* (W. H. Allen), London, 1951, p. 140.
154. *Hansard*, May 19, 1943, Vol. 389, col. 1198; Dr. Weizmann, *Trial and Error*, p. 536.
155. *Ibid.*
156. *Protocol of the XXII. Zionist Congress* (1946), p. 340 (Dr. Weizmann's statement).
157. *Hansard*, May 23, 1939, Vol. 347, col. 2168f.
158. *Israel*, pp. 20/21.
159. *Political Report*, 1946, p. 13.
160. See p. 119.
161. *A Short History of Zionism* (Frederick Muller Ltd.), London, 1951, p. 181.
162. *Hansard*, May 19, 1943, Vol. 389, col. 1196.
163. Should read 1939.
164. *Second World War*, IV, 849.
165. *Political Report*, 1946, p. 13.
166. Vladimir Jabotinsky, *The Jewish War Front* (George Allen and Unwin), London, 1940, p. 183.
167. *Ibid.*, p. 181.
168. Hurewitz, *Struggle for Palestine*, p. 138.
169. Speech at the Conference of the "American Jewish Conference", Pittsburgh, December 4, 1944, in *The American Jewish Conference, Proceedings of the Second Session* (ed. by Alexander S. Kohanski), New York, 1945, p. 224.
This probably refers to Horthy's offer to Britain and the U.S.A. via the Red Cross in Switzerland to release Jews in possession of visa to Palestine and elsewhere. (See p. 134.)
170. "The Morgenthau Diaries" in *Collier's*, November 1, 1947, p. 65.—President Roosevelt expressed his negative attitude towards

the *White Paper* in a statement which he authorized Dr. Stephen S. Wise and Dr. Abba Hillel Silver to make to the National Conference on Palestine in Washington (March 9, 1944): "The President authorized us to say that the American Government has never given its approval to the White Paper of 1939" (*American Jewish Year Book,* 1944/1945, Vol. 46, p. 174).
171. *Second World War,* V, 602.
172. *Struggle for Palestine,* p. 172.
173. *Hansard,* August 1, 1946, Vol. 426, col. 1248.
174. See p. 120.
175. See p. 123.
176. Dr. Weizmann, *Trial and Error,* p. 522.
177. *Second World War,* III, 658.
178. pp. 31-40.
179. *Political Report,* 1946, p. 38.
180. *Second World War,* VI, 596/597.
181. *Ibid.,* pp. 600/601.
182. p. 38.
183. The official War Office announcement in *Times,* September 20, 1944, p. 3.—In Britain were two committees. The "Committee for a Jewish Army", headed by Lord Strabolgi and Capt. Jeremiah Halpern, and the "Committee for a Jewish Fighting Force", headed by Colonel Victor Cazalet.
184. Statement of the Jewish Agency, in *Zionist Review,* September 22, 1944, p. 1.
185. September 20, 1944, p. 5.
186. *Hansard,* September 28, 1944, Vol. 403, col. 474.
187. *Second World War,* VI, 461.
188. *Hansard,* May 2, 1945, Vol. 410, col. 1509.
189. *Political Report,* 1946, p. 40.
190. *Second World War,* VI, pp. 96/97.
191. *Ibid.,* p. 96.
192. *Ibid.,* IV, 681.

193. See p. 132.
194. *Secret Roads,* p. 13.
195. Dr. Weizmann, *Trial and Error,* p. 522.
196. *Ibid.*
197. *Hansard,* August 20, 1940, Vol. 364, col. 1169-1170.
198. *Zionist Review,* September 12, 1941, p. 1.
199. *Political Report,* 1946, p. 14.
200. *Ibid.,* p. 17; *Trial and Error,* p. 536.
201. *Political Report,* 1946, p. 17.
202. *Ibid.,* p. 21.
203. *Trial and Error,* p. 539.
204. *Victory,* p. 182.
205. *Ibid.,* p. 183.
206. *Ibid.,* p. 186.
207. Litvinoff, *Ben Gurion,* p. 153.
208. See for instance *The New Judaea,* Vol. XXI, February-March, 1945, pp. 61/62.

209. *Second World War*, III, pp. 287/288.
210. *Ibid.*, p. 294.
211. *Ibid.*, p. 293/294.
212. *Ibid.*, p. 294.
213. *Ibid.*, p. 295.
214. *Hansard*, February 27, 1945, Vol. 408, col. 1279.
215. *Ibid.*, col. 1275/1276.
216. *Ibid.*, col. 1285.
217. *Ibid.*, col. 1289.
218. *Ibid.*
219. See pp. 138-139, and Dr. Weizmann, *Trial and Error*, p.526.
220. See p. 139.
221. *Hansard*, August 1, 1946, Vol. 426, col. 1261.
222 *Ibid.*, February 27, 1945, Vol. 408, col. 1290.
223. *Second World War*, VI, 306.
224. See p. 139.
225. *Hansard*, August 1, 1946, Vol. 426, col. 1258.
226. January 26, 1949, Vol. 460, col. 956.
227. W. H. Thompson, *I Was Churchill's Shadow* (ed. Christopher Johnson), London, 1954, p. 21.
228. Sacher, *Israel*, p. 36.
229. See p. 124.
230. *Hansard* (Lords), July 28, 1943, Vol. 128, col. 838.
231. See p. 126.
232. See p. 129.
233. *Ibid.*
234. See p. 124.
235. *J.C.*, March 13, 1942, p. 10.—See also p. 124.
236. Sacher, *Israel*, p. 30.
237. *Ibid.*
238. See p. 141.
239. *Congress Weekly* (New York), September 24, 1943, Vol. 10, No. 27, p. 13.
240. *Second World War*, VI, 597.—See also p. 147.
241. *Challenging Years*, pp. 274-279.
242. Henry Morgenthau, Jr., "The Morgenthau Diaries", in *Collier's*, November 1, 1947, pp. 22/23.
243. *Ibid.*, p. 22.
244. *Ibid.*—On the War Refugee Board, see p. 127f.
245. Harry S. Truman, *Year of Decisions* (Hodder and Stoughton), London, 1955, p. 72.
246. "The Morgenthau Diaries", *Ibid.*
247. The Minutes of that Conference (ed. by Alexander S. Kohanski), New York, 1945, p. 139.
248. van Paasen, *The Forgotten Ally*, Preface.
249. Dr. Weizmann, *Trial and Error*, p. 533.
250. *Memorandum Submitted to the United Nations Conference on International Organisation, San Francisco, by the Jewish Agency for Palestine*, April 1945, reproduced in *Palestine Jewish Year Book*, 1944/1945, Vol. 1, 320.

251. *Hansard*, August 1, 1946, Vol. 426, col. 1252.—Churchill was not isolated in expressing after the war his surprise at the true extent of the massacres. Jews and non-Jews shared equally in this as for instance appears from a statement by Emanuel Neumann, American Member of the World Executive of the Jewish Agency, and then President of the Zionist Organisation of America in *The American Jewish Year Book*, III, 27.

### Great Britain

1. " Anti-Semitism ", in *Encyclopædia Britannica*, Eleventh Edition, II, 134-146.
2. See Chapter II, p. 46f.
3. See p. 52.
4. See p. 58.
5. *J.C.*, December 2, 1904, p. 12.
6. Speech to the Achei Brith Society, Manchester, January 7, 1906. (*J.C.*, January 12, 1906, p. 44.)
7. See p. 64.
8. *Hansard*, July 3, 1905, Vol. 148, col. 875/876.
9. *Ibid.*, July 10, 1905, Vol. 149, col. 154/155.
10. *Ibid.*, col. 159-161.
11. *J.C.*, July 14, 1905, p. 7.
12. *Protocol* VII, 85.
13. See p. 186, 188.
14. *Hansard*, July 3, 1905, Vol. 148, col. 860; see also p. 76.
15. *Ibid.*, April 28, 1911, Vol. 24, col. 2170.
16. *Ibid.*
17. *J.C.*, August 25, 1911, p. 8.
18. *Ibid.*
19. *Ibid.*
20. These events are described in " Churchill and the Trade Unions " by George Isaacs, in *Churchill by His Contemporaries*, pp. 368-373
21. *Hansard*, August 11, 1911, Vol. 29, col. 188.
22. Reproduced in *J.C.*, August 25, 1911, p. 8.
23. *Ibid.*, p. 5.
24. August 26, 1911. Leader.
25. Maurice Simon, " Anti-Semitism in England ", in *The Jewish Review*, London, November 1911, Vol. II, No. 10, p. 303.
26. *J.C.*, August 25, 1911, p. 11.
27. *Ibid.*
28. *Ibid.*, p. 8, quoting the *Western Mail*.
29. *Ibid.*, p. 9.
30. *Ibid.*, September 1, 1911, p. 5.
31. See pp. 167-168 and Dr. Oskar K. Rabinowicz, " Sir Winston Churchill and the South Wales Riots ", in *J.C.*, December 3, 1954, p. 15.
32. *Ibid.*, September 8, 1911, p. 11.
33. *Ibid.*, November 24, 1911, p. 17.
34. *Ibid.*, October 20, 1911, p. 15.
35. November 3, 1911, p. 8.

36. See pp. 37, 80, 192.
37. *Hansard*, July 10, 1936, Vol. 314, col. 1547-1634.
38. *Ibid.*, col. 1617/1618, 1624, 1628.
39. *J.C.*, July 31, 1936, p. 7.
40. *Hansard*, July 30, 1936, Vol. 315, col. 1706.
41. *Ibid.*, col. 1753.
42. The events of this day are fully described in *J.C.*, October 9, 1936, pp. 7 and 22.
43. *J.C.*, October 16, 1936, pp. 28, 29.
44. See p. 170.
45. "The Communist Schism", in *Step by Step* (ed. 1939), p. 73.
46. *Hansard*, November 9, 1936, Vol. 317, col. 660.—See for text of the Bill *The Times*, November 11, 1936, p. 9.
47. *Hansard* (Lords), December 16, 1936, Vol. 103, col. 972.
48. *The Times*, December 4, 1936, p. 18.—See also the description of the events in 1936 in Britain and the reference to Churchill's speech in Harry Schneiderman, "Review of the Year 5697", in *American Jewish Year Book*, 1937/1938, Vol. 39, pp. 292-298.
49. A full description of that battle in *The Great War*, II, 833-896.
50. See pp. 33-34.
51. "Ephesian" (Bechhofer Robert), *Winston Churchill*, London, 1940, pp. 223-225; *The Times*, July 18, 1923, p. 5; December 11, 1923, p. 5; and December 12, 1923, p. 7.—The whole case has recently been re-told in *Hatred, Ridicule and Contempt* by Joseph Dean (Constable & Co. Ltd.), London, 1953. (A condensed extract from this book of this case was published in the London *Evening Standard*, December 5, 1953, p. 9, by Joseph Dean.)
52. This and the whole aspect of the writings of those days is excellently described and refuted by Lucien Wolf in *The Myth of the Jewish Menace in World Affairs or The Truth about the Forged Protocols of the Elders of Zion* (The Macmillan Company), London, 1921.
53. *The Truth About "The Protocols". A Literary Forgery.* From *The Times* of August 16, 17 and 18, 1921. (The Times, Printing House Square), London, 1921.
54. *The Times*, July 18, 1923, p. 5.
55. *Ibid.*, where the action is recorded in great detail and from where the quotations which follow below were taken.
56. *J.C.*, July 20, 1923, p. 8.
57. For the full text of the sentence see p. 177.
58. *The Times*, December 11, 1923, p. 5, and December 12, 1923, p. 5, from where the quotations which follow were taken.
59. It is interesting to note that this action was revived by the Nazis and prominently featured by them during World War II in their campaign of abuse against Churchill. (See for instance Franz Rose, *Das ist Churchill* (J. F. Lehmanns Verlag), Muenchen/Berlin 1940, pp. 57/58.)

CHAPTER IV
The Solution

1. See p. 86.
2. *Ibid.*
3. See about these negotiations, Herzl's *Diaries* (German edition), Berlin, 1923, III, 295-298 and 307-309; also Oskar K. Rabinowicz, "Herzl and England", in *Jewish Social Studies*, New York, Vol. XIII. No. 1, pp. 25-46.
4. About these negotiations see Herzl's *Diaries* (same ed.), III, 412f., 437, Herzl's speech at the 6th Zionist Congress in *Protocol* VI, 7-9; Dr. Oskar K. Rabinowicz, "New Light on the East Africa Scheme", in *The Rebirth of Israel: A Memorial Tribute to Paul Goodman*, edited by Israel Cohen (Edward Goldston & Son Ltd.), London, 1952, pp. 77-97; the same author, *Fifty Years of Zionism* (Robert Anscombe & Co. Ltd.), London, 1952 (2nd ed.), pp. 48-64.
5. *Trial and Error*, p. 111.
6. *Hansard*, June 20, 1904, Vol. 136, col. 561-579.—See also p. 63.
7. *Protocol* VI, p. 327.
8. *Report of the East Africa Commission*, p. 3.
9. *J.C.*, December 23, 1904, p. 11.
10. *Report of the East Africa Commission*, p. 4.
11. See p. 63.
12. *Protocol* VII, 133.
13. *J.C.*, August 25, 1905, p. 17.
14. See p. 74.
15. *J.C.*, September 15, 1905, p. 24.
16. *Ibid.*, May 5, 1905, p. 33.
17. See pp. 72-74.
18. See pp. 37, 198.
19. See p. 65.
20. *Hansard*, July 10, 1905, Vol. 149, col. 178.
21. *Evening News*, Glasgow, February 28, 1930. ("Our Task for Peace in Palestine".)
22. *J.C.*, January 5, 1906, p. 16.
23. The documents regarding the East Africa scheme are in the Foreign Office Archives under No. F.O.2 (785), East Africa, 1903; Africa 10 (1904), Command Paper 2163; F.O.2 (835, 846, 849, 850), East Africa, 1904.
24. Alfred L. Lyttelton, Colonial Secretary in Balfour's Government.
25. The newly appointed Colonial Secretary under whom Churchill then served as Under-Secretary for the Colonies. Lord Elgin gave his consent to Churchill's letter. (See p. 191.)
26. *J.C.*, January 19, 1906, p. 33.
27. *Ibid.*, p. 31.
28. *Ibid.*, February 2, 1906, p. 24.
29. *Ibid.*, January 12, 1906, p. 44.
30. Blanche E. C. Dugdale, *Arthur James Balfour* (Hutchinson & Co.), London, 1936, I, 433-436. See also Dr. Weizmann, *Trial and Error*, pp. 142-145.
31. January 19, 1906, p. 9.—See also pp. 80, 172.

32.  *Report of the East Africa Commission*, p. 4; reprinted in *J.C.*, June 16, 1905, p. 15.
33.  *Hansard*, June 22, 1906, Vol. 159, col. 642.
34.  *J.C.*, June 7, 1907, p. 23; *Ibid.*, June 14, p. 26; *Ibid.*, June 21, pp. 8, 17.
35.  *American Jewish Year Book*, 1907-1908, p. 539.
36.  *J.C.*, December 13, 1907, p. 28.
37.  *Ibid.*
38.  *Ibid.*, June 14, 1907, p. 26; *Ibid.*, July 12, 1907, p. 33; *American Jewish Year Book*, 1907-1908, p. 539.
39.  *J.C.*, December 13, 1907, p. 30.
40.  *Ibid.*, p. 28.
41.  *Annual Register*, 1907 (Longmans, Green & Co.), London, 1908, p. 426.
42.  Published by Hodder and Stoughton, London, 1908.
43.  pp. 45-65.
44.  p. 45.
45.  An interesting short sketch about the history and efforts of I.T.O. was given by Israel Zangwill in his presidential address to the Inter-University Jewish Students Federation, held at Jews' College, London, on November 26, 1922.  He referred therein to Churchill's declaration of sympathy with the objects of I.T.O. (See *J.C.*, December 1, 1922, p. 28.)
46.  The phrase is used in an article " Protestrabbiner ", signed " H." (which undoubtedly stands for " Herzl "), in *Die Welt*, Vienna, July 16, 1897, No. 7, p. 1.
47.  *J.C.*, February 7, 1908, p. 26.
48.  *J.C.*, May 27, 1921, p. 21.
49.  Should read thirteen years ago.

ABBREVIATIONS

AFTERMATH = *The Aftermath.  A Sequel to The World Crisis*, by Winston S. Churchill.  Macmillan & Co. Ltd., London, 1941.
AMERICAN JEWISH YEAR BOOK = An annual published by the Jewish Publication Society of America, Philadelphia.
Broad, CHURCHILL = *Winston Churchill*, by Lewis Broad. Hutchinson & Co. Ltd., London, 1941.
CONGRESS WEEKLY = A weekly published by the American Jewish Congress, New York.
CHURCHILL BY HIS CONTEMPORARIES = *Churchill by His Contemporaries*, edited by Charles Eade. Hutchinson & Co. Ltd., London, 1953.
CHURCHILL, SERVANT OF CROWN AND COMMONWEALTH = *Winston Spencer Churchill, Servant of Crown and Commonwealth.  A Tribute by Various Hands Presented to him on his Eightieth Birthday*, edited by Sir James Marchant.  Cassell & Co. Ltd., London, 1954.
DUBNOW, I, II, III, ETC. = *Weltgeschichte des jüdischen Volkes*, by Simon Dubnow.  Ten volumes.  Jüdischer Verlag, Berlin, 1925-1929.
F.O. = Foreign Office, London.

FINAL SUMMARY REPORT = *Final Summary Report of the Executive Director, War Refugee Board.* Washington, September 15th, 1945.

GREAT CONTEMPORARIES = *Great Contemporaries,* by Winston S. Churchill. Odhams Press Limited, London, 1949.

GREAT WAR, I, II, ETC. = *The Great War,* by Winston S. Churchill. Three volumes. George Newnes Ltd., London.

GREENBERG, JEWS IN RUSSIA = *The Jews in Russia* by Louis Greenberg. Two volumes. Yale University Press, 1944 and 1951.

Hirschmann, LIFE LINE = *Life Line to a Promised Land,* by Ira A. Hirschmann. The Vanguard Press, Inc., New York, 1946.

Hurewitz, STRUGGLE FOR PALESTINE = *The Struggle for Palestine,* by J. C. Hurewitz. W. W. Norton & Co. Inc., New York, 1950.

ILLUSTRATED SUNDAY HERALD = Issue of that weekly (now extinct) of February 8th, 1920.

INTO BATTLE = *Into Battle. Speeches* by Winston S. Churchill. Compiled by Randolph S. Churchill. Cassell & Co. Ltd., London, 1941.

I.T.O. = Jewish Territorial Organization.

J.C. = *The Jewish Chronicle,* London.

JEWISH CASE = *The Jewish Case Before the Anglo-American Committee of Inquiry on Palestine as Presented by the Jewish Agency for Palestine. Statements and Memoranda.* The Jewish Agency for Palestine, Jerusalem, 1947.

JEWISH YEAR BOOK = An annual published now by the Jewish Chronicle Publications, London.

Kimche, SECRET ROADS = *The Secret Roads,* by Jon and David Kimche. Secker and Warburg, London, 1954.

Litvinoff, BEN-GURION = *Ben-Gurion of Israel,* by Barnet Litvinoff. Weidenfeld and Nicolson, London, 1954.

LORD RANDOLPH CHURCHILL = *Lord Randolph Churchill,* by Winston S. Churchill. Two volumes. Macmillan & Co., London, 1906.

MARLBOROUGH, I, II, ETC. = *Marlborough, His Life and Times,* by Winston Churchill. Four volumes. George G. Harrap & Co. Ltd., London, 1933-1938.

MY EARLY LIFE = *My Early Life, A Roving Commission,* by Winston S. Churchill. Macmillan & Co. Ltd., London, 1941.

Martin, LASKI = *Harold Laski, A Biographical Memoir,* by Kingsley Martin. Victor Gollancz Ltd., London, 1953.

ONWARDS TO VICTORY = *Onwards to Victory, War Speeches,* 1943, by Winston S. Churchill. Compiled by Charles Eade. Cassell & Co. Ltd., London, 1946.

PALESTINE YEAR BOOK, I, II, ETC. = *The Palestine Year Book and Israeli Annual.* Published by the Zionist Organization of America, New York, I (1944/45), II (1945/46), III (1947/48), IV (1948/49).

PROTOCOL, I, II, III, ETC. = Official *Protocols* of the I, II, III, etc. Zionist Congress.

POLITICAL REPORT = *Political Report of the London Office of the Executive of the Jewish Agency, Submitted to the Twenty-Second Zionist Congress.* London, 1946.

216

Roth, Short History = *Short History of the Jewish People* by Cecil Roth. East and West Library, London, 1948.

Rufus Isaacs=*Rufus Isaacs, First Marquess of Reading*, by His Son the Marquess of Reading. Hutchinson & Co., London, 1942.

Report of the East Africa Commission = *Report of the Work of the Commission Sent out by the Zionist Organisation to Examine the Territory Offered by H.M. Government to the Organisation for the Purposes of a Jewish Settlement in British East Africa.* London, 1905.

Trial and Error = *Trial and Error, The Autobiography* of Chaim Weizmann. Hamish Hamilton, London, 1949.

Survey of International Affairs = This survey is published for the British Institute of International Affairs since 1925 by the Oxford University Press.

Step by Step = *Step by Step, 1936-1939*, by Winston S. Churchill. Macmillan & Co. Ltd., London, 1942.

Sacher, Israel = *Israel, the Establishment of a State*, by Harry Sacher. George Weidenfeld & Nicolson, London, 1952.

Second World War, I, II, III, etc. = *The Second World War*, by Winston S. Churchill. Six volumes. Cassell & Co. Ltd., London, 1948-1954.

Stemming the Tide = *Stemming the Tide, Speeches 1951 and 1952*, by Winston S. Churchill. Edited by Randolph S. Churchill. Cassell & Co. Ltd., London, 1953.

Survey of Palestine, I, II = *A Survey of Palestine, Prepared in December 1945 and January 1946 for the Information of the Anglo-American Committee of Inquiry.* Two volumes. The Government Printer, Palestine.

Thoughts and Adventures=*Thoughts and Adventures*, by Winston S. Churchill. Macmillan & Co. Ltd., London, 1942.

Unrelenting Struggle = *The Unrelenting Struggle, War Speeches* by Winston S. Churchill. Compiled by Charles Eade. Cassell and Co. Ltd., London, 1942.

van Passen, Forgotten Ally = *The Forgotten Ally*, by Pierre van Passen. The Dial Press, New York, 1943.

Victory=*Victory, War Speeches, 1945*, by Winston S. Churchill. Compiled by Charles Eade. Cassell & Co. Ltd., London, 1946.

Wise, Challenging Years=*Challenging Years, The Autobiography of Stephen Wise.* G. P. Putnam's Sons, New York, 1949.

" Zionism versus Bolshevism " = " Zionism versus Bolshevism, a Struggle for the Soul of the Jewish People ", by Winston S. Churchill, in *The Illustrated Sunday Herald*, February 8th, 1920.

# INDEX

218

East - End (London, see also Whitechapel), 46, 54, 60, 62, 64, 70, 77, 172-175, 201
Easterman, Alexander Levvey, 205
Ebbw Vale, 167, 170
Eden, Sir Anthony, 97, 112, 113, 115, 130-135, 153, 158, 161, 205
Egypt, 26, 114, 120, 154, 186
Eichmann, Adolf, 133
E.L.A.S., 136, 208
Elgin, Earl of, 189, 191, 193, 214
Emergency Conference to Save the Jewish People of Europe, 128
Emmott, A., 76, 78, 166
Empire (see also British Empire), 115-117, 121, 161, 187, 190-193
Encyclopaedia Britannica, 211
End of the Beginning, The (Churchill), 9
" Enemies to the Left " (Churchill), 203
England, English (see also Britain), 51, 52, 65, 72, 79, 81-83, 87, 95, 98, 135, 161, 166, 175, 183, 193, 200
English Speaking Union, 198
English Zionist Federation, 124, 152, 193, 194
" Ephesian " (Bechhofer), 213.
Essays on Antisemitism (Pinson), 202
Europe (Continent), 16, 35, 72, 80, 92, 104-112, 115-119, 121, 124-126, 128, 129, 131, 132, 136, 140, 141, 144, 146, 147, 152, 153, 160, 162, 164, 166, 173, 185, 192
" Europe in Suspense " (Churchill), 203
Europe United (Churchill), 9
Evans-Gordon, Major William Eden, 46, 56-58, 61, 193, 200
Evening News (Glasgow), 214
Evening Standard (London), 213
Everest, Mrs., 20
Evian, 115

Exodus (see also Bible, Old Testament), 26

Fascism, Fasicsts, 173
Fascist, The, (London), 173
Fifty Years of Zionism: A Historical Analysis of Dr. Weizmann's " Trial and Error " (Rabinowicz), 213
" Fight Against Anti-Semitism in Soviet Russia " (Steinberg), 203
Final Summary Report (War Refugee Board), 133, 135, 136, 206-208
Finburgh, S., 74, 187
Finlay, Sir Robert B., 59, 67, 76, 165
First Lord of the Admiralty, 171, 179, 181
First Lord of the Treasury, 75, 139
Forces (British), 108, 118-123, 149, 157, 167-170
Forces (Jewish, see also Jewish Army, Jewish Brigade), 108, 120, 121, 146-149
Foreign Office, 123
Foreign Office Archives, 214
Foreign Secretary, 112, 114, 134, 186, 207
Forgotten Ally, The (van Paassen), 205, 211
France, French, 29, 34, 35, 51, 82, 94, 101, 104, 105, 109, 116, 154, 157, 204
" France Faces a New Crisis " (Churchill), 197
Frankfurter, David, 97
Frederick the Great, 83
Free French Forces, 154
Free Trade, 53
Friends News Sheet (London), 196
Friendship towards Jews, 16, 19, 20, 118, 119, 136, 137, 139, 146, 147, 158, 161, 184, 189
" Friendship with Germany " (Churchill), 203
Fripp, Sir Alfred, 179
Future of the Jews, The (Lynx), 203

221

222

224

Parliament, 21, 36, 38, 46, 49-53, 62, 63, 67, 70, 71, 76, 78, 80-82, 85, 95, 101, 102, 104, 105, 109, 112-118, 124, 125, 134, 140, 142, 143, 145, 149, 150, 152, 153, 155, 156, 158, 165-167, 174, 193, 194, 199, 200, 205
Parliamentary Oath, 21
Partition of Palestine, 139, 140, 144, 156, 158, 159
*Patria*, S.S., 141, 145, 206
Peake, Osbert, 113-117
Pentateuch (see also Bible, Old Testament), 26, 32
*Persécution des Juifs en France, La,* (Monneray), 204
Persia, 116
" Personal Contacts " (Churchill), 196
Petlura, Simon, 91, 92
Pinson, Koppel S., 202
Pittsburgh, 209
*Plain English* (London), 175-178, 182
" Plain Word to the Nazis, A " (Churchill), 203
Pogroms (see also Atrocities), 36, 110, 164, 170, 202
Poland, Polish, Poles, 96, 101, 104, 105, 110, 111, 116, 134, 141, 149, 150, 153-155, 157, 204, 207
*Political Report of the Jewish Agency for Palestine to the XXII. Zionist Congress,* 135, 146, 148, 153, 205-210
Pollack, Stephen W., 9
Poor Law, 68
Porat-Pirotinsky, 208
Port of London Bill, 62
Portugal, 135
Post-War Plans, 107-109, 111, 112, 138-140, 145, 151-159
President, see Roosevelt
Press (see also Jewish Press), 118, 119, 127, 165, 168, 179, 185, 186
Prime Minister, 54, 63, 67, 77, 79, 107, 116-119, 121, 123, 124, 138, 139, 142, 146-148, 150, 152, 156, 159, 161, 165,

166, 188, 192, 204
Progressive Party, 43
Promised Land (see also Palestine), 32
Prophet, Prophesy, 23, 31
" Protestants, 27, 95
" Protestrabbiner " (Herzl), 214
*Protocols of the Elders of Zion,* 176
*Protocols* of the Zionist Congresses: VI, 212, VII, 212, 213, XXII, 209
Prussia, Prussians, 83, 98, 104
Przemysl, 110
Public Order Bill, 174
Putnam's Sons, G.B., 10

Quickswood, Lord, 21

Rabinowicz, Dr. Oskar K., 212, 213
Racial persecution (see also Anti-Semitism, Atrocities, Pogroms), 83, 87
Radek, Karl B., 40
Rapallo, 176
" Rape of Austria " (Churchill), 203
Rath, vom, see vom Rath
Rathbone, Miss Eleanor, 127
Rathenau, Dr. Walter, 176
"Reaction to Overseas Events" (Jelenko), 206
Reade, Winwood, 22
Reading, Lord (see also Isaacs, Rufus), 38, 39, 198
*Rebirth of Israel, The, A Memorial Tribute to Paul Goodman* (Cohen), 213
Red Cross (see also International Red Cross), 209
Red Sea, 114
Redeemer (see also Prophet, Bible, Old Testament), 23
Refugees, 52, 67, 74, 79, 80, 101, 102, 113-118, 121, 122, 124-130, 133, 135, 136, 141, 142, 144, 160, 162, 164, 167, 190
Rehovoth, 197
Religion, 20-22, 25, 26, 28, 83, 87, 95, 175, 192

228

230

231